# From Hitler to Codreanu

This book examines fascist ideology in seven leaders of parties and movements in the interwar period.

It makes use of the conceptual morphological approach, focused on core and adjacent concepts, as well as on the interlinkages between them. With such an approach, the book seeks to offer an innovative perspective on fascism and arrive at a conceptual configuration of fascist ideology, capable of highlighting its main concepts and combinations. Furthermore, it examines the major texts of seven leaders from Germany, Italy, the UK, Portugal, Spain, France and Romania – Adolf Hitler, Benito Mussolini, Oswald Mosley, Rolão Preto, Primo de Rivera, Marcel Déat, and Corneliu Codreanu. With the conceptual approach, the book reasserts the possibility of finding a definition of generic fascism at the same time as depicting the ideological varieties espoused by each leader.

This title will be of interest to students and scholars of fascism, extremism and the far right.

**Carlos Manuel Martins** holds a PhD from the University of Lisbon, Portugal. His doctorate research revolved around the ideology of historical fascism and fascist leaders. He is now preparing postdoctoral research on the Contemporary Radical Right.

# Routledge Studies in Social and Political Thought

150 Hegel and Contemporary Practical Philosophy
   Beyond Kantian-Constructivism
   James Gledhill and Sebastian Stein

151 A Marxist Theory of Ideology
   Praxis, Thought and the Social World
   Andrea Sau

152 Stupidity in Politics
   Its Unavoidability and Potential
   Nobutaka Otobe

153 Political Correctness: A Sociocultural Black Hole
   Thomas Tsakalakis

154 The Individual After Modernity: A Sociological Perspective
   Mira Marody

155 The Politics of Well-Being
   Towards a More Ethical World
   Anthony M. Clohesy

156 From Hitler to Codreanu
   The Ideology of Fascist Leaders
   Carlos Manuel Martins

157 The Fascist Temptation
   Creating a Political Community of Experience
   David Ohana

For a full list of titles in this series, please visit www.routledge.com/series/RSSPT

# From Hitler to Codreanu
The Ideology of Fascist Leaders

Carlos Manuel Martins

LONDON AND NEW YORK

First published 2021
by Routledge
2 Park Square, Milton Park, Abingdon, Oxon OX14 4RN

and by Routledge
52 Vanderbilt Avenue, New York, NY 10017

*Routledge is an imprint of the Taylor & Francis Group, an informa business*

© 2021 Carlos Manuel Martins

The right of Carlos Manuel Martins to be identified as author of this work has been asserted by him in accordance with sections 77 and 78 of the Copyright, Designs and Patents Act 1988.

All rights reserved. No part of this book may be reprinted or reproduced or utilised in any form or by any electronic, mechanical, or other means, now known or hereafter invented, including photocopying and recording, or in any information storage or retrieval system, without permission in writing from the publishers.

*Trademark notice*: Product or corporate names may be trademarks or registered trademarks, and are used only for identification and explanation without intent to infringe.

*British Library Cataloguing-in-Publication Data*
A catalogue record for this book is available from the British Library

*Library of Congress Cataloging-in-Publication Data*
A catalog record has been requested for this book

ISBN: 978-0-367-61558-1 (hbk)
ISBN: 978-1-003-10604-3 (ebk)

Typeset in Times New Roman
by MPS Limited, Dehradun

Printed in the United Kingdom by Henry Ling Limited

This book is dedicated to my family, especially my mother.

# Contents

*Acknowledgements* x
*List of Abbreviations* xi

**Introduction: fascist leaders, generic fascism and the conceptual approach**   1

*Taking fascist ideology seriously 1*
*Why the leaders? 3*
*The search for a 'generic fascism' and new concerns about ideological fluidity 4*
*The conceptual morphological approach 6*
*Fascism and the conceptual morphological approach 9*
*Methodology and primary sources 11*
*Notes 15*
*List of references 17*

**1 The conceptual structure of 'generic fascism': seven core concepts**   20

*Main interpretations and definitions of fascism 21*
*The core concepts of fascism 23*
*Concluding remarks 40*
*Notes 40*
*List of references 45*

**2 Adolf Hitler and German national socialism: racial struggle as the basis of a worldview**   48

*Hitler and the Nazi party 48*
*Adolf Hitler amid the ideological struggles of his time 50*
*The conceptual core of Mein Kampf 51*
*Other important features of the configuration 62*

viii *Contents*

> *Concluding remarks 66*
> *Notes 67*
> *List of references 70*

3 **Oswald Mosley and the British Union of Fascists: the ideological synthesis of 'Greater Britain'** 72

> *Mosley and the BUF 72*
> *Oswald Mosley amid the ideological struggles of his time 74*
> *The conceptual core of Greater Britain 75*
> *Other important features of the configuration 86*
> *Concluding remarks 89*
> *Notes 90*
> *List of references 92*

4 **Francisco Rolão Preto and Portuguese national syndicalism: corporatism and the construction of an alternative modernity** 94

> *Rolão Preto and NS 94*
> *Rolão Preto amid the ideological struggles of his time 96*
> *The conceptual core of Rolão Preto's texts 97*
> *Other important features of the configuration 106*
> *Concluding remarks 110*
> *Notes 111*
> *List of references 114*

5 **José António Primo de Rivera and the Spanish Falange: the historical mission of the Spanish nation** 116

> *Primo de Rivera and the FE de las JONS 116*
> *Primo de Rivera amid the ideological struggles of his time 118*
> *The conceptual core of Primo de Rivera 120*
> *Other important features of the configuration 129*
> *Concluding remarks 132*
> *Notes 133*
> *List of references 137*

6 **Corneliu Codreanu and the iron guard: the Manichean battle between good and evil** 139

> *Corneliu Codreanu and the GF 139*
> *Corneliu Codreanu amid the ideological struggles of his time 141*
> *The conceptual core of Pentru Legionari 143*
> *Other Important features of the configuration 153*

*Concluding remarks 156*
*Notes 157*
*List of references 160*

7 **Marcel Déat and the French RNP: the European Revolution and the New Party** 162

*Marcel Déat and the RNP 164*
*Marcel Déat amid the ideological struggles of his time 165*
*The conceptual core of Le Parti Unique 167*
*Other important features of the configuration 175*
*Concluding remarks 180*
*Notes 180*
*List of references 183*

8 **Benito Mussolini and Italian Fascism: the creation of a new conceptual configuration** 185

*Benito Mussolini, fascism and the political milieu of Italy in the 20$^{th}$ century 186*
*The conceptual reconfigurations of Mussolini during the formative years of Fascism 190*
*Concluding remarks 200*
*Notes 201*
*List of references 204*

9 **Final considerations about the conceptual configuration of generic fascism** 206

*The core concepts of fascism 206*
*Interlinkages 213*
*The adjacent concept of order 214*
*One marginal concept: liberty 215*
*Permeability and rejections 216*
*Contradictions and tensions 216*
*Concluding remarks: a definition of fascism 217*
*Notes 218*
*List of references 219*

**Conclusion** 222

*Index* 224

# Acknowledgements

I acknowledge my debt to several people who help me though the writing of this work. Among them, I would like to highlight Professor António Costa Pinto, Professor Goffredo Adinolfi, Professor Michael Freeden, and Professor Aristotle Kallis.

# List of Abbreviations

| | |
|---|---|
| ANI | Associazione Nazionalista Italiana |
| BUF | British Union of Fascists |
| CEDA | Confederación Española de Derechas Autónomas |
| CGN | Garda Conştiinţei Naţionale |
| DAP | Deutsch Arbeiterpartei |
| DF | La Dottrina del Fascismo |
| DPP | Os Doze Princípios da Produção |
| DZP | Deutsche Zentrumspartei |
| FE | Falange Española |
| FE de las JONS | Falange Española de las Juntas de Ofensiva Nacional Sindicalista |
| FIC | Fasci Italiani di Combattimento |
| GB | The Greater Britain |
| GF | Garda de Fier |
| IBS | Irish Blue Shirts |
| IL | Integralismo Lusitano |
| LAM | Legiunea Arhanghelului Mihail |
| LANC | Liga Apărării Naţional Creştine |
| LVF | Légion des volontaires français contre le bolchévisme |
| MF | Mouvement Franciste |
| MK | Mein Kampf |
| MSR | Mouvement Social Révolutionnaire |
| NL | Nacionalismo Lusitano |
| NS | Nacional Sindicalismo |
| NSDAP | Nationalsozialistische Deutsche Arbeiterpartei |
| PL | Pentru Legionari |
| PNF | Partito Nazionale Fascista |
| PNL | Partidul Naţional Liberal |
| PPF | Parti Populaire Français |
| PSI | Partito Socialista Italiano |
| PU | Le Parti Unique |
| RNP | Rassemblement National Populaire |
| SNSP | Svenska nationalsocialistiska partiet |

| | |
|---|---|
| SA | Sturmabteilung |
| SFIO | Section Française de l'Internationale Ouvrière |
| SPD | Sozialdemokratische Partei Deutschland |
| SS | Schutzstaffel |
| TPT | Totul pentru Țară |
| UN | União Nacional |

# Introduction
Fascist Leaders, Generic Fascism and the Conceptual Approach

**Taking fascist ideology seriously**

Researchers have approached fascism in the most varied ways since time immemorial, some of which are apparently irreconcilable. According to Salvatore Garau, academic studies about fascism are divided into two main approaches: the first that pays particular attention to ideology and sees it as a crucial element to understand fascism, and the second that holds ideology to be less important, if not totally irrelevant.[1] While the latter approach was most prominent in the years that immediately followed World War II, the former began to gain importance in the 1960s and can now be considered the predominant approach. Undoubtedly, this early tendency to downplay fascist ideology was due to the legacy of destruction largely caused by the Axis regimes, and the impression that to take the content of fascism seriously might be a form of somehow rehabilitating it. Nevertheless, the 1960s witnessed a crucial change thanks to the contribution of historians like Eugen Weber and Ernst Nolte, who were among the first who dared to approach this ideology by taking its content at face value.

Several decades have passed since this turning point. Most contemporary studies on fascism take its ideological content seriously while approaching it in a manner that is similar to the scrutiny of other ideologies. In this context, we can only agree with Adrian Lyttelton when he concluded that 'the greatest advance [in studies about fascism] has certainly come from taking fascist values and ideology seriously'.[2] While it is true that fascism is oftentimes seen as too irrational and prone to prioritise action over thought (something that fascists themselves often acknowledged), this should not prevent researchers from analyzing it with the same methodology and approaches used with other ideologies.

This statement is corroborated by quoting Salvatore Garau once again.[3] According to the author, there are three different perspectives through which ideologies can be understood: as a metapolitical drive (which, in the case of fascism, is an impetus to regenerate the nation); as a mentality (which, in fascism, is a mentality prone to violent direct action); and a doctrinal core composed of political concepts. Assuming that the metapolitical drive and the mentality are the features that give fascism an irrational component, its doctrinal core is where we can find content that is as coherent and as rational as that of any other ideology. This view believes that the task of the scholar is to discover where the doctrinal core is to be found (whether in texts, books, or speeches) and decide how to interpret it.

As already mentioned, the last decades were quite fruitful with regard to innovative studies about fascist ideology and the phenomenon of fascism as a whole. For this reason, Stein Ugelvik Larsen proposed a strategy towards a theoretical synthesis of fascism. Such synthesis should be able not so much to arrive at new findings, but rather to summarise and reunite previous conclusions. He suggested an inventory with several entries related to different topics, each of them with a group of questions that are important to have in mind when building a theoretical synthesis. One of these entries is 'Ideology' and it includes questions addressing the items that make up the ideology, its internal logic, and the prominence of each item. Some of the questions that Larsen proposed are:

> What are the most important items in the minimum list and how can one find substitutes? How are different items on the ideology minimum weighted against each other? Is racism more important than anti-communism? May a fascist ideological profile be ordered according to the rank of items? What are the items within the ideology that are in contradiction with each other? Which items can be left out without destroying the 'fascist taint'?[4]

Larsen viewed these questions as the starting point for a work aiming to bring together the most important findings of the past decades. Such a goal assumes that the existing books and essays have already found an answer to most of these questions, leaving to the researcher the task of gathering what is most relevant in a theory that synthesises the fundamental tenets. Nevertheless, and in spite of the important contribution of Larsen's text, it is legitimate to suppose that there are still new findings that can be made by researchers who choose innovative approaches and methods. After all, in a field of studies as vast as that of fascism, we can hardly afford to conclude that everything has already been discovered or thought through before.

Thus, we argue here that previous researches have not exhausted the pertinence of a study exclusively focused on fascist leaders. The leaders of fascist parties, as is about to be argued, can be valuable sources of information to help us complement what is already known about this ideology. This will contribute to find new answers to some of the questions posed by Larsen, rather than just summarizing conclusions to which others have arrived before.

## Why the leaders?

According to Eatwell, when individual fascists are chosen as subjects of study, it is common for the attention to be placed on renowned thinkers who somehow contributed to the development of fascism. That is the case, for instance, of A. James Gregor and his in-depth analysis of thinkers like Giovanni Gentile, Sergio Panunzio, Ugo Spirito, and Julius Evola. However, Eatwell notes that leaders themselves are usually not the ones chosen to be studied.[5] This can either be a consequence of the still-prevalent idea that fascist chiefs were but opportunistic liars, or simply of the idea that political leaders in general, due to the tactical twists and turns that they are forced to do, are not the individuals best suited for a study focused on the supposedly stable content of an ideology.

However, the opposite is argued here. If one bears in mind that few political parties gave such importance to the cult of the leader as did fascist parties, it is easy to conclude that one cannot understand fascism without paying due attention to the individual that was the target of worship and obedience. According to Stanley Payne, 'because of their [fascist parties'] authoritarian principles, they required a strong leader—with at least some degree of ability—more than did more liberal forces'.[6] The adage 'Mussolini is always right', enthusiastically repeated by the fascist militants that surrounded the Italian dictator, is a perfect example of this principle of subordination to a charismatic guide who supposedly had all the answers to the problems faced by the nation. To think that one can downplay the political ideology shared by these individuals is not the wisest attitude to have since, as Mosse wrote, 'describing the movements without the leaders is rather like describing the body without the soul'.[7]

Furthermore, to understand the importance of leaders, it is relevant to mention Pinto and Larsen when they argue that a fourth type of authority can be added to the triad of forms of political legitimation conceived by Max Weber, which included Traditional Authority, Legal Authority, and Charismatic Authority. That fourth type is Ideological Authority and it is based on beliefs. This form of political legitimation takes place when the followers of a leader are expected to fully and publicly adhere to ideological manifestos and obey them in every aspect of life while maintaining belief in the accomplishment of certain goals. Still according to Pinto and Larsen, 'ideology gives its followers the definitive 'reason' for their individual support for the leader, as well as for their willingness to sacrifice themselves in order to fight for the cause'.[8]

Thus, the case for an ideological analysis focused on fascist leaders lies mostly in this Ideological Authority upon which fascist chiefs constructed their legitimacy. Though the leaders themselves might sometimes not be the main producers of ideology within the movement (merely repeating ideas created by some other thinker), their texts and speeches will still contain the fundamental principles of their movement. As Pinto and Larsen recall, 'the 'content' of the leader's 'messianic message' added a great deal to the persuasive manner of his charisma'.[9] To know more about the content of this message is a starting point to draw new conclusions about the ideas of the movement or party as a whole.

Bearing in mind all that has been said about the leaders, the goal of this book is to find out which items were part of their ideology as well as how they were articulated. It is important to note that a research like this must be limited to the epoch that goes from 1919 (when the first fascist movement was founded by Benito Mussolini) to 1945 (when WWII ended with the defeat of fascism). As to spatial limits, the subject of study must be circumscribed to the European continent, where fascism originated and developed. It would not be feasible to go beyond it and study leaders like the Brazilian Plínio Salgado or the Japanese Nakano Seigo, to name but a few.[10] Furthermore, this could render the study inconsistent and lead to discussions about the pertinence of classifying as fascist some of the movements that appeared outside Europe (a discussion that, while interesting, would be sterile to the current purposes).

Before proceeding to the study itself, it is necessary to describe in detail the approach to be used and address some questions related to methodology and primary sources. This also requires a quick overview of the main trends in fascist studies in the last decades, which will help discover which topics have been discussed and the doubts put forward by recent researchers. This will create a more enlightened idea about the questions to which the chosen approach must give an answer.

## The search for a 'generic fascism' and new concerns about ideological fluidity

Roger Griffin was the main responsible for reviving the interest for the definition of a 'fascist minimum' or 'generic fascism' in the 1990s. These two terms have been used to imply that there is a set of definitive features shared by several movements and parties in the interwar period, and this allows them to be gathered under the generic label of 'fascism'. Griffin famously used the Weberian 'ideal-type' approach to come to the conclusion that fascism was 'a genus of political ideology whose mythic core in its various permutations is a palingenetic form of populist ultra-nationalism'.[11] The majority of researchers that followed in the wake of Griffin, in spite of some disagreements, seemed at least to agree with the idea that fascist ideology should be taken seriously and that it was possible to define a set of core features.[12] This led Griffin to state that there finally seemed to be a 'consensus' about the nature of fascism, with which most researchers agreed.[13]

However, Michel Dobry recently criticised Griffin while revealing his skepticism towards approaches that try to reach a definitive definition of fascism through a set of core features. Opposing this method, Dobry believes that the process of ideological definition takes place in the context of a struggle for meaning which has outcomes that cannot be idealised and inserted in a stable and abstract definition. Ideological identity is characterised by constant fluidity, and it is influenced by the conflicts existing in a given context; thus, it is not possible to infer the existence of a stable essence in relation to any ideology whatsoever. Essentialist and historicist approaches are, therefore, ineffective and can lead to misunderstandings and erroneous conclusions, so this author would argue.

This way, Dobry discards treating fascism as 'a species apart, endowed with a radically different nature or essence from that of other authoritarian movements and, more specifically, movements of the radical, conservative or extreme right'.[14] The theoretical inadequacies stemming from the tendency to see in fascism a radically different phenomenon can be overcome if researchers start thinking in 'relational terms'. To adopt a relational perspective means to approach fascism (or any other political ideology, for that matter) not by isolating movements or individuals from their spatial and temporary context, but rather by taking into account their relationship to the competitive social spaces where the struggles for meaning were taking place.

The concerns raised by Dobry were met by authors such as David D. Roberts, who draws from his work to put forward an approach focused on 'fascist interactions'. That is, the interlinkages and negotiations that took place between fascists and other social groups or right wing organizations. António Costa Pinto and Aristotle Kallis attempted a new approach to interactions that revolved around the idea of hybridization. Acknowledging this hybridization, so they argue, opens new paths to the understanding of the competitive nature of right wing politics back in the interwar period, even if it blurs the distinctions between the several varieties of ideologies that authors like Stanley Payne had carefully outlined.[15]

At this point, it is important to note that Roger Griffin himself has always rejected that his approach was an 'essentialist' one, defending it for its heuristic value rather than for the supposed potential to grasp the 'essence' of fascist ideology. As the author explicitly states, 'there is clearly no question of it [his approach] revealing the 'essence' of fascism [...] It is the result of consciously elaborating, formulating and systematizing a pattern 'seen' by me at a largely intuitive or unconscious level'.[16] Nevertheless, Dobry was not the first to see in Griffin's approach a way to (in spite of his intentions) arrive at a static and essentialist definition, a criticism that Philip Morgan, for instance, had previously also made.[17] Besides, the most important aspect of Dobry's criticism is that opting to build an abstraction is, in itself, a wrong starting point when studying political ideologies. This is so because, in this author's perspective, ideologies are inevitably fluid and mutable, and one's ideological positioning is often based on personal perceptions and interpretations or even on the practical goals that one has in mind. Such a picture gets even more complicated if it is also acknowledged that any political positioning may be a response (positive or negative, according to circumstances) to some other positioning already taken by a political competitor. Abstractions, therefore, have no heuristic value at all when it comes to the understanding of such a dynamic subject of study as political ideas, or at least that is what Dobry would argue.

In this context, we do recognise that some of Dobry's concerns are legitimate and that opting to reach an abstract definition can sometimes compromise the understanding of ideological dynamism. That some authors nowadays talk about 'interactions' and 'hybridization' seems to prove that the questions posed by Dobry do hold many valid points. Nevertheless, it is also wise not to take Dobry's criticisms to its ultimate consequences, for this would lead one to conclude that there was never really any phenomenon that we can call 'fascism', but only people or organizations that, for some reason, classified themselves as such. Therefore, this book reiterates the possibility of finding fixity and stability in a definition of fascism, while also acknowledging that ideologies do encompass dynamism, fluidity and reconfigurations.

A 'fixed' definition that encompasses the most important features of fascism can not only serve as a mainstay when trying to identify fascist individuals and organizations but also as a guide in the study of different varieties. To look for fixity in the characterization of fascism is a necessary step for those trying to make sense of the political turmoil of the interwar years, for otherwise it will be impossible to have a clear sense of the different types of authoritarian programs put forward by distinct organisations and what made each of them unique. This way, and since we also acknowledge the mutability and dynamism of ideologies, it is necessary for this study to make use of an approach that is flexible enough to account for both fixity and fluidity. The approach that we need is the so-called conceptual morphological approach, as will be discussed in the next section.

## The conceptual morphological approach

The conceptual morphological approach was put forward by Michael Freeden in his groundbreaking study *Ideologies and Political Theory: A Conceptual Approach*. According to him, 'the thinking encapsulated in ideologies deserves examination in its own right, not merely for what it masks'.[18] Freeden thus aims to interpret and decode the content of ideologies rather than unmasking their social function (which occurs, for instance, with Marxist and Structuralist approaches). The conceptual morphological approach is a semantic approach, for it focuses on the implications and insights of a particular set of political views and the universe of meaning that it constructs whether deliberately or unintentionally. It is neither a genetic approach (for genetic approaches focus on how the ideology came to being and refer to the history of ideas and the history of political thought), nor a functional approach (for it is not focused on roles that an ideology plays in a given society).

Introduction    7

This approach also aims at grasping ideologies as patterns of thought, which implies understanding how they make use of the main unities that compose these patterns, that is, political concepts, which are the 'basic unities of thinking about politics [and] constitute its main foci'.[19] Each ideological pattern represents a unique configuration of concepts carrying a specific meaning and an internal logic. The conceptual morphological approach tries to disentangle these configurations by focusing on the morphology of the interlinkages that take place between concepts. Its objective is not, for instance, to monitor the evolution of a concept over time, but rather to interpret them by locating them in the actual pattern in which they appear. Freeden convincingly argues that 'political concepts acquire meaning not only through accumulative traditions of discourse, and not only through diverse cultural contexts, but also by means of their particular structural position within a configuration with other political concepts'.[20]

Furthermore, Freeden also states that due to the polysemic nature of language, each concept is 'essentially contested', meaning each concept contains multiple meanings and more potential components than the ones that it will actually display in a specific pattern. There is always the possibility of extending and enlarging its meaning. Thus, the emergence of a pattern of thought involves a linguistic struggle for meaning. 'Ideologies are consequently the systems of thought through which specific meaning is conferred upon every political concept in their domain', Freeden writes.[21] When concepts are placed within a coherent and meaningful pattern of thought, they are 'decontested'; that is, they acquire a specific and undisputed meaning in that pattern. Political concepts thus help each other creating meaning through the connections and combinations that are established between them, and such combinations hold the key to the interpretation of ideological content. Decoding the meaning of an ideological configuration therefore implies disentangling the interlinkages between concepts.

Before going back to fascism, it is still necessary to mention the main features of the morphological analysis, which according to Freeden include the following:

1. *Priority,* because in each ideological pattern there is a hierarchy of concepts. Not all concepts have the same relevance or are highlighted in the same manner. For instance, the concept of 'Liberty' is at the core of liberalism (in each of its variants), but has a less relevant status in more conservative ideologies. Oftentimes, conceptual patterns of a given ideology suffer alterations, and some concepts come closer or further away from its core. That is the case of 'Private Propriety', which is central to classical liberalism but seems somehow less relevant in some manifestations of contemporary North-American liberalism (which come close to what a European would call 'social democracy'). Freeden distinguishes between core concepts (the ones that are central

to the ideology and cannot be left out without it being transformed into another ideology) and peripheral concepts. These peripheral concepts can belong to the 'margin' (where we find the concepts that are unsubstantial to the meaning of the core) or to the 'perimeter'. The perimeter exists in interface with time and space and is often expressed through themes and ideas in a phrase rather than just in one or two words. It represents the point in which ideologies lose their purely abstract dimension and come closer to action and practice. In a given context, for instance, a core abstract concept such as 'Nationalism' can lead to a perimeter concept such as 'restriction of immigration', if that is the topic being discussed in that same context.

2. *Proximity,* which refers to the interlinkages between concepts, especially between core and adjacent concepts. These adjacent concepts are placed in the vicinity of core concepts, limiting their possible meanings by helping in their decontestation. Different ideological patterns can display different relations of proximity between core and adjacent concepts, and thus they present completely different decontestations. For instance, if the concept of 'Liberty' is decontested in close proximity with the concept of 'Individual Rights' in a liberal configuration, in the case of a communist and socialist pattern it can be decontested in proximity to concepts such as 'Classless Society'.

3. *Permeability,* which reminds us of the intersections taking place in ideologies, and can have two dimensions. In the first dimension, permeability exists because each concept unfolds in a set of different components which are in themselves political concepts intersecting between each other. In the second dimension, different ideological patterns intersect each other and make use of the same concepts, with more or less relevant distinctions in their decontestations. Because of this, Freeden writes that 'ideologies are not hermetically sealed: they have porous boundaries and will frequently occupy overlapping space'.[22] As an example, one can note that both Liberalism and Democratic Socialism make use of the concept of 'Democracy'. In this study, everytime we use the word 'permeability', we will be refering to this second dimension.

4. *Proportionality,* which refers to the relative space that each conceptual configuration gives to a particular concept. For instance, while the concept of 'Liberty' is both present in Socialism and Liberalism, the latter ideology gives it a relevance that is proportionally greater than in the former.

5. *Internal Contradictions,* which deal with the features that seem to bring some inconsistency to the conceptual configuration. In spite of all the logic constraints, it is inevitable that the complexity of political thinking and the multiple contextual challenges fetch some tensions to ideologies. If we compare an ideology to a room and political concepts to the furniture of that room, the contradictions are like objects that seem out

of place or do not fit well next to another object or piece of furniture. For a configuration to maintain its coherence even when these tensions and contradictions are present, it is necessary to employ a series of logical instruments, which are also used in other moments of the struggle for meaning. One example of a contradiction is found in variants of communist ideology that, in spite of the centrality of 'Internationalism', support the idea of building 'Socialism in one Country'. This apparent contradiction can be solved by returning to the concept of 'Class struggle'. This way, in the context of the struggle between the bourgeoisie and the proletariat, communists could defend Soviet nationalism as a form of resistance against a type of bourgeois internationalism and an attempt to build a fatherland for the workers. Even if Freeden does not assert it explicitly, it is here contended that paying attention to internal contradictions and to the way these contradictions are solved are also important aspects of the morphological analysis of political ideologies. By paying attention to the solving of contradictions, one has better understanding about how an ideological pattern acquires coherent content. One can also learn about the processes of thought that are behind the emergence of a conceptual pattern. The logical reasoning used to solve the contradictions shall tell much about the ideological pattern itself, for such reasoning displays the instruments that are used in other features of a given conceptual configuration.

## Fascism and the conceptual morphological approach

So far, it has been made clear that this study aims to: 1 – take fascist ideology seriously; 2 – place its focus on the items of the ideology, their weight and the internal logic of the ideology, as suggested by Larsen; 3 – see fascist leaders as a source of valuable information about the content of the ideology; and 4 – strive for a new definition of a fixed generic fascism, even while acknowledging that ideological fluidity must be taken into account. It remains to be shown why the conceptual morphological approach is best-suited for all these purposes.

The first author worth mentioning is none other than Roger Griffin who, in spite of having used myths rather than concepts to define fascism, acknowledged the relevance of the theory of 'ideological morphology'. He also recognised that it has 'profound implications' for the previous approaches that tried to define fascism in terms of style or organizational structure, since this theory allows for fascism to be defined 'in terms of ideology'.[23] This theory of 'ideological morphology' is therefore compatible with the Weberian methodology that Griffin himself once used to arrive at his definition of 'generic fascism' and, as we will try to prove, is equally capable of making us come to interesting conclusions of our own.

Furthermore, and while it is not necessary to go into much detail about something that was already discussed, it is worth mentioning once again Salvatore Garau and his distinction between the metapolitical drive, the mentality, and the doctrinal core of ideologies. We argue that this doctrinal core exists in fascism in the same way as in other ideologies and somehow displays some type of coherent content, for the simple reason that no ideology, independently of its irrational features, can totally dispense the employment of some form of rational thinking. It is this doctrinal core, providing that we know how to find it (this subject will be addressed in the next section), that can be analysed with Freeden's approach in order to pinpoint the patterns of thought that were behind the conceptual configurations of fascist leaders. Another argument that justifies the adoption of the said approach is simply that it has not been properly used before, at least not in a thorough way.[24]

Another important feature of this approach is also pointed out by Griffin, who states that the theory of ideological morphology is nominalist and, therefore, 'anti-essentialist' for it recognises the conceptual changes that an ideology can experience. This morphological theory explains why 'every concrete permutation of an ideology is simultaneously unique and the manifestation of a generic 'ism' which may assume radical morphological transformations in its outward appearance without losing its definitional ideological core'.[25] What this means is that the conceptual morphological approach can account both for fixity and fluidity in ideologies. It is able to grasp the main features that are part of the most important traditional ideologies while also accounting for the different and unlimited permutations that they will display thanks to conceptual rearrangements. Furthermore, perimeter concepts, by revealing how an ideology ceases to be abstract and interacts with reality, can also show which themes are part of specific varieties of a major ideology and represent the specific concerns of the society in which the conceptual pattern emerged. For this reason, we can use this approach both to grasp the content of 'generic fascism' and properly scrutinise the several national varieties that emerged in different contexts.

Lastly, this approach also has the advantage of being able to account for the hybridity of right-wing ideologies in the interwar period. Though the limitations of this study do not allow for this point to be developed much further, with this approach it is possible to disentangle the configurations of fascism as well as other radical right ideologies and then compare them and verify how mutual influences led to changes and reconfigurations. In spite of not dealing with this topic as much as it would be interesting to do, this study will contain some chapters that highlight the permeability in the ideology of different leaders – that is, the concepts that overlap with other ideological configurations with which the leader could be waging an ideological battle for meaning.

## Methodology and primary sources

We already know how to grasp the doctrinal core of fascist ideology. Now it is necessary to address the issue of where to find such core. In the first place, it is the goal of this study to disentangle a tentative configuration of generic fascist ideology, a task where the reading of secondary sources and academic texts (though important) is not enough, since it is crucial to read and interpret actual fascist sources that belong to the fascist tradition or to a fascist canon. In this regard, Freeden has once stated that, when trying to define the core of the main ideologies, we are 'deferring to the power of tradition and convention as classifiers of ideologies'.[26] It is thanks to tradition and convention that one can identify and delimit the most important Western ideologies, each of them having established themselves through a set of canonical texts, ideologues, philosophers and sometimes organizations like political parties, collectivities or movements. In the case of fascism, which has erupted in the landscape of Western politics without having produced a traditional core of canonic texts and ended just abruptly as it began, the search for this canonic convention may seem, at first, a fruitless one. However, for the purposes of this study, it is necessary to gather a body of texts that contain the main tenets of fascist ideology.

Therefore, this collection of major fascist sources must include important texts such as *The Doctrine of Fascism* (*La Dottrina del Fascismo* – DF). This notorious text was published in 1932 and was co-authored by the philosopher Giovani Gentile (who wrote the section on the fundamental ideas of fascism) and Mussolini himself (who wrote the section on the political and social doctrine of fascism). It contains the core principles of Italian Fascism, and for this reason it cannot be ignored when discussing the generic fascist configuration. This work does not advocate that the specific features appearing in DF are common to all national permutations of fascism and, due to the existence of diverse factions within Italian Fascism, not even to all the stages of development of the Italian variety. But it would be unwise to leave such an important work aside when trying to grasp the fascist core. Furthermore, other primary sources shall also be used. That is the case, for instance, of the texts that we find in an anthology compiled by Roger Griffin and entitled *Fascism*, which brings together several fascist authors, be they leaders or ideologues. With a thorough reading of these texts, as well as secondary sources, it will be possible to reach a conceptual configuration of generic fascism.

We shall note that this configuration is not meant to be a definitive one, for we acknowledge that it is possible to draw other valid configurations. This generic pattern must be simply seen as one possible interpretation of fascism and not as a definitive map of the ideology. Freeden's methodology is open to a certain degree of subjectivity and to the possibility of mapping different configurations, as long as they are validated by the actual sources. Nevertheless, this study intends to minimise as much as possible this subjectivity by justifying the inclusion of each concept with extensive quotations from fascist texts and references to authoritative secondary sources. This way, the words of fascists themselves shall corroborate the ideological map and assert its validity. Furthermore, the search for generic fascism has an exploratory dimension, for the tentative configuration that will first be drawn shall be subjected to revision according to the conclusions drawn from the analysis of fascist leaders. For this reason, the reader must not assume that they know our final conceptual configuration before reading the conclusion. By choosing this option, we hope to make the reader have a better sense of the exploratory nature of this research, sharing with us the line of reasoning that led to the final conclusions.

In the generic conceptual configuration, both the core concepts and their proximity with adjacent concepts shall be highlighted, as well as the meaning created through their interlinkages (peripheral concepts will only be taken into account in the analyses of individual leaders). Apart from its value as a definition of generic fascism, the configuration shall also be helpful to guide the study of individual leaders. With it in mind, it will be possible to know which concepts and interlinkages to look for in individual permutations. Likewise, it will be possible to know in which aspects each individual configuration is similar to the generic configuration and in which aspects it differs.

As for the analysis of the specific configurations of leaders, an effort was made to include works that could be seen as major and defining texts, something close to the *Quotations of Chairman Mao*, but in the context of fascist ideology. It was necessary to find a text that contained the most important political views and ideas of the leaders. Note that, for the comparison to be feasible, it was decided to choose only texts written before the leader conquered actual executive power (which posed no problem since only Mussolini and Hitler achieved such type of power). Besides, the study will include not only the most famous leaders, like the Italian *Duce* and the German *Fuhrer* (though they could hardly be left out), but also lesser-known leaders of parties from countries that have, for a long time, been ignored.

Each leader and each configuration shall be dealt with in separate chapters. Before mapping their ideology, it will be important to refer to the political context of the time when the text was written (the political organizations that were part of it and the struggles for meaning that were taking place in the social competitive spaces). Thus, each chapter will present the main political concepts being discussed and articulated at that historical moment. The history of the fascist party and the life and works of the leader shall also be briefly mentioned. The mapping of the configuration will then include the description of the core concepts and interlinkages by following a pattern similar to the one found in generic fascism, but also including peripheral concepts, as well as a comparison with the generic configuration whenever that makes sense (comparing priority, proximity and proportionality).

The analysis of the individual configurations also encompasses two other aspects: permeability and the fascist rejections. Permeability is related to the ways in which fascism overlaps with other ideologies, including concepts that were also present in rival parties, oftentimes with distinct decontestations. This aspect is important as it allows us to deal with questions related to the hybridity of ideologies (even though dealing with hybridity is not the main goal of this study). As for the fascist rejections, they refer to the concepts that fascists rejected and the ideologies that they repudiated on the basis of those rejections. This mapping of fascist permeability and rejections in the context of a morphological analysis can only be carried out by remaining close to the texts and not reaching conclusions that are not supported by the words of the leaders.

This idea of 'rejection' is not included in the ideological analysis put forward by Freeden. However, one cannot forget that, for a time, fascism was traditionally defined, at least partially, by its rejections and negations (that is, the ideologies that fascism opposed). Thus, the first attempts to describe fascist ideology usually stressed either the importance of anti-communism or anti-liberalism, and sometimes even anti-conservatism.[27] While this study rejects a definition of fascism exclusively focused on rejections, it still acknowledges the importance of knowing what exactly fascists were opposed to and for this reason this topic shall not be left out.

Note also that this choice to treat each leader separately is a consequence of the characteristics of the conceptual morphological approach. Trying to disentangle an ideological configuration is a task that can only be carried out by looking individually at each bearer of a configuration (be it an individual, a party, a regime, or simply an ideological tradition). The concepts of a given configuration interlink in such a manner that it does not allow for any other feasible option. In other words, if one wants to discover the disposition of the ideological 'room' of, for instance, Adolf Hitler, one must treat Adolf Hitler individually. To not lose sense of the wider scope, as was already mentioned, a final chapter will be later added to discuss the general conclusions that can be drawn from the individual analyses.

It is true that, to a certain extent, this study puts more emphasis in stability and fixity rather than fluidity. Surely, ideological fluidity is dealt with when studying the permutations of different countries, and when acknowledging that different arrangements can stem from different ideological competitive spaces. But the main goal remains – it is still that of finding a single configuration for the leader of each movement. However, we argue that the main tenets of the movement can be grasped by focusing on one major definitive text with core ideas, even if it becomes impossible to account for all the reconfigurations that took place after the writing of the text. To track the full development of the movement would be a task that could endanger the feasibility of this study, and that is why it is preferable to restrict the conceptual analysis to a single text.

14  *Introduction*

The reasons that justify the choice of the leaders will be better explained in each chapter. Throughout this book, it will also be explained how some problems were solved; for instance, the problems that arose when a leader did not have any major work. Nevertheless, we can now reveal which leaders were chosen. Since, at this stage, the generic configuration has not yet been disentangled, it is not possible to identify which movements of the 20s and 30s could be classified as fascists. For this reason, the choices were based on the typology presented by Stanley Payne.[28] Thus, the leaders to be included are the following:

> *Adolf Hitler*, leader of the National Socialist German Workers' Party (*Nationalsozialistische Deutsche Arbeiterpartei* – NSDAP). The focus will be placed on the infamous book *My Struggle* (*Mein Kampf* – MK), which gained an inescapable status among the followers of the Nazi leader since it contained the main political principles that guided Hitler's actions.
> *Oswald Mosley*, leader of the British Union of Fascists (BUF). The goal is to analyse the book *The Greater Britain* (GB) for it was written when Mosley had just converted to fascism and it contains the main tenets and ideological goals of the movement that he was about to lead.
> *Francisco Rolão Preto*, leader of the Portuguese National Syndicalist Movement (*Nacional Sindicalismo* – NS). In this case, Preto does not have one major work. Thus, it was necessary to choose a series of texts and pamphlets written when he was leading his fascist movement. Since all these texts were written around the same time, they easily perform the function of the major work of the other leaders.
> *José Antonio Primo de Rivera*, leader of the Spanish Falange of the Councils of the National Syndicalist Offensive (*Falange Española de las Juntas de Ofensiva Nacional Sindicalista* – FE de las JONS). Since he too does not have one major work and his movement went through different phases, it becomes particularly difficult to disentangle a definitive ideological configuration for this leader. For this reason, it is preferable to recur to an anthology published after his death which contains the most relevant quotations from his speeches and writings. More will be said about this choice in due time.
> *Corneliu Codreanu*, leader of the Romanian Iron Guard (*Garda de Fier* – GF). This leader is the author of *For my Legionaries* (*Pentru Legionari* – PL), which is sometimes referred to as a Romanian version of MK. Given this epithet, it is legitimate to assume that, in this book, one will find the most definitional features of the Romanian variant of fascism.
> *Marcél Déat*, leader of the National Popular Rally (*Rassemblement National Populaire* – RNP). The focus of analysis will be the book *The Unique Party* (*Le Parti Unique* – PU), which was written in 1942, when he was about to convert to fascism and had created a party with the aim of influencing French politics. It is a text that contains important

insights about the thought of this ex-socialist who adhered to fascism. *Benito Mussolini*, leader of the Italian National Fascist Party (*Partito Nazionale Fascista* – PNF). The choice of placing the first fascist leader in the last chapter is due to its specific characteristics. In it, rather than analysing one single text in order to disentangle a fixed configuration, some fundamental moments of the Italian fascist movement will be subject of analysis. With it, the goal is to analyse how Mussolini's configuration developed in the first years of fascism and, in order to accomplish it, it will be necessary to use the *Opera Omnia*, which contain all the texts written by the Italian leader.

The fact that these texts were produced in very different contexts (going from the end of the 10s in the case of Mussolini to the epoch of WWII in the case of Déat) not only does not represent a problem, but rather serves to show how this approach can be used to grasp permutations emerging from the most varied places and times. Independently of when the texts were written, they shall display both the core features of fascism and specific interlinkages that arose due to contextual influence.

Finally, after taking all these steps, the final chapter will draw some general conclusions bearing in mind the analysis of each leader and the guidelines of the generic configuration. In other words, the first goal is to disentangle the ideological disposition of a 'room' that can be called 'generic fascism' and then proceed to the disentangling of the disposition of each leader's 'room'. Then, a final conclusive chapter shall resume all that has been written about the individual leaders and draw some final conclusions about the way fascist leaders structured the ideology of their movement and articulated their concepts. For instance, it will be possible to arrive at some conclusions related to peripheral concepts, contradictions, permeability and rejections. Likewise, there will also be an opportunity to change the initial generic configuration if the analyses of leaders show that the initial configuration is not the most fitted to understand generic fascism. In this final chapter and after altering our generic configuration if that becomes necessary, we will try to use the core concepts to arrive at our own definition of fascism; that is, a sentence (like the one that Griffin arrived at, but probably longer) that contains the key features of fascism. This will be the main contribution that this study of the leaders can bring to this field.

## Notes

1 Salvatore Garau, *Fascism and Ideology: Italy, Britain and Norway* (London, Routledge, 2015), 1.
2 Adrian Lyttelton, 'Concluding Remarks' in António Costa Pinto, Ed., *Rethinking the Nature of Fascism: Comparative Perspectives* (London, Routledge, 2010), 273.
3 Garau, *Fascism and Ideology*, 10–11.

## 16  Introduction

4 Stein Ugelvik Larsen, 'Decomposition and Recomposition of Theories: How to Arrive at Useful Ideas Explaining Fascism' in António Costa Pinto, Ed., *Rethinking the Nature of Fascism: Comparative Perspectives* (London, Routledge, 2010), 40–43.
5 According to Eatwell, 'One key problem in constructing fascist ideology is whether the focus should be mainly on individual fascists (writings and speeches) or whether the emphasis should be on movements and regime policies-the types of problems studied more by historians. Some individuals (usually not leaders) can provide a high level of thought, of interest to the academic political theorist, but it is not clear how, indeed whether, these influenced movements and regimes'. Roger Eatwell, 'Ideologies: Approaches and Trends' in Roger Eatwell and Anthony Wright, Eds., *Contemporary Political Ideologies* (London, Pinter Publishers, 1994), 10.
6 Stanley Payne, *A History of Fascism: 1914–1945* (Madison, University Press of Wisconsin, 1995), 491.
7 George Mosse, *The Fascist Revolution: Toward a General Theory of Fascism* (New York, Howard Fertig Pub, 1999), 37.
8 António Costa Pinto and Stein Ugelvik Larsen, 'Conclusion: Fascism, Dictators, and Charisma' in António Costa Pinto, Roger Eatwell, and Stein Ugelvik Larsen, Eds., *Charisma and Fascism in Interwar Europe* (London: Routledge, 2014), 255.
9 Ibid., 256.
10 To read more about the study of fascism outside Europe, see Stein Ugelvik Larsen (ed.), *Fascism Outside Europe: The European Impulse Against Domestic Conditions in the Diffusion of Global Fascism* (New York: Social Science Monographs, 2001). To read more about Plínio Salgado and Brazilian fascism, see Hélgio Trindade, *Integralismo: o fascismo brasileiro da década de 30* (São Paulo, Difel, 1974). As to Nakano Seigo and Japanese fascism, see Leslie R. Oates, *Populist Nationalism in Pre-War Japan: A Biography of Nakano Seigo* (London, Routledge, 1985).
11 Roger Griffin, *The Nature of Fascism* (London, Routledge, 1993), 44.
12 Nevertheless, we find some major disagreements in works like David Renton, *Fascism: Theory and Practice* (London, Pluto Press, 1999); or Robert Paxton, *The Anatomy of Fascism* (London, Vintage Books, 2005).
13 The complete definition by Griffin is worth quoting in full. According to this author, this consensus accepts that fascism is 'a genuinely revolutionary, trans-class form of anti-liberal, and in the last analysis, anti-conservative nationalism. As such it is an ideology deeply bound up with modernization and modernity, one which has assumed a considerable variety of external forms to adapt itself to the particular historical and national context in which it appears, and has drawn a wide range of cultural and intellectual currents, both left and right, anti-modern and pro-modern, to articulate itself as a body of ideas, slogans, and doctrine. In the inter-war period it manifested itself primarily in the form of an elite-led "armed party" which attempted, mostly unsuccessfully, to generate a populist mass movement through a liturgical style of politics and a programme of radical policies which promised to overcome a threat posed by international socialism, to end the degeneration affecting the nation under liberalism, and to bring about a radical renewal of its social, political and cultural life as part of what was widely imagined to be the new era being inaugurated in Western civilization. The core mobilizing myth of fascism which conditions its ideology, propaganda, style of politics and actions is the vision of the nation's imminent rebirth from decadence' Roger Griffin, 'The Palingenetic Core of Generic Fascist Ideology' in Alessandro Campi, Ed., *Che Cos'è il Fascismo? Interpretazioni e Prospettive di Ricerche* (Roma, Ideazoni, 2003), 97.

14 Michel Dobry, 'Desperately Seeking 'Generic Fascism': Some Discordant Thoughts on the Academic Recycling of Indigenous Categories' in António Costa Pinto, Ed., *Rethinking the Nature of Fascism: Comparative Perspectives*, 75.
15 Payne rigorously distinguishes between what he calls the three faces of authoritarian nationalism in the interwar period, of which fascist movements constituted the most extreme expression. The details of this typology shall not concern us here, but we can mention, for instance, that according to it the Portuguese nationalist parties and organizations in this epoch included an Authoritarian Conservative Right (represented in Salazar in its party, the National Union), a Radical Right (the Integralists) and a Fascist Movement (National Syndicalism). Payne, *A History of Fascism: 1914–1945*, 14–19.
16 Griffin, *The Nature of Fascism*, 19.
17 As the author writes, 'in adopting this approach, fascism to an extent becomes an abstraction, with the attendant risks, in less careful hands, of reification, of treating the 'idea' as a real 'thing', a danger to which all the 'isms' are exposed'. Philip Morgan, *Fascism in Europe, 1919–1945* (London, Routledge, 2003), 1.
18 Michael Freeden, *Ideologies and Political Theory: A Conceptual Approach* (Oxford, Clarendon Press, 1996), 12.
19 Ibid., 5.
20 Ibid., 53.
21 Ibid., 4.
22 Michael Freeden, *Ideology: A Very Short Introduction* (Oxford, Oxford University Press, 2003), 64.
23 Roger Griffin, 'Fascism's New Faces (and New Facelessness) in the 'Post-fascist' Epoch' in Roger Griffin, Werner Loh and Andreas Umland, Eds., *Fascism Past and Present, West and East: An International Debate on Concepts and Cases in the Comparative of the Extreme Right* (Stuttgart, Verlag, 2014), 39.
24 Among the articles that used this approach we find Lena Berggren, 'Intellectual Fascism: Per Engdahl and the Formation of 'New-Swedish Socialism'', *BRILL*, 3 (2), 2014, 69–92; Roger Griffin, 'The post-Fascism of the Alleanza Nazionale: A Case Study in ideological Morphology', *Journal of Political Ideologies*, 1 (2), 1996,123–145.
25 Griffin, 'Fascism's New Faces (and New Facelessness) in the 'Post-fascist' Epoch', 40.
26 Freeden, *Ideology: A Very Short Introduction*, 78.
27 Juan Linz, 'Fascism' in Walter Laqueur, Ed., *Fascism: A Reader's Guide – Analyses, Interpretations, Bibliography* (Berkeley, University of California Press, 1977), 5.
28 Payne, *A History of Fascism*, 15. All the movements that we include appear in the table shown by Payne with the exception of the BUF, which later in the book is also revealed to be a fascist one according to the typology of by this historian.

## List of references

Ball, Terence and Richard Bellamy (ed.), *The Cambridge History of Twentieth-Century Political Thought* (Cambridge, Cambridge University Press, 2008).

Berggren, Lena, 'Intellectual Fascism: Per Engdahl and the Formation of 'New-Swedish Socialism', *BRILL*, 3 (2), 2014, 69–92.

Bosworth, Richard James Boon (ed.), *The Oxford Handbook of Fascism* (Oxford, Oxford University Press, 2010).

Campi, Alessandro (ed.), *Che Cos'è il Fascismo? Interpretazioni e Prospettive di Ricerche* (Roma, Ideazoni, 2003).

18  *Introduction*

Eatwell, Roger, *Fascism: A History* (London, Penguin Books, 1997).
Eatwell, Roger and Anthony Wright (eds.), *Contemporary Political Ideologies* (London, Pinter Publishers, 1994).
Festenstein, Matthew and Michael Kenny (ed.), *Political Ideologies: A Reader and Guide* (Oxford, Oxford University Press, 2005).
Freeden, Michael, *Ideologies and Political Theory: A Conceptual Approach* (Oxford, Clarendon Press, 1996).
Freeden, Michael (ed.), *Reassessing Political Ideologies: The Durability of Dissent* (London, Routledge, 2001).
Freeden, Michael, *Ideology: A Very Short Introduction* (Oxford, Oxford University Press, 2003).
Freeden, Michael, Lyman T. Sargent, and Marc Stears (ed.), *The Oxford Handbook of Political Ideologies* (Oxford, Oxford University Press, 2015).
Garau, Salvatore, *Fascism and Ideology: Italy, Britain and Norway* (London, Routledge, 2015).
Gentile, Emilio, *The Origins of Fascist Ideology: 1918–1925* (New York, Enigma Books, 2005 [1975]).
Gregor, Anthony James, *The Ideology of Fascism* (New York, Free Press, 1969).
Gregor, Anthony James, *Mussolini's Intellectuals: Fascist Social and Political Thought* (Princeton, Princeton University Press, 2005).
Griffin, Roger, *The Nature of Fascism* (London, Routledge, 1993).
Griffin, Roger (ed.), *Fascism* (Oxford, Oxford University, 1995).
Griffin, Roger, 'The Post-Fascism of the Alleanza Nazionale: A Case Study in Ideological Morphology', *Journal of Political Ideologies*, *1* (2), 1996, 123–145.
Griffin, Roger, Werner Loh and Andreas Umland (eds.), *Fascism Past and Present, West and East: An International Debate on Concepts and Cases in the Comparative of the Extreme Right* (Stuttgart, Verlag, 2014).
Griffiths, Richard, *Fascism* (London, Continuum Intl Pub Group, 2006).
Hayes, Paul, *Fascism* (Crows Nest, Australia, Allen & Unwin, 1973).
Heywood, Andrew, *Political Ideologies* (London, Palgrave-Macmillan, 2012).
Iordachi, Constantin, 'Fascism in Interwar East Central and Southeastern Europe: Toward a New Transnational Research Agenda', *East-Central Europe, 37*, 2010, 161–213.
Laqueur, Walter (ed.), *Fascism: A Reader's Guide – Analyses, Interpretations, Bibliography* (Berkeley, University of California Press, 1977).
Laqueur, Walter, *Fascism: Past, Present and Future* (Oxford, Oxford University Press, 1996).
Larsen, Stein Ugelvik (ed.), *Fascism Outside Europe: The European Impulse Against Domestic Conditions in the Diffusion of Global Fascism* (New York, Social Science Monographs, 2001).
Leopold, David, *Contemporary Movements and Ideologies* (New York, McGraw-Hill, 1996).
Mann, Michael, *Fascists* (Cambridge, Cambridge University Press, 2004).
Milza, Pierre, *Les Fascismes* (Paris, Éd. du Seuil, 1991).
Morgan, Philip, *Fascism in Europe, 1919-1945* (London, Routledge, 2003).
Mosse, George, *The Fascist Revolution: Toward a General Theory of Fascism* (New York, Howard Fertig Pub, 1999).
Neiberg, Michael, (ed.), *Fascism* (London, Routledge, 2006).

Nolte, Ernst, *Three Faces of Fascism: Action Française, Italian Fascism, National Socialism* (New York, Holt, Rinehart and Winston, 1966).

Oates, Leslie, *Populist Nationalism in Pre-War Japan: A Biography of Nakano Seigo* (London, Routledge, 1985).

Passmore, Kevin, *Fascism: A Very Short Introduction* (Oxford, Oxford University Press, 2014).

Paxton, Robert, *The Anatomy of Fascism* (London, Vintage Books, 2005).

Payne, Stanley, *A History of Fascism: 1914–1945* (Madison, University Press of Wisconsin, 1995).

Pinto, António Costa (ed.), *Rethinking the Nature of Fascism: Comparative Perspectives* (London, Routledge, 2010).

Pinto, António Costa, *The Nature of Fascism Revisited* (New York, Columbia University Press, 2012).

Pinto, António Costa (ed.), *Corporatism and Fascism: The Corporatist Wave in Europe* (London, Routledge, 2017), 5.

Pinto, António Costa and Aristotle Kallis (ed.), *Rethinking Fascism and Dictatorship in Europe* (London, Palgrave Macmillan, 2014).

Pinto, António Costa, Roger Eatwell, and Stein Ugelvik Larsen (ed.), *Charisma and Fascism in Interwar Europe* (London: Routledge, 2014).

Renton, David, *Fascism: Theory and Practice* (London, Pluto Press, 1999).

Roberts, David, *Fascist Interactions: Proposals for a New Approach to Fascism and Its Era, 1919–1945* (New York, Berghahn, 2016).

Sargent, Lyman Tower, *Contemporary Political Ideologies: A Comparative Analysis* (Boston, Wadsworth Publishing, 2009).

Steger, Manfred, *The Rise of the Global Imaginary: Political Ideologies from the French Revolution* (2008).

Trindade, Hélgio, *Integralismo: o fascismo brasileiro da década de 30* (São Paulo, Difel, 1974).

Vincent, Andrew, *Modern Political Ideologies* (New York, Wiley-Blackwell, 2010).

Weber, Eugen, *Varieties of Fascism* (Florida, Krieger Pub Co., 1982 [1964]).

# 1 The conceptual structure of 'generic fascism'

Seven core concepts

The first fascist organization was officially formed on 23 March 1919 in Milan. Its name was *Fasci Italiani di Combattimento* and it was led by former socialist Benito Mussolini. After months of stagnation, the movement began to grow in 1920, benefiting from the political turmoil of the time and the fear of a revolutionary uprising by socialist forces. Fascist squads and their violent methods were viewed as effective defense against the supposed perils brought about by the left, especially in rural areas. After a few years, Fascism became so relevant that Benito Mussolini had enough political capital to be appointed Prime Minister in October 1922. This was after a sham demonstration that became known as the 'March on Rome'. It is still highly debatable whether the 1919 program of this organization already contained a fully-formed permutation of fascist ideology or if the conceptual configuration of this ideology was still in the making. Roger Griffin, for instance, sees the *Fasci* as the first political movement that displayed a variant of 'palingenetic ultra-nationalism'. Emilio Gentile, on the other hand, contends that what came to be understood as fascist ideology was only completely formed in October 1921, when the movement was transformed into a party.

For our purposes, while we also consider that fascist ideology was still in formation (as shall be seen in a later chapter), we nevertheless use the date of 23 March 1919 as the the beginning of historical fascism. For this reason, this date marks the beginning of the period to which our attention must be turned in the search for a generic fascism. As to the milestone that marks its end, we place it at the end of the month of April 1945, because the leader of Nazi Germany Adolf Hitler took his own life on 30 April 1930, just a few days after the death of his ally Benito Mussolini. Even if the dissolution of the Third Reich would officially only happen on 23 May 1945, the death of the German leader demarcates in practice the end of the era of fascism, a denouement which came about with the complete defeat of the Axis regimes in a world war that fascists themselves had seen as a fundamental step to complete their goals of European renewal.

Before proceeding to displaying our preliminary generic configuration, it is necessary to briefly account for the most relevant interpretations of fascism that came to light during the preceding decades, as these may be important to have in mind when trying to reach conclusions about the concepts that define this ideology.

## Main interpretations and definitions of fascism

Fascism caught the attention of observers from the moment it appeared. However, during the era of interwar fascism, the majority of the authors who tried to make sense of this phenomenon lacked the objective distance that is often necessary to produce a careful research. Furthermore, their goals were practical rather than theoretical, since they had the purpose of defeating a political force that endangered the type of society that they envisioned to create or maintain. At the time, political goals were more important than academic research, and for this reason the first theories that tried to explain fascism have limited value to this study.

Italian historian Renzo de Felici became known for synthetising the most important theories of those early days. According to him, it is possible to point out three main interpretations. The Liberal interpretation, held by intellectuals such as Benedetto Croce, tended to see fascism as a 'moral disease' and a parenthesis that interrupted the march towards progress that western societies had been witnessing since the 19th century.[1] The 'radical democratic' interpretation (as it is called by de Felici), on the other hand, saw fascism as the product of the development of some countries and of the imperfections of their elites.[2] As for Marxist interpretations, they are too complex to be mentioned in full detail, but it can be said that they generally tried to make sense of fascism by relating it to the class struggle between the bourgeoisie and the proletariat in that specific stage of capitalism.[3] The writings of the Frankfurt School are also worth mentioning, as they fused Marxism with psychoanalysis, proposing an interpretation of fascism focused on sexual repression and the alienation of modern industrialised societies.[4]

One characteristic that all these theories seemed to have in common was the tendency to downplay fascist ideology and see it as an irrelevant component, even if there are some exceptions like the texts by the Marxist thinker Antonio Gramsci. Even in the period that immediately followed WWII, most studies still displayed a tendency to overlook ideology. Some of them also lacked objectivity and academic rigour since they emerged during the Cold War and were affected by ideological bias. One interpretation, which was undoubtedly influenced by this environment, was the theory of Totalitarianism, which sought to establish a parallel between the Nazi and the Soviet regimes and contended that Nazism represented a whole new form of ruling in which the state mobilised the masses trough ideology and regulated every aspect of the intimate life of the citizens by appealing to a major historical goal (whether racial struggle, class struggle, or any other).[5]

The first groundbreaking studies that placed their focus on ideology were produced in the 60s by authors such as Eugen Weber, George Mosse and A. James Gregor. Worthy of a more detailed mentioning is Ernst Nolte's *The Three Faces of Fascism*, who concluded that fascism is 'anti-Marxism which seeks to destroy the enemy by the evolvement of a radically-opposed and yet related ideology and by the use of almost identical and yet typically modified methods, always, however within the unyielding framework of national self-assertion and autonomy'.[6] After this impactful study, other works emerged, such as the ones by Zeev Sternhell, who wrote about the origins of fascism in the intellectual milieu of the revolt against decadence that began in 19th century France. However, researchers like Gilbert Allardyce still showed skepticism about the feasibility of trying to define a wider phenomenon called 'fascism', defending that the word could only really be applied to the movement and regime that existed within the Italian borders.

It was in this context that Roger Griffin wrote the groundbreaking book-which was already mentioned, *The Nature of Fascism*. Published in the 90s, it reasserted the possibility of using an operative definition of 'generic fascism' that could encompass permutations of the ideology that emerged outside of Italy. He also famously defined fascism as a 'palingenetic form of populist ultra-nationalism'.[7] In the years that followed, several other researchers developed their own definition, each proposing relevant points of agreement and disagreement to Griffin's theory. Thus, Stanley Payne developed a typological description of fascism that included ideology and goals, the fascist negations, and features of style and organisation.[8] Roger Eatwell concluded that fascism 'sought to create a 'new man' (especially an elite) who would forge a holistic nation and radical Third Way state'.[9] Philip Morgan, on the other hand, stated that 'fascist movements were radical hypernationalist cross-class movements with a distinctive militarist organization and activist political style', and that they sought the regeneration of the nation through violent means and often with the goal of territorial expansionism.[10] As for Michael Mann, he defined fascism as 'the pursuit of a transcendent and cleansing nation-statism through paramilitarism', thus pinpointing five fundamental components: nationalism, cult of the state, transcendence, cleansing, and paramiltarism.[11] One final author that can be added to this list of important researchers is Aristotle Kallis, who sought to construct an explanatory model that took into account not only ideological principles but also cultural, social, and political factors, to grasp the outcomes of specific regimes (for instance, according to Kallis's typology, the way fascist movements came to power and the type of alliances they made could influence the progress of the regime).[12]

All the authors and definitions in the last paragraph will be important, since the generic configuration will be partially based on their conclusions. This does not mean that only secondary sources will be used (nor even that these will be the only secondary sources that will be used) but that, in the works of these authors, one finds a relevant theoretical body that shall help to sustain the conclusions that are about to be presented.

## The core concepts of fascism

At this point, we are ready to present the first tentative configuration of generic fascism. Since the conceptual approach leaves some room to the personal choices and the subjectivity of the researcher, we recognise that this configuration is open to debate and contestation. Nevertheless, to try to minimise as much as possible this subjectivity, we shall always remain close to the actual fascist sources and avoid drawing conclusions that are not supported by the words of fascists themselves. Each concept that is included will be justified with a discussion about its centrality in the fascist configuration.

The preliminary conceptual configuration of generic fascism is composed of the following seven core concepts: **Nation**, **State**, **Corporatism**, **Revolution**, **Authority**, **Violence** and **Empire**.[13] In the following sections, these concepts will be discussed separately. Adjacent concepts, which will be presented alongside the discussion of core concepts, will also be paid due attention. Finally, the interlinkages that take place within this conceptual configuration shall also be pinpointed: both the interlinkages between core concepts as well as the interlinkages between core and adjacent concepts.

### *Nation*

Apart from Roger Griffin, who saw ultra-nationalism as a core component of fascist ideology, all other definitions include this concept or at least some type of reference to the **Nation**. This is so because nationalism is one of the most obvious elements of fascism; that is, one of those concepts that cannot be left out without this ideology being transformed into something else. Such a statement is an uncontroversial one and virtually every researcher would agree with it. Therefore, we consider the **Nation** as a core concept of fascist ideology because all the goals held by fascism were related to the revitalization of the national community, implying a commitment to the national cause on the part of fascist followers. This means that, in the conceptual configuration of fascism, all the other concepts somehow interlink with and contribute to further understanding how fascists conceived the **Nation** and which type of transformations they wanted to perform in it.

Paying attention to the words of fascists themselves is enough to prove the importance of nationalism. Let us mention, for instance, the members of the Austrian Heimwehr, who met in 1930 to swear allegiance to the so called Korneuburger Oath.[14] In this event, they declared complete commitment to their fatherland, swearing that 'we want to reconstruct Austria from anew! [...] We demand from every comrade the indisputable faith in the fatherland'.[15] Examples of fascist nationalism are found in the most diverse variants, from the British fascists and their motto 'Britain first' to the French leader Jacques Doriot, who was obsessively preoccupied with the survival of the French nation in the face of the supposed menace of Stalinism. Around the time of the March on Rome, Mussolini declared that 'our myth is the nation, our myth is the greatness of the nation! And to this myth, this greatness, which we want to translate into a total reality, we subordinate everything else'.[16]

The first two adjacent concepts that we find in the vicinity of this core concept are 'Organicism' and 'Holism'. 'Organicism' refers to a worldview which sees the universe as a living organism in which all its parts play a significant function for the survival of the whole.[17] In an organicist view of the world, all sectors of society have a structured relationship between each other and the roles and rights of individuals are delimited according to the duties that everyone must fulfill. The interlinkage between the core concept of **Nation** and the adjacent concept of 'Organicism' is what allows us to conclude that fascists see the national community as a living organism dependent on the correct functioning of its vital members to survive. In some permutations of fascist ideology, the concept of 'Integralism' is used with a meaning that is similar to that of 'Organicism'.

As for the concept of 'Holism', Eatwell reminds us that 'fascism sought to homogenise the nation, rather than celebrate diversity within it'.[18] 'Holism' means seeing the **Nation** as a homogeneous entity that is devoid of internal conflicts and that transcends divisions and contradictions. This transcendental and holistic characterization of the **Nation** is perceptible in DF. According to the author of this text, the **Nation** is an idealistic and transcendental entity which unites all the values of one people, as well as the historical consciousness that that people has of itself. The **Nation** transcends materialism and acquires a spiritual dimension, for it is not constituted by 'race, nor a region geographically identified, but rather a lineage perpetuating itself historically, a multitude united by an idea, which is a will of existence and power: conscience of itself, personality'.[19]

Furthermore, the concept of 'People' is also in the vicinity of the **Nation** and it refers to the homogeneous group that inhabits it. According to Kevin Passmore, this reference to the 'People' in fascist ideology does not presuppose the existence of social cleavages within the community and can be used to appeal to any group that may feel discontented with the political establishment.[20] The 'People' is also conceived as a major force driving the **Nation** onwards. Nowhere else did this concept acquire such a relevance than in Germany, where we find the concept of 'Volk' (which can be translated as 'people') and the *Volkisch* culture. This 'Volk' was idealised as an abstract entity that surpassed time and space, and encompassed the most important characteristics of the German people, including the connection to the soil and to a timeless culture.[21]

The 'Volk' belonged to a higher idealised reality and possessed a cultural and civilisational superiority that distinguished them from any other people on earth. This adjacent concept was often used in German National Socialism, as it becomes evident if we look at Nazi periodicals like the *People's Observer* (*Völkischer Beobachter*). Even in the so-called 'left-wing' fascism of the Strasser brothers, there are references to this *Völkischer* community, for instance, when Otto Strasser states that the new Germany 'must be anchored deeply in the Volkisch nature of the German, and hence exhibit qualities which are familiar to us from the German past and from German prehistory'.[22]

Interlinking with the concept of 'People'. there is the adjacent concept of 'Race', which does not have the same preponderancy in all national permutations. However, and even if the significance of racism in the case of Italian fascism remains controversial (one of the passages from DF even seems to reject it), we find several other variants outside of Germany in which this adjacent concept is given much prominence. That is the case, for instance, of the Norwegian Vidkun Quisling, leader of the Naadjacency of the State and asserts that thesjonal Samling (NS), who warned his followers that the influence of supposedly inferior races represented a peril to the superior Nordic race. As he said, 'Our civilization, created and borne forward by the Nordic race and by Nordic elements in other races is now threatened by the devastating activities of inferior races'.[23] Likewise, Hungarian fascist Szálasi Ferenc, leader of the Arrow Cross Party, developed the concept of 'Hungarism', which attributed a mystic past and mystic qualities to the Magyar people, a race supposedly displaying the best elements of European and Asian races.[24]

It is legitimate for us to assert that fascism is inherently racist, even when it does not explicitly use this concept (even when it seems to reject it), as the decontestation of the **Nation** as an organic unity leaves no doubt about the animosity towards elements that are seen as foreigner. Nevertheless, this concept is not necessarily decontested in proximity to concepts and themes coming from Social Darwinist thought or from the ideology of the authors that contributed to the development of racist thought in the Western world (such as Gobineau, Édouard Drumont or Houston Stewart Chamberlain). But while these Darwinist features may be more evident in the configuration of German fascism, the concept of 'Race' still appears in the configuration of generic fascism, even if sometimes it remains in the periphery. When Mussolini's regime formally adopted racism, which happened in the second half of the 30s, the official version of Fascist ideology witnessed a process of reconfiguration in which this peripheral concept traveled from the margin to a place closer to the core.

## *State*

Several definitions of fascist ideology include the **State** as a fundamental concept, which is the case of Payne's typology. More importantly, Michael Mann included the cult of the **State** as one of the five distinctive features of fascism. According to him, the **State** in fascism 'involved both goal and organisational form. Fascists worshiped state power'.[25] Therefore, this is a core concept because fascism implied a reconceptualization of the **State** and an alteration of the functions that were attributed to it in liberal ideology.

26  *The conceptual structure of 'generic fascism'*

To alter the nature of the liberal **State** and strengthen its powers was a core goal of all varieties of fascism, independently of how far the different variants thought that this strengthening should go (something which could vary substantially).

It is thus hardly surprising that in texts by fascists such as Jacques Doriot we find the expression of the desire for a powerful **State**. As he says,

> If we had a State able to carry out this recovery it would be one strong enough to reorganise France and the Empire. It would restructure the economy of France by creating professional organizations which regulate problems of production. It would reorganise France into large economic-administrative regions. Once its authority had been restored it would be strong enough to decentralise the outmoded and antiquated system of administration, which is now stifling the country instead of stimulating activity.[26]

The core concepts of **Nation** and **State** interlink and both have in their vicinity the adjacent concepts of 'Organicism' and 'Holism', which we have already discussed. This happens because fascists conceive the **State** as the instrument necessary for the **Nation** to achieve conciliation between its opposite parts. If fascism sees the **Nation** as an organic entity, the **State** is the instrument that allows for it to organise according to organicist principles. Furthermore, the DF also acknowledges the interlinkage between **Nation** and **State** when its author says that 'it is the state which transcends the brief limits of individual life and represents the imminent consciousness of the nation'.[27]

The **State** also has the function of conducting the economic, political, spiritual, and social life of the **Nation**. For this reason, it also interlinks with adjacent concepts such as 'Order' (for it must have the function of restoring harmony in the national territory) and 'Dirigisme', for it has the function of directing the political and economic tasks. According to French fascist George Valois, founder of *Le Faisceau,* 'Dirigisme' means 'a unitary national State which provides over the rational organization of production based on a systematic collaboration of science, and industry in turn provides the basis for social justice'.[28]

In another dimension, authors like Emilio Gentile and Michael Burleigh associate the **State** with the concept of 'Totalitarianism'. Even though this term was first created by anti-fascists, it was appropriated by some fascists, who used it in a more positive way.[29] The concept of 'Totalitarianism' thus relates to the notion that the community should be unified and be turned into cohesive wholeness through the use of a strong **State** that allows no dissent. This notion is perhaps best noticed in the notorious quote attributed to Mussolini: 'All within the state, nothing outside the state, nothing against the state'. The goal of the Totalitarian **State** in fascist ideology is to synthetise and unite all the opposites within it, reinserting all the fragmented parts in a new whole, which is an aim also mentioned several times by the authors of DF. According to them, the **State** must thus be a 'synthesis and unity of all values'.[30]

As already mentioned, the concept of 'Totalitarianism' was also the base of a theory that was particularly popular during the Cold War. While not accepting the main implications of this theory, we still see this concept as an important one to help understand fascism and the role that fascists intended to attribute to their new type of **State**. Contrary to what is traditionally held by this theory, we also believe that the concept can be applied to the Italian variant of fascism and not only to German National Socialism. Independently of the practical goals of the regime, Italian Fascism, after all, had totalitarian goals, just like many other fascist organizations that were never able to conquer executive power. David D. Roberts had recently also acknowledged the importance of the concept of 'Totalitarianism', going as far as seeing it as the main category that distinguishes fascism from other competing ideologies of the time. According to him, the choice of departing towards a totalitarian direction was the main feature that characterised fascism at a time when the right was divided on the lines of the binomial authoritarianism-totalitarianism. While the generic configuration of our book does not hold this concept to have such centrality in fascist ideology, it still places it (at least for now) in the adjacency of the **State** and asserts that the totalitarian goals of fascism are particularly important to have a clearer idea of the precise decontestation of this core concept.

## *Corporatism*

In his typology of fascism, Stanley Payne states that one of the most important goals of this ideology is the 'organization of a new highly regulated, multiclass, integrated national economic structure' that many times referred to a national corporatist organization of society.[31] Therefore, we choose to insert the concept of **Corporatism** in the generic configuration because it holds the key to understanding how fascists envisioned the restructuring of the national community on a political and (most importantly) economic level. As shall be seen, by constituting an alternative to both capitalism and communism, **Corporatism** is the concept that explains why fascists were believed to be constructing what Roger Eatwell called a radical 'Third Way'.

Nevertheless, it must be noted that this concept was at the time a highly contested one. Several ideologies made use of it, inserting it in configurations which had slightly different meanings. The importance of the battle for meaning surrounding this concept is evident if we evoke the many authors that wrote about it, a group in which stands out, for instance, the Romanian thinker Mihail Manoilesco (himself not a fascist but a proponent of radical right ideologies), who even wrote that 'the twentieth century will be the century of corporatism just as the nineteenth century was the century of liberalism'. Nevertheless, the concept of **Corporatism** can have distinct functions within different configurations: there are differences, for instance, between Catholic corporatism (influenced by Leon XIII's encyclical *Rerum Novarum* and relying less on the power of the state) and fascist corporatism, not to mention that some varieties of left wing socialism and many other ideologies have also developed their own version of **Corporatism**.[32]

Therefore, it is important to know not only what **Corporatism** means in general, but also the interlinkages that surround it in the specific context of fascist ideology. Philippe Schmitter, after discussing several possible definitions of **Corporatism**, decided to describe it as

> a system of interest representation in which the constituent units are organised into a limited number of singular, compulsory, noncompetitive, hierarchically ordered and functionally differentiated categories. These constituent unities are created, or at least recognised or licensed, by **State** power and are granted a 'deliberate representational monopoly within their respective categories in exchange for observing certain controls on their selection of leaders and articulation of demands and support.[33]

In a first dimension, fascist **Corporatism** interlinks with the core concept of **State** and with the adjacent concepts of 'Organicism' and 'Holism', for it represents a 'vision of political community in which the component parts of society harmoniously combine'.[34] Also according to Costa Pinto, 'A central ideal of corporatist thinkers was the organic nature of society in the political and economic sphere'.[35] The central idea surrounding this concept is that it is not only possible but necessary to create a form of 'Organic-State' that expresses a corporatist nature and shall be a new form of political representation. In the words of Alexander Raven Thomson, ideologue of British fascism, the **Corporate State** 'is the organic form through which the nation can find expression [...] It is also the means of self-expression of the nation as a corporate whole in the attainment of its national destiny'.[36]

The adjacent concept 'Class Conciliation' also appears in its vicinity, for the defense of a corporatist system was accompanied by the attempt to convert workers to nationalist ideas. Fascist leaders and ideologues, rather than rejecting working class demands or downsizing the concern for their situation, preferred to appeal to the workers on the basis that their needs would best be met within the scope of the national community than with the help of communist or socialist ideologies. This is evident when Elias Simojoki of the Finish Patriotic People's Movement (*Isänmaallinen kansanliike* – IKL) stated that the new society will be one where 'class hatred has been eradicated' and that the most important mission of the national movement is to 'win the soul of the working people back to the Fatherland'.[37]

Rejecting both capitalist laissez-faire and the Soviet planned economy, fascists also used the adjacent concept of 'Dirigisme' for they wanted the

**State** to organise and conduct the economic activity of the **Nation** without falling into complete economic **State** control. At the time, many believed that fascism (or other ideologies which also incorporated the concept of corporatism within their configuration) 'would provide the means to solve the problems of both liberalism and socialism in a new synthesis that would resolve the spiritual crisis of Europe, as well as the economic split between capitalism and socialism'.[38] Among the main fascist economic goals are to harmonise, control, and direct the national production. In the words of Raven Thomson, the 'balanced system of co-operation between the factors of economic life must emerge from the present conflict between producer and consumer, debtor and creditor, employer and worker'.[39]

It is important to note, however, that the highly contested nature of this concept made it a controversial one even among the different variants of fascism within the same country. That happened even in the case of Italian fascism. However, when it comes to **Corporatism** in the Italian regime, the best text to mention is not the DF, but rather the *Charter of Labour* (*Carta del Lavoro*), a piece of legislation promulgated by the Fascist Grand Council in 1927 with the goal of installing a **Corporatist** system in Italy. This document explicitly created a set of institutions which should have a role to play in harmonizing the different elements of the organic **Nation**. For instance, in Article 5, there is a mention of the Magistracy of Labour, which is 'the organ with which the State intervenes and regulates the controversy of labor, whether they concern the observance of the pacts and the other existing norms, or the determination of new working conditions'.[40] This piece of legislation became very influential and many movements in different countries adopted its most important features in their programs, sometimes practically copying what was written in the original document. Thus, the concept of **Corporatism** is relevant not only to understanding the conceptual configuration of fascism, but also the transnational relations that took place between different varieties of fascism.[41]

At this point, it is relevant to mention that, as it is generally acknowledged by most researchers, many variants of fascism made little use of the concept of **Corporatism,** often defending instead an economic structure that they could either call 'national socialist' or 'national syndicalist', which did not necessarily correspond to the type of organization displayed in the *Carta del Lavoro*. Such assertion should be enough to exclude this concept from our list of core features of fascism. However, and since the alternative concepts played a function that was very similar to **Corporatism** in the permutations in which they appear, we still argue that it is important to reserve a space for some correspondent concept in the generic configuration of fascism. For now, and for the sake of convenience, we will still use the concept of **Corporatism**, even though we are aware that this is one of the features that may need revision after the analysis of the leaders.

### Revolution

According to Eugen Weber, when writing specifically about Nazism, 'The Nazi revolution held out the ultimate revolutionary promise: changer la vie'.[42] This assertion, however, is not applicable to the German variant only. According to Payne, 'Fascism was the most revolutionary form of nationalism in Europe at that point in history', which means that the goal of 'changing life' was indeed a common feature of the permutations of fascist ideology emerging during the interwar period.[43] At the core of the ideological goals of fascism, there was a deep desire to transform society and carry out profound changes concerning societal norms, values, and beliefs. We shall call this desire for social transformation '**Revolution**' (something which fascists themselves often did too) and we will consider it a core concept of the fascist configuration. **Revolution** is a core concept for it holds the key to understanding what kind of transformations fascists considered to be among their primary goals.

To understand what kind of **Revolution** fascists aimed at, it is first important to notice that, according to Payne, this was characterised 'by its culture of philosophical idealism, willpower, vitalism, and mysticism'.[44] Thus, there was a mystic and spiritual side to fascism that rose above material and worldly matters which is expressed, for instance, by Belgian leader Léon Dégrelle, when he says that 'it is only the quality and vibrancy of the soul which matters, the capacity for giving oneself unstintingly, its will to place an ideal above all other considerations in a spirit of total disinterest'.[45] This spiritualism is also evident in the DF, when its author writes that 'to Fascism, the world is not this material world which appears at the surface in which man is an individual separated from everyone else and standing alone'.[46] This feature gave fascist **Revolution** a meaning that is absent from other rival ideological configurations. Furthermore, this core concept closely interlinks with the core concept of **Nation,** for every alteration to be performed implied a change in the way the national community lived. This national and spiritual side of fascist revolutionary goals led Elias Simojoki to write about a 'revolution of the Finnish Heart'.[47]

The best description of the fascist **Revolution** is found in Roger Griffin, who famously used the word 'Palingenesis' to define its nature. This term, 'deriving from *palin* (again, anew) and *genesis* (creation, birth), refers to the sense of a new start or of regeneration after a phase of crisis or decline which can be associated just as much with mystical (for example the Second Coming) as secular realities (for example the New Germany)'.[48] Thus, in the context of a secular political ideology, 'Palingenesis' refers to the idea of inaugurating a new society, bringing about a turning point in the history of a society. The term thus implies an idea of rebirth and, even though it is not usually seen as a traditional political concept (Griffin calls it a 'myth'), with the lack of a better word to express the idea that is meant to be contained in it, it shall be here considered as an adjacent concept. Thus, the main difference between our generic configuration and Griffin's definition is that the concept is not placed at the core of fascist ideology, but rather in its adjacency, in this manner serving to delimit the meaning of the 'palingenetic **Revolution**'.

Still according to Griffin, the palingenetic conception of the **Revolution** implies the perception that the **Nation** is facing a current state of crisis and decadence.[49] However, fascist ideology is not limited to the acknowledgment of such decay nor to inevitable pessimism, for it envisions a solution for such crisis. It is precisely the conception of the national rebirth as a solution to the crisis of decadence that places the concept of **Revolution** at the core of fascism, for the rebirth is seen as a fundamental transformation of national communities and even as the dawn of a new era. Furthermore, fascists somehow conceived the present state of decay as containing the seeds or at least the foreshadowing of the new era that is dawning: the crisis reaches such overwhelming proportions that it could not but represent a catharsis after which the new society would appear.

It follows that two main features are contained in the idea of 'Palingenesis': crisis and rebirth. Liberalism, parliamentary democracy, individualism, moral degradation, free press, and the power of money are among the main causes of decay (in some racist variants, this moral corruption was also attributed to Jewish influence). A.K. Chesterton, member of the BUF, summarises this sense of decay in a paragraph which is worth quoting in full:

> Evidence of national neurosis today is only too abundant. The almost unbelievable shifts and stratagems and blundering follies of modern democratic governments represent one of its facets. The brazen and suicidal rampages of vested interests represent another. The astounding depravity of the Press represents a third. Evidence even more direct is supplied by the facile and poisonous Utopianism of the post-war period: the meaningless catchwords and slogans, the advocacy of the brave new world by human leeches sticking frantically to the bald old order, the failure of the Conservative to conserve, the inability of the progressive to progress, the murder of the intellect by the intellectuals, and above all the hanging, drawing and quartering of Peace by pacifists who in the frenzy of their hysteria howl and dance and shriek for war. All these things indicate something more than a mental or spiritual stammer; they indicate a strongly entrenched neurosis which is the spirit's cancer and the trumpeter of death.[50]

As to the idea of rebirth, it implied the surpassing of the failures of the present era, including both liberal individualism and soviet collectivism, to achieve a new type of society in which fascist principles would play a crucial role. José Streel, chief ideologue of the Belgian Rexist movement, said that, 'We are witnessing the crystallisation of what historians call the century of

32  *The conceptual structure of 'generic fascism'*

fascism or national socialism, on par with the great periods of the Middle Ages, the Renaissance, the ancient régime, and the liberal epoch'.[51]

In the vicinity of **Revolution**, we also find the adjacent concept of 'New Man', which was considered by Roger Eatwell to be one of the core ideological goals of fascism.[52] This refers to a new type of man that must surpass the flaws of present society and is reinserted in the entire national community. In this context, E. Gunther Grundel claims that 'the creative dynamic, the basic quality of the Germanic-Western cultural soul, is awakening in the dawn of its fourth day the creation of a new type of human being'.[53] This search for the 'New Man' should also 'magnify men [...] imposing virility as the ultimate quality of the type of man to be configured'.[54] Virility and masculinity are thus crucial ideas to understanding how fascists conceived the 'New Man': they wanted to recover masculinist conceptions and mentalities that, according to them, had been affected by social decay.

Ugo Spirito's thought gives us some glimpses about this adjacent concept, for he defends that fascism must create a 'homo corporativus', which was supposed to substitute the 'homo economicus' of liberalism and to be fully integrated in the community where he belonged.[55] The new fascist man would reacquire his strength and vitality through connection with the other elements of the groups of which he was part and from which he was kept separated by Liberal individualism. 'He is not a person in his own right, and not the embodiment of a class, but of his people. He does not live for himself but as an integral part of a living whole', according to E. Gunther Grundel.[56] In DF, we learn that the 'New Man' should acknowledge a set of eternal and transcendental values, which surpass the limits of time and space. Acquiring knowledge about history and its eternal laws, the 'New Man' could be aware of eternal ideals and reject materialism, and thus be able to live in a modern world and face contemporary challenges while recognizing the ideals that surpass one given historical moment.

Besides, it is also relevant to note the adjacent concept of 'Cult of Youth', for young age was seen by fascists as the virile epoch in which people are most committed to sacrifice and enact revolutionary change. Thus, fascist regimes normally created organisations that were destined to convert the young to the national cause (think of the Hitler Youth or the Italian Balilla) and praised the value of youth in songs like the Fascist hymn, 'Giovenezza', which mentions the 'Spring of Youth' ('Primavera di Belezza'). 'Youth symbolised vigour and action [...] This was the classical ideal of beauty, which had become the manly stereotype', said historian George Mosse.[57] This conception of youth is also noticeable, for instance, in the words of Sven Olof Lindhom, leader of the Swedish National Socialist Party (*Svenska nationalsocialistiska partiet* - SNSP), when he said that, 'During youth, this is how it happens: one strives for much and the ideal elevates high. If, as adult men, we had adopted this perspective, maybe it would not have had strength enough'.[58] Also, the leader of the Irish Blue Shirts (IBS), Eoin O'Duffy, states proudly that 'the Young Blueshirt is the expression of the new Ireland'.[59]

## Authority

Stanley Payne affirms that 'there was a general tendency to exalt leadership, hierarchy, and subordination, so that all fascist movements came to espouse variants of a *Führerprinzip,* deferring to the creative function of leadership'.[60] For this reason, this historian includes in his typology the tendency towards an authoritarian charismatic, personal style of command as a fundamental feature of style and organisation. However, we argue that the authoritarian features of fascism were noticeable not only in the style of leadership but also as a principle that is fundamental to understanding the organisation of society in a fascist worldview. Thus, we consider **Authority** to be a core concept of fascist ideology for it denotes an interpretation of society as a hierarchical place where discipline as a matter of principle must be maintained for those whose role is to obey and be led (the choice of this word, therefore, is not related to the binomium authoritarianism/totalitarianism). The concept of 'Hierarchy' is found in the adjacency of this core concept, and it is noticeable, for instance, in one of the most notorious fascist mottos during the Italian regime: 'believe, obey, fight' ("credere, obbedire, combattere").

Two other adjacent concepts must be mentioned when one talks about **Authority**: 'Leader' and 'Elites'. The 'Leader' refers to the charismatic chief who embodies the destiny of the **Nation** and its eternal core values, the person who shall be followed in times of crisis and despair. Let us not forget what is written by Sven Olof Lindholm when he said that 'if the people is certain that the leader performs his task maturely, that he understands them and takes care of their affairs with duty and no bargains, then no one shall miss democracy'.[61] Fascist ideology aims to create a bond between the population and the leader, for this is a necessary component for social transformation to occur. Obedience must be shown towards a leader who rises above the masses and who at the same time represents their aspirations. Furthermore, this leader must be a charismatic one and display extraordinary personal features, so that he is able to arouse an emotional commitment among the masses.

British fascist William Joyce (also known as Lord Haw Haw) shows us an example of this cult of the leader when he praises the deeds of Adolf Hitler: 'throughout the whole of his life as a leader, Adolf Hitler has shown his love for the working people [...] that this hope [for Britain's redemption] and this belief shall not prove vain there are two guarantees, for me sufficient: the greatness of Adolf Hitler and the Greater Glory of the Almighty God'.[62] German National Socialist Gottfried Benn also discussed the concept of Leader, which, according to him, represents the true disruptive element of the new ideology and the one that can bring about social transformation, for 'the leader is not the embodiment of power, and certainly not conceived as a principle of terror, but as the highest spiritual principle'.[63]

34  *The conceptual structure of 'generic fascism'*

As to the concept of 'Elites', it refers to the supposedly superior people that are destined to lead society in the fascist worldview. According to the author of DF, Italian society should be conducted by a restricted and clairvoyant group of a selected few with enough prescience to know what is best for the people as a whole. The reason why these elites would be able to command the **Nation** lay in their supposed spiritual elevation: they would be in touch with higher spiritual values and would be conscious of the historical destiny of the national community. However, one of the specific features of fascist ideology is that it does not aim to defend the interests of the established 'Elites', but rather to create a whole new elite capable of substituting the weak and decadent 'Elites' of the Liberal epoch. The emergence of the new elite is, therefore, one of the features of the palingenetic social transformation that is at the core of fascist ideology. In this sense, **Authority** interlinks with **Revolution** mostly thanks to this adjacent concept and this interlinkage carries two specific layers of meaning: the fascist **Revolution** had elitist goals (since it meant to create a new elite) but it was also elitist in its method (for the **Revolution** itself would have to be led and carried out by the ascendant new elite).

Mario Piazzesi, who was one of the participants of the March on Rome, noted in his diary how a new group, coming from an ascending petit-bourgeoisie, was willing to become a new elite in post-WWI Italy: 'New classes are forming who are leap-frogging the political and economic generations of before the war, most of them belonging to the small and middling bourgeoisie and artisan class. These have held military rank and have no intention of being absorbed back into the anonymous masses'.[64] In other cases, such as German Nazism, the concept of 'Elite' interlinks with concept of 'Race', for what the Nazis aimed at was the selection of the best members of Aryan breed to create an aristocracy of blood: that is evident, for instance, in the book *Blood and Soil* by German author Walter Darré.

*Violence*

The concept of **Violence** in fascist ideology was initially placed in its periphery but would later move to the core and, so we argue, stayed there from then onwards. The trajectory of this concept may perhaps be explained by the environment in which the Italian fascist movement evolved. Influenced by the ideas of ex-veteran soldiers who fought in WWI, fascist ideology developed its potential for violence in a context of struggle against working class insurgency and bitter fights against enemies coming from the Communist left.[65] The punitive expeditions organised by Fascist Squads soon acquired notoriety for its destructive nature. Allen Douglas, for instance, has no qualms in stressing the importance of **Violence** to the development of fascist ideology:

*The conceptual structure of 'generic fascism'* 35

Fascism, violence and storm troopers: in the popular mind the three are inseparable. The same could be said, on a more sophisticated plane, of the scholarly discourse on fascism. In an area in which so little consensus reigns, this seems to be one of the few points of near-universal agreement. Most catalogues of 'fascist minima' have, for example, included paramilitary formations; and fascism has been seen to have a predilection for violence both on the level of ideology and that of tactics.[66]

However, oftentimes fascists themselves claimed not to praise **Violence** for **Violence's** sake but only use it in cases of self-defense. It was Mussolini himself who wrote that fascist squads 'do not preach violence for the sake of violence, but reply to all violence by passing to the counterattack'.[67] Such a statement coming from the very first leader of fascism could at a first glance be interpreted as a sign that fascism, contrary to general perception, did not make such a big use of this concept and reserved the calls for violence to acts of self-defense.

Nevertheless, one must not forget that such justifications could often be distorted rationalisations destined to present as self-protection acts that could very well be pure and simple aggressions. Thus, some caution is needed whenever one finds this type of explanations, for this is a case in which one should not be so naïve as to take fascist affirmations at face value. Besides, the importance of the concept of **Violence** can also be noticeable in cases when, while not explicitly using the word, fascists make use of adjacent concepts and terms like 'Fight', 'Battle' and 'Struggle'. Such warlike vocabulary to describe political activity shows that fascists saw the world as a place of struggle, with militants oftentimes compared to soldiers on a fight against materialism and decadence. It is within this scope that one can conclude that 'fascism is distinguished from liberalism by the aestheticisation of struggle and the glorification of paramilitary violence as primary features of political action'.[68] **Violence** is, therefore, a core concept, for 'fascism is a philosophy of political action that ascribes value to absolute violence in the political realm'.[69]

According to our conceptual configuration, this concept can have three dimensions in fascist ideology, each of them interlinking with different adjacent concepts: **Violence** as a pragmatic instrument; **Violence** as a force of creation, and **Violence** as a principle of life itself. In the first dimension, **Violence** is defended as something that must be used with the practical goal of defeating the enemies of the **Nation**, be they ethnic or political enemies. One finds here in its vicinity the adjacent concept of 'Eliminationism', which refers to a drive for purging the enemies of the **Nation** and the violent removal of all the elements that supposedly endanger its survival.[70] It is the proximity between the core concepts of **Violence** and **Nation** (seen as an organic unity) that allows the adjacent concept of 'Eliminationism' to acquire such relevance in this conceptual pattern: the need for the **Nation** to preserve its homogeneity implies the removal of dangerous elements at any cost.

The implicit urge for the cleansing of the **Nation** is found, for instance, in the words of Gustav Celmins, leader of the Latvian Perkon Krust, when he argued for a homogenised country and wrote that 'we assume that the only place in the world where Latvians can settle is Latvia. Other peoples have their own countries [...] In one word – in a Latvian Latvia there will only be Latvians'.[71] Likewise, we find similar instigations by Ante Pavelic, leader of the Croatian Ustash movement, who defended vehemently the purging of practitioners of Orthodox religion. However, nowhere else than in Himmler's Poznan Speech is it possible to find such an accurate description of the necessity of eliminating enemies in a meticulous and systematic way.[72]

As for the second dimension, **Violence** as a force of creation, it interlinks with the core concept of **Revolution**. Violence was closely related to the palingenetic transformation of society and the creation of the 'New Man'. Thus, violent acts supposedly had a cathartic component that enabled the cleansing of the national community. It is taken for granted that this concept in fascism was influenced by the writings of the French Georges Sorel who, in the beginning of the 20th century, praised **Violence** as a crucial element of revolutionary change. However, while we do not deny the importance of Sorel's thought, it is evident that the insertion of this concept in the fascist configuration gives it a unique meaning, which differs from that of the French thinker.

In this dimension, 'War' also becomes an adjacent concept and it seems to be surrounding the core concept in some of the most important varieties of fascism. This ideology idealised war as an event with the potential not only to destroy but also to create. Even before the founding of the fascist movement, futurist writer Filippo Tomaso Marinetti wrote, 'We will glorify war-the world's only hygiene'. 'War' should be capable of creating bonds between the soldiers, a new national unity and the awareness about a common destiny'. In the DF, one also finds a rejection of Pacifism, when the author says that Fascism 'rejects Pacifism, behind which there is renunciation of struggle and cowardice in face of sacrifice. Only war brings human energies to maximum tension and gives a seal of nobility to the peoples who have the virtue of facing it'.[73]

It was Goebbels himself who, when referring to World War II, said that 'every birth brings pain. But amid the pain there is already the joy of a new life [...] The significance of the war has grown as its scale has increased. It is relentlessly at work, shattering old forms and ideas, and directing the eyes of human beings to new, greater objectives'.[74] Thus, according to the mastermind of German propaganda, the war that the country was engaged in was a moment in history that was powerful enough to purge the national life and bring the necessary rebirth. Likewise, the praise for combat as a form for bringing national cohesion and unity led a fascist like Sven Olof Lindholm to speak about a 'soldier socialism', which referred to the comradery that was created in the trenches. This notion, which is also present in fascists whose countries actually participated in the war, oftentimes reflected a nostalgia for the time of WWI and for the trenches, where class barriers supposedly vanished.

Nonetheless, it is in its third dimension that the concept of **Violence** truly reveals itself to be a core one, that is, it is as a principle of life that the concept becomes important to understand how fascists saw the world. According to them, **Violence** was part of life itself, being that the world is a place of struggle and battle in which only the strongest could and should survive, and even in the constant comparisons of fascist followers to soldiers one finds evidence of such a worldview. Thus, **Violence** is positively evaluated in fascist ideology and is regarded as a component of society that one should not renegade, but rather accept and live in accordance to it. In the fascist worldview, the principle of struggle underlies all aspects of society. The best adjacent concept that we can here refer to is 'Social Darwinism', a term to refer to the group of ideas that, at the beginning of the twentieth century, applied Darwin's conclusions about the survival of the species to the organisation of societies.[75] Even if Darwinist ideas varied depending on the ideologies that made use of them, it can be generally said that they refer to the notion that, in society, the ones who are stronger deserve to receive some benefits because of it.

In this dimension, we also find recurrent themes and ideas such as that of 'Virility', which can be considered here as an adjacent concept and which closely interlinks with the concept of 'New Man', already found in the vicinity of **Revolution**. Fascists valued manhood, while despising what they saw as feminine traits of personality, because the former was necessary to survive in a world where violence was a constant component. The recurrent cult of heroes and soldiers in fascist liturgy cannot be disassociated from this conception of male values. Let us lastly point out that the idea of 'Sacrifice' was also prevalent in fascist discourse as an example of the ultimate act of heroism in the fight for the survival of the **Nation**. For instance, Romanian fascist Ion Mota, writing about the Spanish Civil War (where he eventually died), says that 'we die here for the defense of our ancestral law, for the happiness of our Romanian people, for its rebirth through the struggle of the legion'.[76] Sacrifice was positively seen as a supreme act of abnegation that was in accordance with a view that conceived the world as a place full of inevitable struggles.

## *Empire*

Lastly, this configuration of generic fascism includes the concept of **Empire**, which in its crudest sense refers to the acquisition of new territories that are supposed to be dominated by a more powerful country. This component of fascist ideology was also acknowledged by Payne, who included it in his typological definition by writing that fascists had 'the goal of empire, expansion or a radical change in the nation's relationship with other powers'.[77] The first noticeable aspect of imperialism in fascism is that it was strongly based on ideological goals and not only in materialistic considerations, as had been the case with other empires of past centuries and had been previously envisioned by Conservative and Liberal ideologies.[78]

Thus, the goal of conquering an **Empire** is, for fascists, something more than just attending to the material needs of one people: it is the fulfilment of a mission. For this reason, it is possible to argue that **Empire** is at the core of fascism because in many of its permutations it interlinks with every other core concept: fascist imperialism, in the configurations in which this concept appears, becomes like a corollary of the whole ideology, the best representation of the goal of revitalizing the national community with a palingenetic **Revolution**. The acquisition of new territories is a historical mission that is also capable of creating the environment in which all the members of the **Nation** unite under a single cause and acquire a profound consciousness of their duties. In no other variety of fascism did this concept play as big a role as in the case of German Nazism, in which the conquering of space in Eastern Europe was held to be a crucial goal.

Furthermore, this core concept also interlinks with **Violence** and **Authority**, as is mentioned by Kallis when he writes that 'the legitimization of violence and war and the elitist basis of the fascist worldview opened up new opportunities and offered solutions which previous liberal and conservative regimes were less inclined to subscribe to'.[79] This happened in the first place because the elitist view of fascist ideology could easily fit with the idea of invading foreigner countries and impose upon them a foreigner yoke. Furthermore, the conception of the world as a place of violence and struggle clearly legitimised the fascist goal of invading other countries and engage in wars with them. This will to conquer territories could sometimes even be seen as a unavoidable necessity, as it is written in DF in the following passage: 'To fascism, the tendency to empire, that is, the expansion of the nation, is a manifestation of vitality; its contrary, that is, closeness to home, is a sign of decadence: the peoples that emerge and re-emerge are imperialistic, the peoples that die are renounced'.[80] Conquering an empire was a sign of national vitality and the condition for the most powerful country to survive, at least according to the view of the authors of this text.

In this context, the first adjacent concept that one finds in the vicinity of **Empire** is 'Expansionism'. Likewise, it is important to mention the adjacent concept of 'Irredentism', which was very popular in the beginning of the 20th century. Kornprobst recognises that, while there may be some controversy about the actual meaning of 'Irredentism', there is a consensus that it is 'a particular kind of territory dispute', independently of the claim for the annexation of territory being based on the desires of an ethnic minority or a state. In the context of this book, this concept can be interpreted as the desire held by some nationalists to conquer territories on the basis of real or imaginary historical affiliation. The desire to annex territories thought to have once belonged to the **Nation**, or in which some compatriots still lived, was prevalent in Italian nationalism at the beginning of the century, but it went beyond the borders of this country and still played a significant role in the era of fascism, even if this was not the only ideology using this concept.

According to Kallis, 'Instead of being a normative concept referring to populations, fascist irredentism focuses on territory and was exploited as part of the justification for wider expansionist plans'.[81] Fascists could make use of this concept to legitimise the creation of a whole new **Empire**, oftentimes neglecting the claim of uniting a population who shared blood ties (even though this is not always the case since, for instance, Nazi leaders could easily refer to the existence of Germans in a given territory to justify an annexation). One can find examples of 'Irredentism', for instance, in Dimitrije Ljotic, leader of the Serbian Yugoslav National Movement – United Militant Labor Organization (*Združena Borbena Organizacija Rada* – Zbor) and its defense of pan-Serbianism. Likewise, one can mention the case of the Hungarian leader Szálasi Ferenc, who called for the creation of the Hungarian United Territories, 'Stretching from the Carpathians to the Adriatic coast, formed out of Hungary, Slovakia, Ruthenia, Transylvania, Croat-Slovenia, and West-Gyepu'.[82]

However, our understanding of the concept of **Empire** seems to become more complex if one bears in mind that not all fascist permutations use the adjacent concept of 'Expansionism' in the vicinity of this core concept, for its decontestation depended on the historical context of each nation. Thus, in countries which already possessed a notable **Empire** (which was the case of France and Great Britain), the focus was on maintaining and valorization of the territory already acquired rather than on new conquests. In such cases, we find the concept of **Empire** had, in its vicinity, adjacent concepts such as 'Exploration' (of the territory already possessed) or 'political reconfiguration of the empire' (more about this will be discussed when dealing with the case of British fascist leader Oswald Mosley).

Besides, the picture gets even more complicated if one notices that, after all, not all fascist movements made explicit use of the concept of **Empire**. This is recognised by Payne, who acknowledges that it could be absent in some permutations of the ideology. Like it has previously happened with the concept of **Corporatism**, this fact should be enough for one to conclude that **Empire** is not really a core concept in fascism However, one should also not forget to mention that, according to Payne's definition, fascist programs could include the goal of simply performing a 'radical change in the nation's relationship with other powers'.[83] In such cases, rather than a claim for territorial acquisition or the maintenance of an **Empire**, fascists would demand an alteration in the realm of international relations to strengthen the influence and respect of the **Nation** in the international arena. Believing that their country had lost the greatness that it once supposedly had, fascists aimed at regaining a lost prestige that supposedly had been lost.

Thus, a fascist aim of performing a change with an international impact was somehow present in all manifestations of the ideology, and one can argue that in several varieties it will be found a concept performing a function that it is similar to that of **Empire**. For this reason, for now, we believe that it is important to reserve a space for such a concept in the fascist configuration and, for the sake of convenience, we will still call it **Empire**. Nevertheless, we acknowledge that this is one of the concepts that may need revision after the study of the leaders and that it can even be left out if its status as a core fascist feature does not hold up.

## Concluding remarks

These seven concepts configure our preliminary core of fascist ideology. They cannot be analyzed separately for it is due to their interlinkages that the meaning of the fascist configuration is created. One cannot, for instance, understand the concept of **Nation** if one doesn't take into account that the national community must be kept united by a strong **Corporate State** and be ruled by **Authoritarian** new elites, who are bent on the creation of a **Revolution** through **Violent** means and the construction of a new **Empire** (or the maintenance of an **Empire** already in existence). Furthermore, these core concepts cannot be isolated from the adjacent concepts which also help them acquire meaning and specific decontestations. These core concepts acquire their meaning both from the interlinkages between themselves and the complex interlinkages with the adjacent concepts we mentioned.

## Notes

1 It is possible to find Crocce's reflections on fascism in Benedetto Crocce, *Scritti e Discorsi Politici* (Bari, Laterza, 1973).
2 These interpretations are found, for instance, in William McGovern, *From Luther to Hitler: The History of Fascist-Nazi Political Philosophy* (Boston, Houghton Mifflin Company, 1941); and Friedrich Meinecke, *The German Catastrophe: Reflections and Recollections* (Boston, Beacon Press, 1963 [1946]).
3 Marxist works are too numerous for us to mention them in detail, but we can refer to David Beetham, *Marxists in Face of Fascism: Writings by Marxists on Fascism from the Inter-War Period* (Manchester, Manchester University Press, 1983).
4 See, for instance, Erich Fromm, *The Fear of Freedom* (London, Routledge, 1942); Wilhelm Reich, *The Mass Psychology of Fascism* (New York, Orgone Institute Press, 1946).
5 Some examples include Zbigniew Brzezinski and Carl Joachim Friedrich, *Totalitarian Dictatorship and Autocracy* (Cambridge, Massachusetts, Harvard University Press, 1965); Hannah Arendt, *The Origins of Totalitarianism* (San Diego, California, Harcourt Brace, 1973).
6 Ernst Nolte, *Three Faces of Fascism: Action Française, Italian Fascism, National Socialism* (New York, Holt, Rinehart and Winston, 1966), 20.
7 Roger Griffin, *The Nature of Fascism* (London, Routledge, 1993), 44.
8 Stanley Payne, *A History of Fascism: 1914–1945* (Madison, University Press of Wisconsin, 1995), 7.
9 Roger Eatwell, *Fascism: A History* (London: Penguin Books, 1997), xxiv.
10 Philip Morgan, *Fascism in Europe, 1919–1945* (London, Routledge, 2003), 13–14.
11 Michael Mann, *Fascists* (Cambridge, Cambridge University Press, 2004), 13.
12 Aristotle Kalllis, 'The Regime-Model of Fascism: A Typology', *European History Quarterly*, 30 (2000), 77–107.

*The conceptual structure of 'generic fascism'* 41

13 From now on, we will write the core concepts in bold and with a capital letter, while adjacent concepts will be written between quotation marks and also with a capital letter.
14 The Heimwehr was a paramilitary group that would later be absorbed by the Fatherland Front that was created by Austrian dictator Kurt Von Schuschnigg, thus knowing a fate that was similar to many ultranationalist organizations under authoritarian conservative dictatorships. To read more on Austrian fascism, see Gerhard Botz, 'The Coming of the Dolfuss-Schuschnig and the Stages of its Development' in António Costa Pinto and Aristotle Kallis, Eds., *Rethinking Fascism and Dictatorship in Europe* (London, Palgrave Macmillan, 2014).
15 Translated by the author from the original in German, 'Wir wollen Österreich von Grund aus erneuern! [...] Wir fordern von jedem Kameraden den unverzagten Glauben ans Vaterland'. Unless it is indicated otherwise, all the translations to be presented were made by the author.
16 cf. Roger Griffin, 'Introduction' in Cyprian Blamires and Paul Jackson, Ed., *World Fascism: A Historical Encyclopedia* (Santa Barbara, AB CLIO, 2006), 4.
17 The term 'organicism' refers to 'concepts of society in which its various sectors are held to bear a structured relationship to each other that serves to define and delimit their roles and rights, taking precedence over the identities and rights of individuals' Stanley Payne, *A History of Fascism: 1914–1945* (Madison, University of Wisconsin Press, 1995), 13.
18 Roger Eatwell, *Fascism: A History* (London, Penguin Books, 1997), xxiv.
19 Translated from the original in Italian: 'Non razza, né regione geograficamente individuata, ma schiatta storicamente perpetuantesi, moltitudine unificata da una idea, che è volontà di esistenza e di potenza: coscienza di sé, personalità'. Benito Mussolini, 'La Dottrina Del Fascismo' in Duilio Susmel and Edoardo Susmel, Ed., *Opera Omnia*, Vol. XXXIV (Firenze, La Fenice, 1961), 120.
20 Fascists 'do not see the people as an economic or social class – they do not, for example, mean the petty bourgeoisie. Rather, the term 'people' can be used to express the anti-establishment sentiments of any group – from discontented workers to wealthy capitalists' Kevin Passmore, *Fascism: A Very Short Introduction* (Oxford, Oxford University Press, 2014), 28.
21 'Völkisch thought was mystical in tone, embracing at best a kind of highly abstract rationalism divorced from analytic thinking. It was ontologically grounded in a concept of nature which flowed from a "higher reality" of the cosmos to man, becoming crystallized in the landscape, environment, and life of the people. Such an attitude rejected Christianity in favor of a pantheistic sense of the cosmos and of nature, credited with creating special conditions and unique human potential. The very landscape of Germany supposedly elicited superior cultural characteristics. The Volk thus became the intermediary and expression of a transcendental essence and was the basis of all that was good in Germany or any higher good that might be developed. For Germans to be truly free and capable of superior achievement, life and thought had to be thoroughly grounded in the Volk and purged of extraneous and corrupting influences'. Stanley Payne, *A History of Fascism: 1914–1945* (Madison, University of Wisconsin Press, 1995), 52.
22 Otto Strasser, 'The German Knight as the Key to Europe's Recovery', in Roger Griffin, Ed., *Fascism* (Oxford, Oxford University Press, 1995), 115.
23 Vidkun Quisling, 'The Nordic Revival', in Griffin, Ed., *Fascism*, 209.
24 To read more on Hungarian fascism, see Nicholas Nagy-Talavera, *The Green Shirts and the Others: A History of Fascism in Hungary and Romania*, (New York, Hoover Institution Press, 1970).
25 Mann, *Fascists*, 14.
26 Jacques Doriot, 'Saving France', in Griffin, Ed., *Fascism*, 199.

42  *The conceptual structure of 'generic fascism'*

27 Translated from the original in Italian: 'È lo Stato che trascendendo il limite breve delle vite individuali rappresenta la coscienza della nazione' Benito Mussolini 'La Dottrina Del Fascismo', 129.
28 George Valois, 'Empty Portfolios', in Griffin, Ed., *Fascism,* 198.
29 'Italian Fascists eulogized the state, which they believed was necessary to create a true Italian nation. Italian Fascists even employed the term "totalitarianism" positively, pointing, after Mussolini's March on Rome in 1922, to the new state which had risen above parochial and political divisions' Roger Eatwell, *Fascism: A History*, xxii.
30 Translated from the original in Italian: 'sintesi e unità di ogni valore'. Benito Mussolini 'La Dottrina Del Fascismo', 129.
31 Payne, *A History of Fascism*, 7.
32 According to Pinto, 'Corporatism became a powerful ideological and institutional device against liberal democracy during the first half of the twentieth century [...] During the interwar period corporatism permeated the main political families of the conservative and authoritarian political right: from the Catholic Parties and Social Catholicism to radical right royalists and fascists, not to speak of Durkheiminian solidarists and supporters of technocratic governments associated with state-led modernized policies'. António Costa Pinto, *Corporatism and Fascism: The Corporatist Wave in Europe* (London, Routledge, 2017), 5.
33 Philippe C. Schmitter, 'Still the Century of Corporatism?', *The Review of Politics*, 36 (1), 1974, 93–94.
34 Alfred Stepan, *The State and Society. Peru in Comparative Perspective* (Princeton, Princeton University Press, 1978), 215.
35 Pinto, *Corporatism and Fascism*, 5.
36 Alexander Raven Thomson, *The Coming Corporate State* (London, Black House Publishing Ltd, 1937), 35.
37 Elias Simojoki, 'The Revolution of the Finnish Heart', in Griffin, Ed., *Fascism*, 214.
38 Payne, *A History of Fascism*, 13.
39 Thomson, *The Coming Corporate State*, 19.
40 Translated from the original in Italian: 'La Magistratura del Lavoro è l'organo con cui lo Stato interviene a regolare le controversie del lavoro, sia che vertano sull'osservanza dei patti e delle alter norme esistenti, sia che vertano sulla determinazione di nuove condizioni di lavoro'. The text is available in the following site: http://www.historia.unimi.it/sezione/fonti/codificazione/cartalavoro.pdf
41 To read more on transnational approaches and the concept of Corporatism, see Matteo Pasetti, 'The Fascist Labor Charter and its Transnational Spread', in António Costa Pinto, Ed., *Corporatism and Fascism: The Corporatist Wave in Europe* (London, Routledge, 2017), 60–77.
42 Eugen Weber, 'Revolution? Counterrevolution? What Revolution?', *Journal of Contemporary History*, 9 (2), 23.
43 Payne, *A History of Fascism*, 487.
44 Ibid., 487.
45 Leon Dégrelle, 'The Revolution of Souls', in Roger Griffin, Ed., *Fascism*, 205.
46 Translated from the original in Italian: 'Il mondo per il fascismo non è questo mondo materiale che appare alla superficie, in cui l'uomo è un individuo separato da tutti gli altri e per sé stante' Benito Mussolini 'La Dottrina Del Fascismo', 117.
47 Elias Simojoki, 'The Revolution of the Finnish Heart', in Roger Griffin, Ed., *Fascism*, 214.
48 Griffin, *The Nature of Fascism*, 33.
49 In the context of 'Palingenesis', 'the perceived corruption, anarchy, oppressiveness, iniquities or decadence of the present, rather than being seen as immutable

*The conceptual structure of 'generic fascism'* 43

and thus to be endured indefinitely with stoic courage or bleak pessimism, are perceived as having reached their peak and interpreted as the sure sign that one era is nearing its end and a new order is about to emerge'. Griffin, *The Nature of Fascism*, 33.
50 A. K. Chesterton, 'A Spiritual Typhus', in Griffin, Ed., *Fascism*, 179.
51 José Streel, 'Fascism's Century', in Griffin, Ed., *Fascism*, 207.
52 Jorge Dagnino, Matthew Feldman and Paul Stocker, *The New Man in Radical Right Ideology and Practice, 1919–1945* (London, Bloomsbury, 2017).
53 E. Gunther Grundel, 'The New Human Synthesis' in Griffin, Ed., *Fascism*, 207.
54 Translated from the original in French: 'La construction de l'homme noveau devait magnifier l'homme, en tant qu'individu sexué, la virilité, s'imposant comme la qualité par excellence du type d'individu à configurer'. Marie Anne Matard-Bonucci, 'Homme Noveau entre dictadure et totalitarisme (1922–1945)' in Marie-Anne Matard-Bonucci and Pierre Milza, Eds., *L'Homme Noveau Dans l'Europe fasciste (1922–1945)* (Paris, Fayard, 2004), 9.
55 'According to Ugo Spirito, corporative institutions should have favored a relationship of coessentiality between the individual and the State until an organic identity between these two identities was achieved'. Piero Bini, 'Corporative Economics and the Making of Economic Policy in Italy during the Interwar Years (1922–1940)' in Monika Alcouffe and Bertram Schefold, Eds., Business Cycles in Economic Thought: A History (London, Routledge, 2017), 145.
56 E. Gunther Grundel, 'The New Human Synthesis' in Griffin, Ed., *Fascism*, 207.
57 George Mosse, *The Fascist Revolution: Toward a General Theory of Fascism* (New York, Howard Fertig Pub, 1999), 71.
58 Translated from the original in Swedish: 'I ungdomen gör man så – man ser klart, man syftar långt och sätter idealen högt. Om vi först som äldre män hade tillägnat oss denna åskådning, så hade den kanske ej blivit tillräckligt stark'. Sven OLof Lindholm, *Svensk Friehtskamp* (1943), 17.
59 Eon O'Duffy, 'The New Corporate Ireland', in Griffin, Ed., *Fascism*, 183.
60 Payne, *A History of Fascism*, 102.
61 Lindholm, *Svensk Friehtskamp*, 18.
62 William Joyce, 'Hitler Shows the way' in Griffin, Ed., *Fascism*, 181.
63 Gottfried Benn, 'The New Breed of Germany' in Griffin, Ed., *Fascism*, 136.
64 Mario Piazzesi, 'The Squadristi as the Revolutionaries of the New Italy' in Griffin, Ed., *Fascism*, 39.
65 Notice, for instance, the effusive description of a battle by fascist leader Italo Balbo, which shows how much Violence was cherished by fascists: 'I [then] announced to [the chief of police] that I would burn down and destroy the houses of all Socialists in Ravenna if he did not give me within half an hour the means required for transporting the Fascists elsewhere. It was a dramatic moment. I demanded a whole fleet of trucks. The police officers completely lost their heads; but after half an hour they told me where I could find trucks already filled with gasoline. Some of them actually belonged to the office of the chief of police. My ostensible reason was that I wanted to get the exasperated Fascists out of town; in reality, I was organizing a 'column of fire'... to extend our reprisals throughout the province... We went through... all the towns and centres in the provinces of Forlì and Ravenna and burned all the Red buildings... It was a terrible night. Our passage was marked by huge columns of fire and smoke' Patricia Knight, *Mussolini and Fascism* (London, Routledge, 2003), 26.
66 Allen Douglas, 'Violence and Fascism: The Case of the Faisceau', *Journal of Contemporary History*, 19 (4), 1984, 689.
67 Payne, *A History of Fascism*, 102.

44  *The conceptual structure of 'generic fascism'*

68 Daniel Woodley, *Fascism and Political Theory: Critical Perspectives on Fascist Ideology* (London, Routledge, 2010), 105.
69 Federico Finchelstein, *Transatlantic Fascism: Ideology, Violence, and the Sacred in Argentina and Italy, 1919–1945* (Durham, Duke University Press Books, 2010), 17.
70 It 'refers to any ideological and political campaign geared towards physically *removing* a group from the community; and this process of removal may involve a series of techniques, ranging from persecution to confinement to physical expulsion to murder, or any combination thereof'. Aristotle Kallis, *Genocide and Fascism* (London, Routledge, 2009), 6. See also Daniel Goldhagen, *Hitler's Willing Executioners, Ordinary Germans and the Holocaust* (New York, Alfred A. Knopf, 1996).
71 Gustav Celmins, 'A Latvian Latvia' in Griffin, Ed., *Fascism*, 218.
72 In Himmler's words, 'Today I am going to refer quite frankly to a very grave chapter. We can mention it now among ourselves quite openly and yet we shall never talk about it in public. I'm referring to the evacuation of the Jews, the extermination of the Jewish people. Most of you will know what it is like to see 100 corpses lying side by side or 500 or 1,000 of them. To have coped with this and—except for cases of human weakness—to have remained decent, that has made us tough. This is an unwritten—never to be written—and yet glorious page in our history. For we know how difficult we would have made it for ourselves if, on top of the bombing raids, the burdens and the deprivations of the war, we still had Jews today'. Peter Longerich, *Heinrich Himmler* (Oxford, Oxford University Press, 2012), 689.
73 Translated from the original in Italian: 'Respinge quindi il pacifismo che nasconde una rinuncia alla lotta e una viltà di fronte al sacrificio. Solo la guerra porta al massimo di tensione tutte le energie umane e imprime un sigillo di nobiltà ai popoli che hanno la virtù di affrontarla'. Benito Mussolini 'La Dottrina Del Fascismo', 124.
74 Joseph Goebbels, 'The True Meaning of War' in Griffin, Ed., *Fascism*, 159.
75 According to Payne, fascists believed that 'violence possessed a certain positive and therapeutic value in and of itself, that a certain amount of continuing violent struggle, along the lines of Sorelianism and extreme Social Darwinism, was necessary for the health of national society". Payne, *A History of Fascism*, 66.
76 Ion Mota, 'The Romanian Legionaries' Mission in Spain' in Griffin, Ed., *Fascism*, 220.
77 Payne, *A History of Fascism*, 7.
78 This is also mentioned by Kallis, when he states that 'if we remove these elements [ideology] from our interpretation of fascist foreigner policies, then fascist expansionism is deprived of an overall explanation for its specific choices and methods,' Aristotle Kallis, *Fascist Ideology: Territory and Expansionism in Italy and Germany, 1922–1945* (London, Routledge, 2000), 199.However, such view is not held by Richard J Bosworth, *Mussolini* (Oxford, Oxford University Press, 2002). In this book, fascist expansionism is seen as a continuation of Liberal colonialism rather than as something ideologically different. As it is argued in this book, our own view is closer to that of Kallis.
79 Kallis, *Fascist Ideology*, 199.
80 Benito Mussolini, 'La Dottrina Del Fascismo', 132.
81 Kallis, *Fascist Ideology*, 117.
82 Szálasi Ferenc, 'Hungarism' in Griffin, Ed., *Fascism*, 225.
83 Payne, *A History of Fascism*, 7.

# List of references

Alcouffe, Monika and Bertram Schefold (eds.), *Business Cycles in Economic Thought: A History* (London, Routledge, 2017).
Allardyce, Gilbert. 'What Fascism Is Not: Thoughts on the Deflation of a Concept', *The American Historical Review, 84* (2), 1979, 367–388.
Arendt, Hannah, *The Origins of Totalitarianism* (San Diego, California, Harcourt Brace, 1973).
Beetham, David, *Marxists in Face of Fascism: Writings by Marxists on Fascism from the Inter-War Period* (Manchester, Manchester University Press, 1983).
Blamires, Cyprian and Paul Jackson (eds.), *World Fascism: A Historical Encyclopedia* (Santa Barbara, AB CLIO, 2006).
Brzezinski, Zbigniew and Carl Joachim Friedrich, *Totalitarian Dictatorship and Autocracy* (Cambridge, Massachusetts, Harvard University Press, 1965).
Burleigh, Michael, *The Third Reich: A New History* (New York, Hill and Wang, 2001).
Crocce, Benedetto, *Scritti e Discorsi Politici* (Bari, Laterza, 1973).
Dagnino, Jorge, Matthew Feldman and Paul Stocker, *The New Man in Radical Right Ideology and Practice, 1919-1945* (London, Bloomsbury, 2017).
Darré, Richard Walter, *Blut Und Boden Ein Grundgedanke Des Nationalsozialismus* (Berlin, Reichsdruckerei, 1936).
Eatwell, Roger, *Fascism: A History* (London, Penguin Books, 1997).
Felici, Renzo de, *Le Interpretazioni Del Fascismo* (Bari, Laterza, 2017 [1967]).
Finchelstein, Federico, *Transatlantic Fascism: Ideology, Violence, and the Sacred in Argentina and Italy, 1919-1945* (Durham, Duke University Press Books, 2010).
Fromm, Erich, *The Fear of Freedom* (London, Routledge,1942).
Gentile, Emilio and Robert Mallett. 'The Sacralisation of Politics: Definitions, Interpretations and Reflections on the Question of Secular Religion and Totalitarianism', *Totalitarian Movements and Political Religions, 1* (1), 2000, 18–55.
Gentile, Emilio, *Chi é Fascista* (Bari, Laterza, 2019).
Goldhagen, Daniel, *Hitler's Willing Executioners, Ordinary Germans and the Holocaust* (New York, Alfred A. Knopf, 1996).
Gramsci, Antonio, *Selections from the Prison Notebooks of Antonio Gramsci* (New York, International Publishers, 1992 [1971]).
Gregor, Anthony James, *The Ideology of Fascism* (New York, Free Press, 1969).
Griffin, Roger, *The Nature of Fascism* (London, Routledge, 1993).
Griffin, Roger (ed.), *Fascism* (Oxford, Oxford University Press, 1995).
Haynes, Rebecca and Martin Rady (eds.), *In the Shadow of Hitler: Personalities of the Right in Central and Eastern Europe* (London, I.B.Tauris Publishers, 2011).
Kalllis, Aristotle, 'The Regime-Model of Fascism: A Typology', *European History Quarterly, 30*, 2000, 77–107.
Kallis, Aristotle, *Genocide and Fascism* (London, Routledge, 2009).
Kallis, Aristotle, *Fascist Ideology: Territory and Expansionism in Italy and Germany, 1922-1945* (London, Routledge, 2000).
Kornprobst, Markus, *Irredentism in European Politics: Argumentation, Compromise and Norms* (Cambridge, Cambridge University Press, 2008).
Knight, Patricia, *Mussolini and Fascism* (London, Routledge, 2003).
Lindholm, Sven Olof, *Svensk Friehtskamp* (1943).

Lampe, John and Mark Mazower, *Ideologies and National Identities: The Case of Twentieth-Century Southeastern Europe* (New York, CEU Press, 2004).
Longerich, Peter, *Heinrich Himmler* (Oxford, Oxford University Press, 2012).
Mann, Michael, *Fascists* (Cambridge, Cambridge University Press, 2004).
Matard-Bonucci, Marie Anne and Pierre Milza (eds.), *L'Homme Noveau Dans l'Europe fasciste (1922–1945)* (Paris, Fayard, 2004).
McGovern, William, *From Luther to Hitler: The History of Fascist-Nazi Political Philosophy* (Boston, Houghton Mifflin Company, 1941).
Meinecke, Friedrich, *The German Catastrophe: Reflections and Recollections* (Boston, Beacon Press, 1963 [1946]).
Mosse, George, *The Crisis of German Ideology: Intellectual Origins of the Third Reich* (New York, Grosset and Dunlap, 1964).
Mosse, George, *The Fascist Revolution: Toward a General Theory of Fascism* (New York, Howard Fertig Pub, 1999).
Morgan, Philip, *Fascism in Europe, 1919–1945* (London, Routledge, 2003).
Mussolini, Benito, 'La Dottrina Del Fascismo' in Duilio Susmel and Edoardo Susmel, Eds., *Opera Omnia*, Vol. XXXIV (Firenze, La Fenice, 1961), 120.
Nagy-Talavera, Nicholas, *The Green Shirts and the Others: A History of Fascism in Hungary and Romania* (New York, Hoover Institution Press, 1970).
Nolte, Ernst, *Three Faces of Fascism: Action Française, Italian Fascism, National Socialism* (New York, Holt, Rinehart and Winston, 1966).
Passmore, Kevin, *Fascism: A Very Short Introduction* (Oxford, Oxford University Press, 2014).
Payne, Stanley, *A History of Fascism: 1914–1945* (Madison, University Press of Wisconsin, 1995).
Pinto, António Costa and Aristotle Kallis (eds.), *Rethinking Fascism and Dictatorship in Europe* (London, Palgrave Macmillan, 2014).
Pinto, António Costa (ed.), *Corporatism and Fascism: The Corporatist Wave in Europe* (London, Routledge, 2017).
Poliakov, Leon, *Aryan Myth: A History of Racist and Nationalist Ideas in Europe* (New York, Basic Books, 1974).
Reich, Wilhelm, *The Mass Psychology of Fascism* (New York, Orgone Institute Press, 1946).
Roberts, David, *Fascist Interactions: Proposals for a New Approach to Fascism and Its Era, 1919–1945* (New York, Berghahn, 2016).
Sorel, Georges, *Reflections on Violence*. Edited by Jeremy Jennings (Cambridge, Cambridge University Press, 1999 [1908]).
Stepan, Albert, *The State and Society. Peru in Comparative Perspective* (Princeton, Princeton University Press, 1978).
Sternhell, Zeev, *Ni Droite Ni Gauche. L'idéologie Fasciste En France* (Pari, Éditions du Seuill, 1983).
Sternhell, Zeev, *The Birth of Fascist Ideology* (Princeton, Princeton University Press, 1994).
Thomson, Alexander Raven, *The Coming Corporate State* (London, Black House Publishing Ltd, 1937).
Tomasevich, Jozon, *War and Revolution in Yugoslavia, 1941–1945: Occupation and Collaboration* (Stanford, Stanford University Press, 2001).
Weber, Eugen, *Varieties of Fascism* (Florida, Krieger Pub Co., 1982 [1964]).

Weber, Eugen, '*Revolution? Counterrolution? What Revolution?*', *Journal of Contemporary History*, 9 (2), 1974, 3–47.
Woodley, Daniel, *Fascism and Political Theory: Critical Perspectives on Fascist Ideology* (London, Routledge, 2010).
Yeomans, Rory, *Visions of Annihilation: The Ustasha Regime and the Cultural Politics of Fascism, 1941–1945* (Pittsburgh, University of Pittsburgh Press, 2013).

# 2 Adolf Hitler and German national socialism

Racial struggle as the basis of a worldview

Arguably the most (in)famous fascist leader who ever lived, Adolf Hitler owes his bad reputation to the visceral racial hatred which was at the core of his ideology and is (rightly so) repudiated in an almost universal way. Mainly due to the legacy of violence and cruelty of the Nazi Holocaust, many in the past, even in academic circles, have tried to approach Hitler by stressing the abhorrent features of his personality. However, we shall not be concerned with 'psychotic' or 'psychopathic' theories.[1] We argue, therefore, that Hitler's worldview (or *weltanschauung*, to employ the German word that he himself used) must be approached as any other ideological configuration, without this meaning that the researcher in any way approves or condones the content of his thought.[2] This is the most effective way of approaching the ideas that, given the importance and charisma of this leader, were behind the practices of both the Nazi party and regime.

## Hitler and the Nazi party

Adolf Hitler was born in the Austrian town of Braunau am Inn on 20 April 1889 to a middle class family whose parental figure, Alois Hitler, was a civil servant in the Austro-Hungarian Empire. He spent a great part of his formative years in Linz and later moved to Vienne, hoping to succeed as a painter, even though he was rejected by the Academy of Fine Arts not much later. In 1913, Hitler moved to the German city of Munich and, at the beginning of World War I, enlisted in the Bavarian Army. When the world conflict was coming to an end, the future Nazi leader was hospitalised in the German town of Pasewalk after being blinded in battle. According to his own accounts, the surrender of Germany left him with the sense that an outrageous act of treason and cowardice had been committed, which exacerbated his nationalism and his desire for retribution. In the following year, after returning to Munich, Hitler was ordered by his army superiors to infiltrate a new nationalist political party by the name of German Workers' Party (*Deutsch Arbeiterpartei* – DAP). This was established by Anton Drexler on 5 January 1919. What happened next is well known: given the permission to speak during a meeting, Hitler's charisma impressed Drexler so much that he invited him to join his party. From then onwards, Hitler's life intertwined with the history of this party.

While gaining notoriety among Bavarian Right-Wing circles due to his militancy, Hitler acquired notoriety that surpassed that of Drexler himself. His influence among the followers was so big that he was able to become the leader of the party in 1921, more than one year after its name was changed to National Socialist German Workers' Party (*Nationalsozialistische Deutsche Arbeiterpartei* – NSDAP). The first major setback of his political career came after the failed Beer Hall Putsch, which took place in Munich on the night of 8 November 1923. In this attempt, Hitler sought to depose the Bavarian regional government and exert pressure on the Berlin government to put an end to the republic then in existence. Such violent methods matched the practices and structures of the Nazi party, which had already created one paramilitary organisation with the goal of fighting rivals (known as the *Sturmabteilung* – SA), and would later also create the *Schutzstaffel* (SS).

After being imprisoned for a short period of time and having confronted Gregor Strasser, who tried to dispute the leadership of the movement with him, Hitler established himself as the unchallenged leader of National Socialism and, this time, decided to obtain political power through legal means. However, for a while, his party seemed not to have particularly good electoral results for, in those years, Germany was apparently satisfied with the so called Weimar Republic, a democratic state that had been founded in 1919 and in which the centre-left Social Democratic Party (Sozialdemokratische Partei Deutschland – SPD) and the center-right Centre Party (*Deutsche Zentrumspartei* – DZP) played the most important roles with regard to parliamentary politics. However, after the Great Depression of 1929, in the Federal elections of 1930, the conditions had changed and the NSDAP conquered 107 seats in the Reichstag. At this time, some of the most important members of the party, who would later acquire worldwide fame, were already relevant political figures of Nazism: that is the case, for instance, of Joseph Goebbels (who would later be Minister of Propaganda), Herman Göring (one of the key personalities of the future regime) and Heinrich Himmler (leader of the SS).

What happened next needs not take us too long to describe. It suffices to say that, in the first few years of the 1930s, democracy in Germany quickly began to deteriorate due to the crisis caused by the Great Depression and the fact that chancellor Heinrich Brüning started taking measures by emergency decree (without the need of parliamentary approval). After his resignation, conservative politician Franz Von Papen and General Kurt Von Schleicher led two ephemeral governments, after which President Paul Von Hindenburg finally accepted to give Hitler the position of Chancellor. His government included only two more members of the Nazi Party. Nevertheless, the date of 31 January 1933 (the so called *Machtergreifung*) was celebrated by Nazis as the beginning of a new era. This date is also seen by historians as the beginning of the Third Reich, that is, the Nazi Regime in Germany. For the purposes of this book, which does not deal with the regime, it is enough to mention that it came to an end in 1945, after Germany lost a war which began by the will of its deranged leader. Adolf Hitler took his own life in Berlin on April 30 of that year, ten days after his 56th birthday.

## Adolf Hitler amid the ideological struggles of his time

The formation and development of the NSDAP happened in a context of ideological dispute among several right-wing organisations and individuals (mostly active in the region of Bavaria), and involved concepts and themes such as 'Volk', 'Lebensraum', 'Anti-Semitism' and even 'Anti-Communism. 'Volk' nationalism, which highlighted ethnocentric and mystic views about the German people and their connection to soil, was a current of populist thought that had gained widespread approval before WWI and was even more relevant when Hitler began his rise to power.[3] Several intellectuals concerned with spiritual rebirth, such as Oswald Spengler and Ernst Jünger, frequently dwelled on this concept, hoping to find in the mystic features of the German people a solution for the supposed national decay.

The notion of 'Lebensraum' (or 'Vital Space') was already in use in the 19th century, but it was reconfigured in the 20th century in order to signify the 'geographical space that the German people needed to conquer in order to survive'. It became a frequent theme in right wing circles after the country's defeat in WWI and increasingly acquired racist traits, mostly because the desire for conquering new territories carried with it a strong contempt against the supposedly inferior peoples of Eastern Europe. As to the concept of 'Anti-Semitism', in fact, it makes part of the European history in the last centuries and not just of 20th century Germany. However, the hatred against the Jews acquired particularly virulent traits in the right wing organizations of this country, mainly after the war, when conspiracy theories attributed Germany's debacle to an elite of powerful Jews that had supposedly plotted against the country. These conspiracies were part of the 'stab in the back' myth, and sometimes they were reinforced by forgeries such as *The Protocols of The Elders of Zion*, a Russian text that supposedly displayed a secret plan by the Jews to rule over the world.

It is also crucial to note the importance of 'Anti-Communism'. Most of the sentiments against communism came as a reaction against the short-lived Bavarian Soviet Republic of 1918–1919, which was violently fought by reactionary groups, among which were the *Freikorps* (paramilitary militias mainly composed of war veterans). Even after the defeat of this revolutionary attempt, right wing organisations persisted in the idea of fighting communism, by force if necessary, even though the extent of the call for violent action varied depending on the ideology and organisations. Thus, from Alfred Hugenberg's conservative nationalism to Hitler's German variety of fascism, the right seemed to agree on the topic of anti-communism, even if the acceptance of these ideas (as well as that of anti-Semitism) in the German population at large depended on economic and social context and varied over the years.

In this context, one of the important competitive battles for ideological meaning was related to the construction of a political programme that could not only defeat Marxism but also present an alternative to it and reconquer the masses and the working class back to nationalism. There was an idea that Marxism could not be simply defeated, but rather fought with an alternative ideology that offered solutions to the segments of the German population that needed them. It was in this milieu of ultranationalist themes that Hitler forged his ideological *Weltschauung*, trying to reach a definitive decontested meaning in a core conceptual configuration that included themes and ideas being disputed by rivals and allies alike. Unsurprisingly, *My Struggle* (*Mein Kampf*-MF) is here chosen as the most indicated text to disentangle Hitler's conceptual configuration. As it is known, this is a miscellany of autobiographical accounts and political manifesto that came to be considered a must-read book for all Germans under the Third Reich (even if very few people actually read it). In spite of being poorly written and badly structured, it is still the best option to fulfil the function that is here needed.

According to historian Ian Kershaw, 'The book did provide, however garbled the presentation, an uncompromising statement of Hitler's political principles, his 'world-view', his sense of his own 'mission', his 'vision' of society, and his long-term aim'.[4] Thus, even if this book does not present a well-defined plan and does not propose any actual political measures, it still displays the basic principles that were behind Hitler's thought and the way how he interpreted the world. The book was divided into two parts, the first of which had a more autobiographical content. It was written in 1924, when Hitler was imprisoned after the failure of the so-called Beer Hall Putsch. Max Amman, a Nazi business manager, would publish this first part in 1925 and the second one (more focused on ideological and political issues) in 1926.

The ideological content of the book does not reveal much originality; it rather represents Hitler's foray into the battle for decontestations that was taking place among right wing groups. In a period of ideological permeability between nationalist groups and parties, Hitler made an effort to be the one setting a definitive configuration for the main themes and ideas that worried those ideologically close to him.

## The conceptual core of *Mein Kampf*

To make reading more enjoyable, the core concepts in this chapter and the ones that follow will not be presented in such a schematised way as in the previous chapter, and more than one concept can be discussed in the same section. Nevertheless, whenever it is necessary, it will be clearly mentioned which concepts are being discussed.

### Race and racial struggle

It is true that Hitler, just as it happens in the case of the generic configuration, strongly emphasises the concept of Nation. This becomes obvious in the first pages of the book, when he narrates how he became a nationalist from a young age, after first encountering the study of history. As he states, 'First, I became a nationalist. Second, I learned to understand and grasp the true meaning of history'.[5] Nationalism thus appears as a key concept to understand the world in Hitler's *Weltanschauung*; it is the concept that is at the basis of his interpretation of history. The Nation is seen as a homogeneous entity, and for this reason he rejects federal rivalries and religious divisions within Germany, refusing to foster strife between Protestants and Catholics, since the enemies of the national community only gain more power when 'Catholics and Protestants are fighting with one another to their hearts' content'.[6] According to the Nazi leader, the truth is that 'for the future of the world, however, it does not matter which of the two triumphs over the other, the Catholic or the Protestant.'

With both being part of German history, the practitioners of both religions should unite to fight a common enemy, like they did in some pivotal moments in the history of the party. That was the case of 1923, when 'the most devoted Protestant could stand side by side with the most devoted Catholic in our ranks without having his conscience disturbed in the slightest as far as concerned his religious convictions'.[7] This way, one can conclude that the adjacent concept of 'Holism' appears in Hitler's configuration just like in generic fascism, which becomes even more evident if one mentions that he also considered the rivalries between German federal states as quarrels that only gave more strength to its enemies.

In Hitler's mind, the only feature which should be used to create divisions among the people living in Germany is that of 'Race'. The concept of 'Race' which plays a role that is more important here than in the generic configuration. In fact, this concept appears in the vicinity of the Nation and, due to its importance, at times it almost seems to take its place in the core. 'Race' closely interlinks with another adjacent concept: 'People' (expressed by the use of the German word 'Volk'). The words 'Volk' and 'Rasse' are used several times throughout the book and, at least in a first impression, they seem to have an interchangeable meaning.[8]

In Hitler's eyes, the world is understood through the lenses of racial distinctions, and his racism contained four main ideas: there were lesser and superior races; the Aryans are superior; there must be a struggle against the dangerous lesser races; and racial purity must be preserved.[9] According to the Nazi leader, the world was divided into three different types of races: 'founders of culture, bearers of culture, and destroyers of culture'. The first are responsible for the creation of 'all the great civilisations of the past' and for making humanity reach a 'superior level of existence'. In his own words, all that we admire in the world to-day, its science, its art, its technical developments and discoveries, are the products of the creative activities of a few peoples, and it may be true that their first beginnings must be attributed to one race. The maintenance of civilization is wholly dependent on such peoples. Should they perish, all that makes this earth beautiful will descend with them into the grave.[10]

The most superior race that ever existed and still exists is the Aryan race, which is described by Hitler as the 'Prometheus of humanity'. This is the race who created civilisation and 'laid the groundwork and erected the walls of every great structure in human culture'. Aryans have 'furnished the great building-stones and plans for the edifices of all human progress'.[11] If such a race were to disappear 'profound darkness will descend on the earth'. The races who belong to the second rank in the hierarchy, the bearers of culture, among which one finds the Japanese, are the ones who can assimilate the technical and scientific knowledge created by superior races, but are not capable of creating anything if left without the influence of 'the enormous scientific and technical achievements of Europe and America, that is to say, of Aryan peoples'. Thus, Hitler is sure that, if the influence of the Western world ceased abruptly, 'the present progress of Japan in science and technique might still last for a short duration, but within a few decades the inspiration would dry up'.[12] As to the races who are at the bottom of the hierarchy, the contempt that the Nazi leader displays towards them is better perceived if one looks at his hatred towards the Jews, of which we will talk more later.

As to the adjacent concept of 'Racial Struggle', it is key to grasp the way he conceived historical evolution. According to him, the struggle between races is something natural, which derives from the very characteristics that each race possesses, just like what happens with animal species: 'the fox remains always a fox, the goose remains a goose, and the tiger will retain the character of a tiger'. Because of that, 'it would be impossible to find a fox which has a kindly and protective disposition towards geese, just as no cat exists which has a friendly disposition towards mice'.[13] The fight between these species is a question of vital instincts, will to survive, and it 'does not arise from a feeling of mutual antipathy but rather from hunger and love'. Human races are perceived no differently from animals in nature, and the enmity between them is seen as having a biological origin.

In their fight for survival, the Aryans became the most important creator of culture for 'as soon as Fate brings them face to face with special circumstances, their powers begin to develop progressively and to be manifested in tangible form'.[14] This race was capable of creating an everlasting culture due to various factors, since 'civilisations are almost always conditioned by the soil, the climate and the people they subjugate'. Nevertheless, the 'last factor – that of the character of the people – is the most decisive one'.[15] Therefore, according to the Nazi leader, and in spite of the several elements that contributed to the development of civilisation, it would not be possible for this superior race to become the 'standard-bearer of human progress' were it not for the features that it naturally possessed.

Lastly, when it comes to 'racial purity', Hitler thought that it was absolutely necessary to preserve by any means the characteristics of the Aryan race that allowed its survival. The Nazi leader strictly opposes miscegenation since 'all the great civilisations of the past became decadent because the originally creative race died out, as a result of contamination of the blood'.[16] Such 'urge for the maintenance of the unmixed breed' was something that once again was present in nature itself for it 'is a phenomenon that prevails throughout the whole of the natural world'.[17] Even in nature, 'each animal mates only with one of its own species' and the 'crossing between two breeds' gives origin to a being which is 'superior to the parent which stands in the biologically lower order of being, but not so high as the higher parent'. For this reason, it will necessarily 'succumb in any struggle against the higher species'.[18]

From this Hitler concludes that:

> If Nature does not wish that weaker individuals should mate with the stronger, she wishes even less that a superior race should intermingle with an inferior one; because in such a case all her efforts, throughout hundreds of thousands of years, to establish an evolutionary higher stage of being, may thus be rendered futile.[19]

Miscegenation is therefore one of the causes of racial degeneration, a 'sin against blood', and must be avoided at all costs. Besides, if the Aryan now face the possibility of extinction, that is because, in the past, they 'neglected to maintain his own racial stock unmixed and therewith lost the right to live in the paradise which he himself had created. He became submerged in the racial mixture and gradually lost his cultural creativeness'.[20]

Finally, we also find the adjacent concept of 'Anti-Semitism' in the vicinity of Nation and 'Race' for, as it is generally known, Hitler considers Jews to be the most dangerous of all the supposedly lesser races and 'the most striking contrast to the Aryan'. Comparing the influence of Jewish people in society to a disease, he goes as far as talking about a 'Jewish contagion' and calling them 'a swarm of rats', a 'pernicious bacillus', and 'parasites', among many other derogatory epithets. Believing that Jews have greatly developed their 'instinct of self-preservation', Hitler nonetheless did not grant them the merit of ever having had a civilisation or having created art because they 'completely lack the most essential pre-requisite of a cultural people, namely the idealistic spirit'.[21] In Hitler's mind, all that the Jews have ever done throughout history was to get hold of the cultures that came from other civilisations, corrupting them. Thus, Jews are not capable of elevated thoughts or actions, and even their apparent racial solidarity among themselves is false and stems from 'herd instinct' for survival.

The absence of an 'idealistic spirit of sacrifice' makes them have a 'brutal egotism' and explains, according to the Nazi leader, why 'the Jewish intellect will never be constructive but always destructive'.[22] Possessing such characteristics, the Jews are bent on the destruction of other cultures, corrupting the civilisations that accept them as their guests for 'wherever he establishes himself the people who grant him hospitality are bound to be bled to death sooner or later'.[23] Likewise incapable of creating their own State and obliged to wander through the world, the Jews survived throughout history by infiltrating other States and 'within the organisation of those States he [the Jew] had formed a State of his own'. Due to their way of surviving, the Jews have also supposedly developed the practice of lying and cunning, for the 'kind of existence which he leads forces the Jew to the systematic use of falsehood'.[24] Being the 'Great Master of Lies', as Hitler calls them by quoting Schopenhauer, Jews supposedly use trickery to corrupt the societies they infiltrate, spreading lies through various ways, including the press.

The Nazi leader places special emphasis on his belief that the Jewish people are not truly a religious community. Instead, this is a lie propagated by Jews themselves to make them be accepted by society. Greater success can be achieved if 'the people who grant him hospitality may be led to believe that the Jew among them is a genuine Frenchman, for instance, or Englishman or German or Italian, who just happens to belong to a religious denomination which is different from that prevailing in these countries'.[25] The Nazi leader even believes that attacking the Jews as if they were a religious group and not a race is one of the reasons so many societies failed to understand their enemy and were destroyed by it.

Because of this, Hitler has no doubt that at the moment in which he was writing the Jews have as their primary goal the destruction of the German Nation and the Aryans. He believes that both Liberalism and Marxism are modern creations of this race and are intended to weaken the national community whether with the talk about 'pacifism', 'democracy', 'cosmopolitism' and 'humanity' (in the case of Liberalism) or with the fostering of class struggle (in the case of Marxism). Having sought the protection of the Bourgeoisie by spreading Liberal ideas, the Jews are now doing the same with the working class by encouraging Marxism, so the Nazi leader believes. In the end, the working people are just victims of one the 'most infamous deceits ever practiced', and since the Jews are behind international capitalism as much as they are behind Marxism, the worker 'is made to fight against capital and thus he is all the more easily brought to fight for capitalist interests'.[26]

Hitler thus sees the corrupt influence of Jews in every sphere of society: in the press (which he calls 'Jewish Press') as well as in the government (mostly composed by the corrupt bourgeoisie that has sold out to the Jews), and believes that powerful members of that lesser race were working in the shadows to destroy Germany. This peril represents the biggest threat against the Aryans and it was to the defeat of the Jews that the superior race must

56  *Adolf Hitler and German national socialism*

devote. His hatred even seems to become a sign of a psychological disorder in the following passage:

> Hence it is that at the present time the Jew is the great agitator for the complete destruction of Germany. Whenever we read of attacks against Germany taking place in any part of the world the Jew is always the instigator. In peace-time, as well as during the War, the Jewish-Marxist stock-exchange Press systematically stirred up hatred against Germany.[27]

*The racial State*

In a passage of his book, Hitler mentions the conceptions of the State that he rejects: the State as 'voluntary association of men who have agreed to set up and obey a ruling authority'; the State 'dependent of same condition' like a 'a uniform system of government'; and the State as 'a means for the realisation of tendencies that arise from a policy of power, on the part of a people who are ethnically homogeneous and speak the same language'.[28] He rejects all these visions because they do not recognise that 'the paramount purpose of the State is to preserve and improve the race'.[29] In Hitler's view 'the fundamental principle is that the State is not an end in itself but the means to an end' and that end is none other than to advance the interests of the best race.[30] The State is worth nothing in itself if it is not animated by the vital will of this race.

Therefore, the adjacent concept of 'Race', which is in the vicinity of Nation, also surrounds the core concept of State and for this reason one can say that what Hitler envisions is a 'Racial State'. This interlinkage occurs because the State is conceived as an instrument that must be submitted to the fulfilment of the needs and goals of the Race. The Aryans need such a State, since a Race needs more than just culture to survive. As he affirms, 'He who talks of the German people as having a mission to fulfil on this earth must know that this cannot be fulfilled except by the building up of a State whose highest purpose is to preserve and promote those nobler elements of our race and of the whole of mankind which have remained unimpaired'.[31] This does not mean that the State is the fundamental prerequisite for cultural progress to take place: as it is already known, that prerequisite in Hitler's mind is always the Race. But the State can play a crucial role if used 'an effective weapon in the service of the great and eternal struggle for existence'.

The Racial State must have at its core a set of racist principles to guide its actions for 'it will be the task of the People's State to make the race the center of the life of the community. It must make sure that the purity of the racial strain will be preserved'.[32] If, for instance, people living in the present are too egoistic to think about the future survival of the Race and of its best elements, it is the function of the State to ensure that 'only those who are healthy shall beget children' and prevent the ones with hereditary diseases from procreating, since it is a crime to 'pass on disease and defects to innocent creatures out of mere egotism'.[33] It must also guarantee that miscegenation does not occur and devotedly zeal for the purity of the Aryans by actively teaching the people about the best practices to have. Furthermore, the State shall also play an important role in other spheres of social life, like educating the youth according to racial principles (including the teaching of history) or the promotion of physical activity in order to improve the Aryan breed.

### Revolution and racial struggle as the key to historical progress

Just like in the generic configuration, the core concept of Revolution in Hitler's ideology relates to a transformation in society that has a spiritual dimension, since he constantly refers to the necessity of inculcating in the masses a 'New Idea', one that would take 'the form of an offensive for the establishment of an entirely new spiritual order of things'.[34] However, to understand the unique features of the Nazi goal of creating a 'New Man', it is important to acknowledge the proximity with the concept of 'Race', for this should be a 'Racial New Man'. Furthermore, the concept of Racial Struggle' is fundamental to show how Hitler conceived progress and the process of historical evolution and transformation. It is thanks to this concept that one can see why he enviosioned his political goals as a revolutionary transformation of a decadent society that would take place according to the laws of history itself. According to the Nazi leader, historical progress occurs in line with the struggle for survival of the superior Aryan race, since struggle is a catalyst for change and for cultural and technological discoveries. 'The process of development towards a higher quality of being' is furthered by the constant struggle that improves the 'powers of resistance in the species'. 'If the case were different' and no improvement occurred, 'the progressive process would cease, and even retrogression might set in'.[35]

Historical progress relates to 'Racial Struggle' in two ways. The fight for survival leads to the creation of tools and inventions that contribute to the progress of humankind, because 'the race that has genius in it needs the occasion and stimulus to bring that genius to expression' and that stimulus can be the struggle. Besides, the subjugation of the lesser races and the enslavement of the weakest is also a catalyst for progress for it can provide the Aryans with the means to construct a higher civilisation. As he says, 'It was not by mere chance that the first forms of civilisation arose where the Aryan came into contact with inferior races, subjugated them and forced them to obey his command', for 'the members of the inferior race became the first mechanical tools in the service of a growing civilisation'.[36]

In sum, the Nazi leader sees historical progress as a ladder that is climbed by the Aryans, who do 'not reach the higher level without first having climbed the lower rungs', that is, without first having to rise above the lesser races.[37] Revolution thus has in its vicinity the important adjacent concept of

58  *Adolf Hitler and German national socialism*

'Social Darwinism', around which there seems to be some strange type of evolutionary ethics.[38] The proximity between the concepts of 'Social Darwinism'/'Racial Struggle' and 'Progress' makes Hitler's configuration acquire a unique understanding of historical transformations and of the forces that drive social change. What most (including the author of this book) would classify as a reactionary ideology that places Racism at its core is presented by Hitler as a worldview with revolutionary garments. To him, seeing the world through the lens of Racism is not only not reactionary, but actually represents the correct way of interpreting the development of societies and understanding the forces that allow for such development.

Lastly, one must also note that, just like in the generic configuration, the 'Cult of Youth' is not absent in the adjacency of Revolution. Hitler sees youth as an age in which the revolutionary spirit can be more easily awakened and which has the vitalism that is necessary to inculcate the race with the will to survive.[39] He is convinced that it is during the time of youth that men 'lay the essential groundwork of their creative thought, wherever that creative thought exists'.[40] Thus, the Racial State must secure and promote the correct development of the young and 'its attention and care must be directed towards the child rather than the adult', for within the former the future of the Aryan race is contained.[41]

### *The authority of the heroic leader*

The core concept of Authority interlinks with the State, for the Racial State must inculcate the notions of discipline and obedience among the masses. In this interlinkage, we find the adjacent concept of 'Hierarchy', just as in the generic configuration. However, more importantly, this concept relates to the organisation of life, society and even the party in a way that goes beyond the power of the State. Thus, the most relevant concepts to be found in its vicinity are 'Leader' and 'Elite', even if Hitler does not always use these words. Instead, he frequently employs terms such as 'hero', 'genius' and 'personality' to refer to people that somehow 'rise beyond the average level of their fellow-men' and for this reason contribute to the progress of history.[42] They are the 'best men' or even 'the most courageous and active elements of its epoch', as Hitler mentions when referring to the type of men that he wants to see involved in his party. Besides, the existence of such outstanding 'men of heroic spirit' is a pre-requisite without which no Revolution can take place, for 'if the struggle on behalf of a *Weltanschauung* is not conducted' by them, within a short period 'it will become impossible to find real fighting followers who are ready to lay down their lives for the cause'.[43]

Without the leadership of such heroic men, the social transformation according to racial principles will simply not be possible, 'for to be a leader means to be able to move the masses'. One of the features that a Leader must exhibit is what Hitler calls the 'rarest phenomenon on this earth'; that is, the union of the 'abilities of theorist and organiser'. A Leader should have a 'very intelligent grasp of the theory underlying a movement' and at the same time 'be a man of psychological insight' that puts ideas into practice and knows how to use human material. Such a marriage of the capacity to understand ideas and organise the masses is a rare feature, one that shall define the true conductor of the Revolution to come. However, one of the important features of Hitler's ideology is that he does not defend the elites that already exist in society, but rather desires that revolutionary activity leads to the discovery of new heroes. Those heroic men may even be hidden among the masses and may seem like ordinary people before some stimulus develops their potential. Thus, it 'will often be found that apparently insignificant persons will nevertheless turn out to be born leaders'.[44]

## *Violence, anti-Semitism and social Darwinism*

In a first dimension, Violence interlinks with the adjacent concept of 'Eliminationism', for Hitler believes that it is necessary to employ force against the enemies and the dangerous elements that imperil the survival of the Race. One finds here once again the adjacent concept of 'Anti-Semitism': since Hitler conceived the Jews as the main enemies of the Aryans, it is naturally for them that he reserves his worst attacks. The extent of his willingness to use Violence against this group of people is best perceived in the following passage:

> At the beginning of the War, or even during the War, if twelve or fifteen thousand of these Jews who were corrupting the nation had been forced to submit to poison-gas, just as hundreds of thousands of our best German workers from every social stratum and from every trade and calling had to face it in the field, then the millions of sacrifices made at the front would not have been in vain.[45]

Apart from this, Violence appears as the key concept that explains life itself and the basis upon which society must rest. In Hitler's view, the world is a place of struggle for survival in which only the strongest have the right to live. As he says, 'Man must realise that a fundamental law of necessity reigns throughout the whole realm of Nature and that his existence is subject to the law of eternal struggle and strife'.[46] In a world that mostly consists of Violence and fights, 'He who would live must fight'. Human societies must accept the existence of this struggle and carry it without any mercy for the ones who prove to be weak, since 'he who does not wish to fight in this world, where permanent struggle is the law of life, has not the right to exist'.[47] It is only the will of nature that some die in waging this struggle. With all this, one finds once again in Hitler's configuration the adjacent concept of 'Social Darwinism', which is inserted in it with a supposedly biological justification.

60  *Adolf Hitler and German national socialism*

Underlying this conception is a notion that the supposed laws of nature are inescapable and also concern human beings, since they too are a part of the natural world. Violence is a force that is biologically determined among animals and humans. As he says, 'Man must not fall into the error of thinking that he was ever meant to become lord and master of Nature', thus asserting that it is best for human beings to accept laws that they cannot alter.[48] With this in mind, it is possible to see why Hitler considered Pacifism to be a 'morbid weakness': it is a dangerous and vain attempt to escape from the inevitable laws of Nature.

Lastly, we recognise that some of the adjacent concepts of the generic configuration also appear in Hitler's book in one way or another. That is the case of 'War', which is viewed by Hitler as an event in which ordinary people come face to face with 'a special situation' and discover a heroic nature that they did not think they possessed. Soldiers, in war, become heroes 'full of determination, undaunted in the presence of Death and manifesting wonderful powers of calm reflection under such circumstances', he says. If war did not exist 'nobody would have thought that the soul of a hero lurked in the body of that beardless youth'.[49] The concept of 'Virility' is noticed whenever Hitler mentions heroic features as being characteristics of males as well as when he scorns what he deems to be the feminine and passive characteristics of cowards and of the masses when they are left unguided. Furthermore, the Violent struggle for survival is in itself seen as a masculine principle that is compared to the 'fight of the male to possess the female'. As to the concept of 'Sacrifice', seen as the ultimate act of honour by a hero in a violent struggle, it is noticeable when Hitler says that 'the readiness to sacrifice one's personal work and, if necessary, even one's life for others shows its most highly developed form in the Aryan race'.[50]

### *Vital space and the survival of the race*

The concept of 'Irredentism' surrounding the core concept of Empire is not lost on Hitler's ideology, for right from the beginning of the book he states that it is necessary to reunite all ethnic Germans under the same State, which included the annexation of Austria. He explicitly affirms that Austria must be 'restored to the Great Motherland', even if 'the union were a matter of economic indifference, and even if it were to be disadvantageous from the economic standpoint'. The defence of German irredentism has a deep meaning in Hitler's ideology, for he believed that, 'German people will have no right to engage in a colonial policy until they shall have brought all their children together in the one State'.[51]

However, Empire mainly manifests itself through the call for the conquering of territory in Eastern Europe, which means that the adjacent concept of 'Expansionism' is in the vicinity of this core concept. Since reconquering the small Empire in the African continent that Germany once

## Adolf Hitler and German national socialism 61

had seemed not to be possible anymore, 'it ought to be an Eastern policy which will have in view the acquisition of such territory as is necessary for our German people'.[52] He also adds that it is fundamental to 'put an end to the perpetual Germanic march towards the South and West of Europe and turn our eyes towards the lands of the East'.[53] The conquering of Eastern Europe is even conceived as the 'territorial policy of the future', thereby distinguishing Nazi Foreign Policy from the one conceived by previous German regimes.

Such an expansionist policy would have the goal of solving the problems which Germany had been facing due to the growth of population, since none of the other solutions mentioned by Hitler seem to him to be feasible: the control of the number of births; internal colonisation; and increasing the exports in the international market. In this sense, one finds the concept of 'Lebensraum' or 'Vital Space' about which we already talked and which refers to the territory that Germany needed. The 'Vital Space is 'that territorial magnitude which gives it the necessary importance to-day and assures the existence of its citizens'.[54] Since what is in stake is the survival of the country itself, 'the right to territory may become a duty' because that is what happen 'when a great nation seems destined to go under unless its territory be extended'.[55]

In the first place, Eastern European territories can give the Aryan Race the food and resources that it needs to survive, since 'only a sufficiently large space on this Earth can assure the independent existence of a people'.[56] Besides, the conquering of such places plays an important role in the German fight against its main enemy, 'the international Jew, who is to-day the absolute master of Russia'.[57] Seeing Russian Bolshevism as a facade behind which the Jews hid, Hitler had no doubts that the Soviet regime represented another Jewish machination destined to conquer the world and that its next goal was to defeat Germany, which is 'the next battlefield for Russian Bolshevism'. Thus, Hitler seemed sure that 'International Jewry' would oppose his foreign policy of expanding eastwards, but he shows no will to retreat because the 'struggle against the Jewish Bolshevization of the world demands that we should declare our position towards Soviet Russia'.[58]

Interestingly enough, we find once again the concept of 'Anti-Semitism' surrounding the core concept of Empire. Hitler's configuration is so dependent on this adjacent concept that it makes a new appearance to justify Nazi imperialism and to give it an ideological interpretation that seems unique when compared to other right wing ideologies that have existed in Germany since before World War I. The goal of defeating the Jews in the Racial struggle and the goal of expanding eastwards were intrinsically linked in his mind, since both represented a necessary task destined to guarantee the survival of the German Nation and the Aryan Race.[59]

62  *Adolf Hitler and German national socialism*

Lastly, notice what Hitler has to say about Russia in the following passage:

> In delivering Russia over to Bolshevism, Fate robbed the Russian people of that intellectual class which had once created the Russian State and were the guarantee of its existence. For the Russian State was not organised by the constructive political talent of the Slav element in Russia, but was much more a marvelous exemplification of the capacity for State-building possessed by the Germanic element in a race of inferior worth.[60]

The Nazi leader clearly believed that every achievement of Russian civilisation in the past was due to the presence of German elements within its people and that, after the Bolshevik Revolution and the triumph of the Jews, such racially superior traits were no longer present in the new elites of the country. For this reason, Russia was now condemned to decay. Besides, the new regime in Russia immediately discarded any possibility of an alliance between Germany and this country, because this would only serve the interests of the Jews.

## Other important features of the configuration

### *Corporatism: a less relevant concept*

We must note that the concept of Corporatism seems not to be given the same priority that it receives in the generic configuration. This lesser relevance may be due to Hitler's depreciation of economic issues or, at least, of economic issues which are not conceived within the scope of racial struggle, which Hitler himself seemed keen to acknowledge. That is what happens, for instance, when he says that 'no improvement can be brought about until it be understood that economics plays only a second or third role, while the main part is played by political, moral and racial factors'.[61] If we move away from Hitler's text just for a moment to analyse the history of Nazism, we can confirm that the Nazi regime never fully adopted a corporatist economic system, thus distancing itself from the Italian regime. However, Nazism did dwell in the theme of Corporatism, albeit tentatively, at a time when the party elites were concerned with social matters during the 20s. This is enough for us to try to find references to this concept in Hitler's book.

Indeed, some of the adjacent concepts that surround Corporatism in the generic configuration are present in Hitler's book, such as 'Class Conciliation'. When discussing the role of National Socialist Trade Unions, Hitler states that 'National Socialist workers and employers are both together the delegates and mandatories of the whole national community'. Workers 'will have to recognise the fact that the economic prosperity of the nation brings with it their own material happiness'; as for the employer, he 'must recognise that the happiness and contentment of his employees are necessary pre-requisites for the existence and development of his own economic prosperity'.[62] Thus, Hitler comes close to defending a Corporatist solution for Germany when he supports a system that conciliates the interests of workers and employers, at the same time that he affirms that 'the trade unions are necessary as building stones for the future economic parliament, which will be made up of chambers representing various professions and occupations'.[63]

Another theme that is important to understand Hitler's views on economics is the so-called 'Social Question', a term which he himself uses and which refers to the problems of poverty and misery in society. The Nazi leader says that 'the attention which I had given to economic problems during my earlier years was more or less confined to considerations arising directly out of the social problem'.[64] Claiming to have formerly lived a life of poverty, he uses his supposed experience to describe the miseries of a poor working class affected by bad working conditions, alcoholism, family dysfunction and problems related to the healthy growth of children, among many others. This concern is accompanied by a contempt for the bourgeois parties who seem to ignore the legitimate claims of the working class, whose plights are thus perpetuated.

However, one must not think that this preoccupation with the 'Social Question' derives from a genuine desire to improve the living conditions of every citizen, for it has its origin in the fear that Marxism might exploit social inequalities to further divide the Nation and push workers against the upper classes. Solving the 'Social Question' is imperative for the workers to regain pride on the Nation they live in, for 'when one half of a nation is sunk in misery and worn out by hard distress, or even depraved or degenerate, that nation presents such an unattractive picture that nobody can feel proud to belong to it'.[65] Hitler's concern for poverty does not come from any commitment to end every type of inequallity, but is born out of the desire to reintegrate the poor in a cohesive national unity in which the workers can also be a source for the best elements of the Aryan racial stock.[66]

*Peripheral concepts*

In the first place, one can note that the concept of 'Liberty' is marginal in Hitler's configuration. The status of this concept is seen when, discussing the role of the State, Hitler asserts that 'a strong national Government can intervene to a considerable degree in the liberties of the individual subject'.[67] Individual freedoms are thus secondary in relation to the ultimate goals of the future Reich and its State. However, as it will be seen in the following sections, in spite of this marginality, the way how Hitler conceived the importance of individual action was more complex and ambiguous than one might at first think.

As to perimeter concepts, they are the ones that exist in intersection with reality and refer to the moments in which Hitler's configuration gains a more concrete and pragmatic dimension. Such perimeter concepts only make sense if we place them in the specific time and space in which Hitler wrote, making them less abstract than the other concepts until here analysed. For instance, in the perimeter of Violence we can find the 'Organisation of Squads', which refers to the actual construction of an organisation destined to use violent acts in the fight against enemies. It is unnecessary to describe in detail all possible perimeter concepts because they are implicit in our analysis of MF, but we can say, for instance, that in the perimeter of Empire it is also found 'Annexation of Austria' and 'Conquering of Eastern Europe', which refer to goals that only make sense in the specific German context in which Hitler wrote.

## *Permeability and rejections*

At first glance, one could conclude that Hitler's configuration permeates with some notions and ideas coming from his rivals on the left, which can be seen in the discussion about the 'Social Question' and in the use of the concept of Revolution. However, it was already observed that the 'Social Question' is secondary in his ideology and, as to the concept of Revolution, it is decontested in a totally different way from the one that is found in left wing ideologies. Thus, it is rather important to verify the permeability with other conservative and radical right ideologies. Two personalities that he specifically mentions are Karl Lueger and Georg Ritter Von Schönerer.

Lueger, leader of the Austrian Christian Social Party 'had a rare gift of insight into human nature and he was very careful not to take men as something better than they were in reality'.[68] It was Lueger's supposed knowledge about human nature that influenced Hitler in his defence of the propagandist measures that he deemed to be adequate for the limited comprehension of the masses. As to Schönerer, a proponent of Pan-Germanism, he was a major figure in the propagation of Germanic Nationalism and of the idea that all Germans must reunite under the same State. However, 'he did not understand that only the broad masses of a nation can make such convictions prevail, which are almost of a religious nature'.[69] In other words, he did not have the same understanding on the nature of the masses as Lueger did, and that was his main weakness. According to Hitler, these two leaders played an important part in the construction of this ideology, even if none of them held a complete view of the problems facing the German people. The way how they conceived nationalism (in the case of Schönerer) and the role of the masses (in the case of Lueger) were therefore incorporated in Hitler's conceptual configuration.

The most important rejections of Hitler's ideology are Liberalism and, of course, Communism. The concept of 'Anti-Semitism' is important to explain both rejections for the leader of Nazism attributes the propagation of these two ideologies to malicious manoeuvres by the Jews. In Liberalism, Hitler rejected individualism, partidary politics, free press, the notion of egalitarian rights and even liberal institutions like the Parliament. As to Communism, Hitler sees it as a tool employed by the Jews to remove workers from the influence of nationalist ideologies and weaken the unity of Germany. Employing a very broad and imprecise definition of Marxism (which also includes the SPD), Hitler sees this ideology as his most dreaded foe and the concept of Revolution is the key to understand this rejection: while it is true that Hitler also uses this concept, he interlinks it with the concept of 'Racial Struggle', and not 'Class Struggle', as communists do. It is the difference in the decontestation that definitively separates the Nazi Revolution from the one that is defended by his ennemies and renders their views irreconcilable.

## *Contradictions: individual/collectivity and people/leader*

Hitler makes a first impression that he holds a collectivist view of society, rejecting individual liberalism. Nevertheless, he also seems to see individual actions as the motor of history and as the creator of all inventions valuable to humanity. As he states, 'Human progress and human cultures are not founded by the multitude. They are exclusively the work of personal genius and personal efficiency'.[70] Thus, there seems to be a contradiction between the concepts of 'Individual' and 'Collectivity' in Hitler's configuration. We argue here that this contradiction is solved thanks to the concept of 'Personality', which is distinguished from the liberal concept of 'Individual' because, in Hitler's view, liberal values can only lead to egoistic actions. 'Personality', on the contrary, is like an entity that rises higher than the rest of the community due to its genius and heroism but is at the same time capable of sacrificing for the collective good of the racial community. 'Personality', therefore, refers to a type of man that is inserted in his racial community and who acts as an individual but in the service of the collective.

When interpreting history, Hitler acknowledges the importance of individual actions, for instance, in the beginning of human civilisation, because 'there can be no doubt that personality was then the sole factor in all decisions and achievements'. However, such achievements were not destined to serve only the interests of the individuals who created them, since they 'were afterwards taken over by the whole of humanity as a matter of course'.[71] Thus, it is true that all important inventions throughout history 'have been produced by the creative powers and capabilities of individuals', but it is also true that 'they serve to elevate the human species and continually to promote its progress', that is, they had a collective value.[72] Hitler's ideology combines individualism and collectivism in a way that ends up not seeming contradictory precisely due to the concept of 'Personality'. With it, he is able to both praise the individual deeds of outstanding men at the same time that he shows his contempt for acts of individualism and egoism that do not serve the whole racial community.[73]

Likewise, there seems to be a contradiction between the concept of 'People' and 'Leader' or, if one prefers, between the concepts of 'Populism' and 'Elitism'. The 'People', or sometimes the 'Masses', are both conceived as a group incapable of doing anything apart from blindly following a 'Leader' and as the group that holds the power to make the Nation go forward. In the first place, Hitler says that 'the broad masses are never able clearly to see the whole stretch of the road lying in front of them without becoming tired and thus losing faith in their ability to complete the task'.[74] These are people 'whose powers of comprehension are limited and will always remain so'.[75] Nevertheless, in another passage, the Nazi leader sees the 'Masses' in a more positive light and states that 'no great idea, no matter how sublime and exalted it may appear, can be realised in practice without the effective power which resides in the popular masses'.[76]

Somehow, it is as if the incapacity of the 'Masses' and their need for a 'Leader' to guide them does not mean that they are not a necessary element to change society. As he says, 'The masses are first set in motion, along a definite direction, by men of superior talents; but then these masses once in motion are like a flywheel inasmuch as they sustain the momentum and steady balance of the offensive'.[77] The 'Masses' need a 'Leader' to initiate a Revolution, but so does the 'Leader' needs the strength that they give to him, so it appears that the 'Leader' and the 'Masses' complement each other in Nazi ideology.

One can note that the tension between elitist and populist themes in Hitler's morphology is never completely solved and is present throughout the entire book (from now on, we shall refer to this contradiction as 'Populism/Elitism' and we will try to see if it also appears in other leaders' configurations). This also means that, in Hitler's ideology, there seems to be a constant tension between the elements that refer to a certain type of egalitarianism among the members of the Race and the elements that clearly refer to elitist conceptions of society. Thus, his supposed concern for the creation of a racial community without 'class distinctions' does not exclude the reverence for the elitist notion of the 'aristocratic principle of Nature'. In Hitler's view, the creation of a homogeneous racial community, in which *old* class differences would disappear, coexists with the goal of creating *new* elites rising above the masses by becoming heroes. This is what explains the tension between 'Populism' and 'Elitism' in his conceptual morphology.

## Concluding remarks

According to Michael Burleigh, 'Hitler took over existing ideas and converted them into a comprehensive programme for a racial new order'.[78] Hitler's configuration is thus far from being original, representing the product of a fierce struggle for meaning that was taking place when the Nazi leader wrote *Mein Kampf*. His conceptual morphology also emerged from the necessity of transforming reactionary concepts and themes and, through specific interlinkages, give them a revolutionary garment, which explains the interlinkage between 'Racial Struggle' and Revolution. This was so because of the necessity of making up an ideological discourse capable of turning the masses and the working class away from Marxism and give them something in alternative: another idea that presented itself as revolutionary.

In spite of some specificities, like the lesser relevance of the concept of Corporatism, it is possible to recognise in this configuration a permutation of fascist ideology. Nevertheless, we do acknowledge that concepts such as 'Race' and 'Racial Struggle' play an important role that is not perceptible in the main generic configuration. These concepts interlink with all the other core concepts and it is not possible to understand Hitler's ideology without them. However, we do not purpose to substitute the concept of Nation for that of Race. We thus still consider that Hitler uses the Nation as his main core concept, even if it is true that to understand his nationalism is crucial to acknowledge that the nation is here defined in terms of race and racial unity.

## Notes

1 The idea that Adolf Hitler was a sincere ideologue rather than a pathological liar was first defended by Hugh Trevor-Roper, 'The Mind of Adolf Hitler' in *Hitler's Table Talk 1941–1944* (London, Enigma Books, 1953). Several decades later, the same ideas was endorsed by Lawrence Birken, *Hitler as Philosophe: Remnants of the Enlightenment in National Socialism* (Santa Barbara, Praeger, 1995), 1–22. This author dismisses the so called 'psychotic' theories on the basis that they are too individualistic and defends an approach that sees Hitler as a philosopher. Lukacs, assessing historiographic representations of Hitler, also rejects the ones who see him as a pure opportunist with pathological problems. See John Lukacs, *The Hitler of History* (New York, Random House, 1997).

2 Rather controversially, Birken states that 'read with an open mind, Hitler indeed appears as a startlingly intelligent thinker who felt compelled to work out an elaborate political philosophy. In particular, if we agree that intellectuals should be judged as much for the questions they ask as for their answers, then Hitler must be regarded as a genuine intellectual'. Birken, *Hitler as Philosophe*, 1. While rejecting Birken's apparent admiration for his subject of study, we do agree on the necessity of studying Hitler's ideas seriously.

3 'By 1900 völkisch concepts had become a relatively formalised ideology, spread by publishing houses, numerous writers and artists, many professors, and thousands of schoolteachers. It seems to have become predominant among teachers and was preached in the classroom, and it also permeated the quasi rebels of the organised youth movement that had sixty thousand members – often the elite of middle- and upper-middle-class youth – by 1914.' Stanley Payne, *A History of Fascism, 1914–1945* (Madison, University of Wisconsin Press, 1995), 53.

4 Ian Kershaw, *Hitler* (New York, W. W. Norton & Company, 2000), 243–244.

5 Adolf Hitler, *Mein Kampf*, Translated by Ralph Manheim (London, Hurst & Blackett LTD, 1939), 22. Note that we are using the translation by Ralph Manheim, which was first published in 1939.

6 Ibid., 429.

7 Ibid., 431.

8 However, authors like Lukacs do claim that there was a slight difference between them, being 'Race' the concept that is used when Hitler wants to talk about the blood ties that unite the people. However, we argue that this distinction does not always seem to hold up, and that there are passages in which the two concepts are

68  *Adolf Hitler and German national socialism*

used with the exact same meaning. Without further ado, we can agree with Weikart, when he states that 'whenever Hitler asserted the primacy of the German *Volk*, he was thinking of it as a racial category'. In Hitler's views, the word 'Volk', just like 'Race', was still defined in relation to blood purity and when he mentioned this concept he was actually interested in 'forging a common language and culture for the German people'. For this reason, he used a word with which several nationalist groups could identify and interpret as a call for racial purity. This was possible for, in the last decades, German *Volkisch* nationalism had clearly acquired racist connotations and was widely interpreted as a form of constructing a 'racial solidarity'.

9 'Hitler's racism therefore consisted of the following elements. Firstly. There were differences in the value of individual races. Secondly, the "Aryans" were the most "valuable" race. Thirdly, if the "Aryan" race interbred with the "less valuable races" it would inevitably decline into extinction, a development which would have to be prevented. Fourthly, not only the "purity" but also the "health" of the "Aryan" race had to be maintained and improved'. Michael Burleigh, *The Racial State: Germany 1933–1945* (Cambridge. Cambridge University Press, 1991), 42.
10 Hitler, *Mein Kampf*, 225.
11 Ibid., 226.
12 Ibid., 227.
13 Ibid., 223.
14 Ibid., 230.
15 Ibid., 226.
16 Ibid., 226.
17 Ibid., 223.
18 Ibid., 222.
19 Ibid., 223.
20 Ibid., 231.
21 Ibid., 235.
22 Ibid., 237.
23 Ibid., 238.
24 Ibid., 238.
25 Ibid., 239.
26 Ibid., 249.
27 Ibid., 476.
28 Ibid., 301–302.
29 Ibid., 304.
30 Ibid., 305.
31 Ibid., 310.
32 Ibid., 314.
33 Ibid., 314–315.
34 Ibid., 142.
35 Ibid., 223.
36 Ibid., 231.
37 Ibid., 230.
38 Richard Weikart was among the first to note that there was a kind of an evolutionary ethics in Hitler's thought regarding social Darwinism and progress. According to him, 'Hitler's ethic was essentially an evolutionary ethic that exalted biological progress above all other moral considerations. [...] This eternal law of struggle, in Hitler's view, produced all that was good in the world. It must continue, if further progress were to be made'. Richard Weikart, *Hitler's Ethic: The Nazi Pursuit of Evolutionary Progress*, 148.

39 'In a speech featured in the film *Triumph of the Will*, he pledged that soon young people would not even be able to imagine the bygone infection of our poisonous party system...Youth, says he, has been consigned to us and has become our bodies and souls' Claudia Koonz, *Nazi Conscience* (Cambridge, Harvard University Press, 2003), 131.
40 Hitler, *Mein Kampf*, 30.
41 Ibid., 314.
42 Ibid., 229.
43 Ibid., 92.
44 Ibid., 442–443.
45 Ibid., 512.
46 Ibid., 194.
47 Ibid., 226.
48 Ibid., 194. Also according to Weikart, 'Hitler believed his ideas were rooted in the laws of nature, which humanity spurned at its peril. He scoffed at those who thought they could transcend nature and set aside its immutable laws, especially its racial laws. Trying to stymie nature in its course would only result in disaster, he explained, since "the man who misjudges and disregards the racial laws [of nature] actually forfeits the happiness that seems destined to be his. He thwarts the triumphal march of the best race and hence also the precondition for all human progress." Conversely, racial awareness and policy based on it would foster improvement of the human species. In the first few pages of this chapter Hitler stressed the importance of racial inequality and racial struggle for his worldview'. Richard Weikart, *Hitler's Ethic: The Nazi Pursuit of Evolutionary Progress*, 59.
49 Hitler, *Mein Kampf*, 229.
50 Ibid., 232.
51 Ibid., 17.
52 Ibid., 508.
53 Ibid., 500.
54 Ibid., 500.
55 Ibid., 500.
56 Ibid., 491.
57 Ibid., 505.
58 Ibid., 490.
59 According to Eberhard Jäckel, 'He had to annihilate the Jews, thus restoring the meaning of history, and with the thus restored, nature-intended struggle for existence, he at the same time had to conquer new living space for the German people. Each of these tasks was inextricably linked to the other. Unless the Jews were annihilated there would very soon no longer be any struggle for living space, nor therefore any culture and consequently nations would die out; not just the German nation, but ultimately all nations. But if, on the other hand, the German people failed to conquer new living space, it would die out because of that and the Jews would triumph'. Eberhard Jäckel, *Hitler's World View: A Blueprint for Power* (Cambridge, Harvard University Press, 1981), 106.
60 Hitler, *Mein Kampf*, 500.
61 Ibid., 181. However, Adam Tooze seems to reject this idea and points out that Hitler did have an economic thought. See Adam Tooze, *Wages of Destruction* (London, Penguin Books, 2008).
62 Hitler, *Mein Kampf*, 459.
63 Ibid., 458–459.
64 Ibid., 456.
65 Ibid., 459.

66 Ibid., 331.
67 Ibid., 341.
68 Ibid., 87.
69 Ibid., 85.
70 Ibid., 270.
71 Ibid., 344.
72 Ibid., 345.
73 Lawrence Birken summarises this question in the following way: 'The German dictator believed that all growth could be traced to individual effort – but only at the service of the common good. He thus tempered what might be taken as a "libertarian" definition of inventiveness with a sombre collectivism. Invention, Hitler believed, was thus the product of individual geniuses of high *personality value*. But personality value was in turn conditioned by the individual's biological (racial) endowments or *race value* so that an economic policy had to be underpinned by a racial policy.' Lawrence Birken, *Hitler as Philosophe*, 56.
74 Hitler, *Mein Kampf*, 198.
75 Ibid., 87.
76 Ibid., 94.
77 Ibid., 94.
78 Burleigh, *The Third Reich*, 305.

## List of references

Birken, Lawrence, *Hitler as Philosophe: Remnants of the Enlightenment in National Socialism* (Santa Barbara, Praeger, 1995).

Bracher, Karl Dietrich, *The German Dictatorship: The Origins, Structure, and Consequences of National Socialism* (Santa Barbara, Prager, 1970).

Broszat, Martin, *The Hitler State: The Foundation and Development of the Internal Structure of the Third Reich* (Harlow, Longman Group, 1981 [1969]).

Bullock, Allan, *Hitler: A Study in Tyranny* (Watford, Odhams Press, 1952).

Burleigh, Michael, *The Third Reich: A New History* (New York, Hill and Wang, 2001).

Dregger, Sebastien, *Conflicts, Compromises and Mutual Self-interest – how the Nazis and the Catholic and Protestant Churches dealt with each other during the Third Reich* (Munich, GRIN Verlage, 2008).

Evans, Richard, *The Third Reich in Power* (London, Penguin, 2006).

Fest, Joachim, *Hitler* (Paris, Gallimard, 1973).

Glaser, Hermann, *The Cultural Roots of National Socialism* (Austin, University of Texas Press, 1978).

Gordon, Sarah Ann, *Hitler, Germans and the Jewish Question* (Princeton University Press, 1984).

Gorlitz, Walter and Herbet Quint, *Adolf Hitler* (Paris, Presses Pocket, 1962).

Griffin, Roger, *The Nature of Fascism* (London, Routledge, 1993).

Heiden, Konrad, *A History of National Socialism* (London, Routledge, 2013 [1934]).

Hildebrand, Klaus, *The Third Reich* (London, G. Allen & Unwin, 1984).

Hilgruber, Andreas, *Germany and The Two World Wars* (Harvard University Press, 1981 [1967]).

Hitler, Adolf, *Mein Kampf*, Translated by Ralph Manheim (London, Hurst & Blackett LTD, 1939).

## Adolf Hitler and German national socialism

Hunt, Richard M. 'Myths, Guilt, and Shame in Pre-Nazi Germany', *Virginia Quarterly Review*, 34, 1958, 355–371.

Jäckel, Eberhard, *Hitler's World View: A Blueprint for Power* (Cambridge, Harvard University Press, 1981).

Kershaw, Ian, *Hitler* (New York, W. W. Norton & Company, 2000, 2001).

Koonz, Claudia, *Nazi Conscience* (Cambridge, Harvard University Press, 2003).

Lukacs, John, *The Hitler of History* (New York, Random House, 1997).

Maser, Werner, *Hitler: Legend, Myth & Reality* (London, Harper & Row, 1973).

Mazower, Mark, *Hitler's Empire: Nazi Rule in Occupied Europe* (London, Penguin Books, 2008).

Mitchell, Allan, *Revolution in Bavaria, 1918–1919: The Eisner Regime and the Soviet Republic* (Princeton, Princeton University Press, 1965).

Mosse, George, *Nazi Culture: Intellectual, Cultural and Social Life in the Third Reich* (New York, Schocken Books, 1966).

Mosse, George, *The Nationalization of the Masses: Political Symbolism and Mass Movements in Germany, from the Napoleonic Wars Through the Third Reich* (New York, Howard Fertig Pub., 1975).

Payne, Stanley, *A History of Fascism, 1914–1945* (Madison, University of Wisconsin Press, 1995).

Steinert, Marlis, *Hitler: A Biography* (New York, W.W. Norton, 1997).

Toland, John, *Hitler* (New York, Doubleday Books, 1976).

Weikart, Richard, *Hitler's Ethic: The Nazi Pursuit of Evolutionary Progress* (London, Palgrave Macmillan, 2009).

Welch, David, *Hitler: Profile of a Dictator* (London, Routledge, 2001).

# 3 Oswald Mosley and the British Union of Fascists

The Ideological Synthesis of 'Greater Britain'

Even if formed in 1932, after the appearance of both Rotha Lintorn-Orman's British Fascists (which lasted from 1923 to 1934) and Arnold Lese's Imperial Fascist League (which lasted from 1929 to 1939), the British Union of Fascists (BUF) was to become the best known example of a fascist organisation in British soil. Its leader was former Labour MP Oswald Mosley, who would continue to play a relevant role in European neo-fascism after WWII, even if not a particularly prominent one in British mainstream politics. Frequently, we come across authors who regret that, had Mosley not let himself be fascinated by fascism, he could have had a remarkable career, for he was considered by many as one of the most promising politicians of his generation. It is precisely such a strange personality that is about to be the focus of this chapter.

## Mosley and the BUF

Oswald Mosley was born on 16 November 1896 in London. After having fought in France during World War I, he entered politics as a Conservative MP. However, he soon became disappointed with the party and began feeling politically closer to Left Wing ideas, eventually joining the Labour Party. It was in 1929, after the elections that led to the formation of the Labour cabinet of Ramsay MacDonald, that Mosley had his first chance to play an impactful role in the politics of his country. Given the task of finding a solution to the problem of unemployment, he conceived a plan which contained a set of interventionist proposals that included the nationalisation of some sectors of the British industry. However, his approach to economic problems clearly collided with that of his colleagues at that time, and he moved away from the party after his proposal was definitely rejected in a Labour congress in October 1930.[1]

However, he was still focused on the goal of finding an alternative economic policy for his country in a time when the effects of the Great Depression were beginning to be felt. For this reason, he found his own New Party in 1931, but this proved incapable of putting forward a political programme impactful enough to influence British politics.[2] Thus, in the general elections of 1931, the New Party did not succeed in winning any seats. By this time, it had become clear to many of his supporters that Mosley was increasingly becoming an admirer of fascism and that the corporatist proposals of the New Party resembled those put into practice by the Italian regime. After a trip to Italy, where he went with the goal of studying the policies of fascism, Mosley came back to the United Kingdom with a clear goal in mind: to create a fascist movement that would be as relevant as the one led by Mussolini.

In 1932, he finally created the BUF which, as was already mentioned, and in spite of its failure, was destined to become the most notorious example of British fascism. In the next few years, his movement would try to make its voice heard in Britain, even if oftentimes unsuccessfully, and managed to get the attention and support of many relevant figures, including the proprietor of the Daily Mail. Among the most notorious personalities that adhered to Mosley's movement, one can mention Alexander Raven Thomson (who became a leading ideologue), William Joyce (later to be known by his nickname Lord Haw Haw) and A.K. Chesterton (who was second cousin to writer G.K. Chesterton).

However, due to the stability of the country's parliamentary democracy, neither the ruling classes nor the Conservative party were prone to establish the same kind of alliances that had led Mussolini and Hitler to power. Besides, the BUF was not even able to participate in the 1935 elections (the last before the war) and Mosley gained a bad reputation after his approximation to the Nazi variant of fascism and the increasingly anti-Semitic tone of his interventions.[6] Furthermore, the credibility of the BUF was severely damaged due to events like the mass meeting known as the Olympia Rally in 1934, in which anti-fascists were violently attacked. Apart from this event, the Battle of Cable Street, which took place in 1936, contributed to strengthen the idea that Mosley was an unreliable and violent politician. This consisted of a clash between Mosley's Black Shirts and their opponents, which happened when the fascist leader provocatively decided to march with his followers through a Jewish neighbourhood and was met with the retaliation of Left Wing militants.[3]

Mosley's goals would soon become definitely impossible to achieve when, after the beginning of World War II, he and some other fascist activists were interned or imprisoned to prevent any act of sabotage in favour of Nazi Germany. Thus, eight years after its formation, the BUF met its dissolution in 1940. Mosley did make a comeback to politics after the conflict and played a relatively relevant role in European neo-fascism, creating in 1948 the Union Movement, a far-right political party that would exist until 1973. However, he was never able to get rid of his image as an anti-Semitic supporter of Hitler and he came to die in 1980 without coming anywhere close to witnessing a fascist revolution in his country.

## Oswald Mosley amid the ideological struggles of his time

It is generally assumed that the United Kingdom lived a period of relative prosperity, social peace and progress during the 20s and that the ideals of democracy and individual liberty have never been at risk. Furthermore, the existence of a hegemonic right wing party, the Conservative Party, contrary to what happened in Germany, seemed to render fierce ideological struggles unnecessary. It is true that some far-right organisations did emerge during the 20s, as was the case of Lintorn-Orman's British Fascists, but they never came close to playing a relevant role. In a context in which democracy was apparently so highly valued, it seems only natural that Mosley's party was destined to become a failure. Independently of the ideological aspects in which he was close to most people on the right, the anti-democratic content of his political programme separated him from them. Such status of the BUF as an outlier that never achieved any success could be enough for one to argue that its study is unnecessary and does not add much to what one needs to know about fascism.

Nevertheless, this apparent insignificance can be misleading for, even if the BUF never attained actual power, it did establish links with other sectors of the dominant right wing sectors, sometimes even having secret meetings with members of the Conservative establishment who were too ashamed to support him publicly. This may be a sign that Mosley's ideology, in the end, was not such an isolated phenomenon in British politics. After all, the BUF and the dominant right wing establishment did share some common concerns and ideological features. That was the case, for instance, of 'Anti-Communism', which was persistent among the British elite at least since the final years of World War I, even if not coated with such violent traits as in Germany. The Conservatives had an attitude of distrust towards the USSR and the fear of a communist revolution was present throughout the 20s. Their concern increased as Labour substituted the Liberals as one of the two dominant parties and also during events like the General Strike of 1926. Likewise, the concept of 'Empire' was relevant in some of the reactionary sectors and individuals of the political right that became active at the beginning of the 30s (and in Winston Churchill as well) to protest against the attempts of giving more self-determination to India. They were as much worried as Mosley about the possibility of the British Empire coming to an end and making England definitely lose its place as a world power. Furthermore, the concept of 'Corporatism' also became highly contested in the first years of the 30s, not only among the political Right. It was seen by many groups as a possible solution to the problems of the liberal market and as an alternative way to reorganise the economic system of the nation.

Martin Pugh goes as far as to say that 'the arguments deployed by fascists enjoyed a lengthy pedigree extending into the Late-Victorian era'.[4] Mosley's ideology must thus be inserted in the ideological context of British politics in which his conceptual configuration emerged, contradicting the classical approaches 'which persistently emphasised the 'alien' character of the BUF in British society and the natural liberalism of Britons'.[5] Rather than being alien to British politics, Mosley's movement is clearly a part of the political milieu of its time and is part of an ideological and political context that should be understood 'not in terms of tight categories but as part of a spectrum'.[6] In this sense, disentangling Mosley's conceptual configuration can be a valuable task for it gives a broader notion of the concepts and ideas that were being discussed and the struggles for meaning that somehow were taking place among some sectors of the British Right (even among the sectors who rejected the authoritarianism of the fascist leader).

To disentangle such a configuration, it shall here be used *The Greater Britain* (GB), a book written in 1932, right after Mosley had formed his movement. Far from being just an enraged tirade against a group of people or a party (like one sometimes find in the most wrathful of Hitler's speeches), this book intends to expose 'the principles for which we fight [and that] can be clearly described in a comprehensive system of politics, of economics, and of life'.[7] This manifold approach to society gives this book a density that is not usually found in most texts by fascist leaders, mainly because of the seriousness with which the author discusses economic matters. In fact, many of the pages of this manifesto are dedicated to the delineation of an economic semi-Keynesian plan that was intended to solve one of the most important problems faced by Britain: the underconsumption caused by the surplus production of modern economy and by the low wages and low standards of living that most workers dealt with.

In sum, this book can be read both as a manifesto and as a political programme that contains the fundamentals of the BUF and Mosley's ideology. One must of course be aware that the analysis of this book in no way allows for the grasping of the ideological complexity of this British fascist movement, for it does not account for the time when the party began to come closer to the German variant of fascism and to explicitly adopt anti-semmitism. Nevertheless, one shall not forget that, independently of some conceptual reconfigurations that the BUF later experienced, many of the principles that guided Mosley and his followers throughout its history are already present in this seminal book, and for this reason the conceptual configuration that is discernable in GB is useful to understand the party as a whole.

## The conceptual core of *Greater Britain*

### *The national corporate state*

It is unsurprising to find the concept of Nation at the core of Mosley's configuration. As he states right in the beginning of GB, 'we are essentially a national movement, and if our policy could be summarised in two words, they would be *Britain First*'.[8] In other words, all the goals espoused by

Mosley are somehow subordinated to the 'national interest as a whole', and to it all the future institutions and organisations of fascism must show 'their ultimate subordination'. Similarly, the adjacent concepts of 'Organicism' and 'Holism' are found in its vicinity, a feature that does not need to take us much time to describe for this happens similarly to the generic configuration. It suffices to say that the leader of the BUF believes that the Nation must be 'organised as the human body' and that 'every part fulfils its function as a member of the whole, performing its separate task, and yet, by performing it, contributing to the welfare of the whole'.[9]

Besides, the Nation closely interlinks with the core concepts of State and Corporatism. The State must represent the interests of the Organic Nation and, for that reason, it shall not tolerate dissent or the existence of parallel interests for 'there is no room for interests which are not the State's interests: laws are futile if they allow such things to be'.[10] Making implicit use of the adjacent concept of 'Totalitarianism', the leader of the BUF goes as far as quoting Benito Mussolini to justify his assertion. As he says, paraphrasing the Italian leader, 'no State within the State can be admitted. All within the State; none outside the State; none against the State'.[11] However, in order to understand how this fascist leader really envisioned the strengthening of State powers, it is important to verify which concrete system he intended to construct.

His main concern was that he believed that the State apparatus that then existed 'was wholly out of date' and had no capacity to deal with the challenges brought by a new era full of dynamism, new technologies, and new processes of mass production. After all, 'our political system dates substantially from 1832 and 'the necessity for a fundamental change exists'.[12] For this reason, he outlines what he considers to be a main reform of the State that shall take place after an eventual seizure of power, and which involves two goals: strengthening the powers of the government, and creating an alternative to a parliamentary system which presently is but a 'power of obstruction' and a place of 'organised obstruction of minorities'. Thus, 'whatever movement or party be entrusted with government must be given absolute power to act'.[13] It would be necessary to inforce the powers of Government and its authority over Parliament, even if this same Parliament still should occasionally meet to scrutinise the work of the Government.

Apart from solving the blockade supposedly caused by sterile debates with the reduction of parliamentary powers, Mosley also wants to solve the obstruction originated by the disagreements between the members of Parliament and local authorities: for this reason, local authorities should be replaced by Fascists M.P.'s. In each region there shall be executive officers at the head of several departments of local government (selected from locally elected Counsels), who on their turn are responsible to the Fascist MP of their area (who is responsible to National Government). With these proposals, Mosley believed to have found a way of constructing an efficient

State, capable of attending the will of the people while avoiding obstructive parliamentary talks: 'the elective principle would thus be combined with executive efficiency and the will of the national majority would prevail over obstructive minorities'.[14] This fascist wished to limit what he saw as a useless parliamentary institution that was not fast and flexible enough to deal with the challenges of modern times and was characterised by democratic practices representing something like a 'too much conversation and too little action' mentality.

Mosley also plans to abolish the House of Commons, for it has outlived its purpose: if it once represented the interests of great landowners, today these people have lost the importance that they once held in society. Thus, the Upper Chamber was no longer necessary. It shall be replaced by a Second Chamber of specialists and men of knowledge. Instead of representing interests which are not relevant anymore, this new Chamber shall include: representatives of the Dominions, Crown Colonies, India, religious thought, the fighting services, Civil Service, education, authorities on foreigner affairs, and those 'who have rendered the State conspicuous service'.[15] A National Council of Corporations shall also be represented in this chamber.

This goal of creating a new State apparatus does not mean that Mosley is not willing to use the existing ones to achieve his aims. On the contrary, he clearly states that 'fascism seeks power by the winning of a parliamentary majority at a general election' and that this 'will be used to confer upon government complete power of action by order'.[16] Instead of choosing between destroying the State apparatus and fully adhering to it, this leader rather opts for a third option: to use the existing apparatus and alter it radically from within. This ambivalent conception of the State also becomes evident in his attitudes towards the British Crown. As he says, 'whatever is good in the past we both respect and venerate. That is why throughout the policy of the movement, we respect and venerate the crown'. The Crown has 'been proven effective and has averted from this empire many a calamity', and therefore it shall not be endangered by the arrival of fascism: on the contrary, it 'is unaffected and indeed is strengthened by fascist policy'.[17]

The third core concept that closely interlinks with the previous two is also the one that reveals the extent of the transformation that Mosley wants to perform in society, a transformation that goes beyond the political system. Corporatism represents a system of economic and social organisation through which the Nation can be organised according to the principles of 'Organicism'. If the Nation is like a human body then it must be 'directed by the central driving brain of government', and that is the reason why the Corporate system must be installed.[18] Besides, Corporatism should also provide the country with the possibility of implementing the solutions that the present State machine cannot offer.

In the first place, the Corporate State should strongly intervene in the economy whenever that is needed, and for this reason one of the first adjacent concepts to be found in the vicinity of Corporatism is 'Dirigisme'.[19] The adjacent concept of 'Order' also make its appearance since the leader of the BUF oftentimes mentions the 'anarchy' of the present, to which Corporatism must put an end. It would also be crucial to think of 'Rationalisation', because Corporatism must be an application of the same principles that were already applied in the economic system, but not yet in the State: 'we have rationalised industry and most other aspects of life, but we have not rationalised the State', he says.[20] Given that new economic practices were already common since the epoch of World War I, it was time for the State apparatus to modernise itself and finally be able to play a role in a system of production that it had not been able to control in recent years.

Unsurprisingly, it is also possible to find the adjacent concept of 'Class Conciliation', for Mosley did not want to further foment the struggles between workers and employers. Instead of a proletarian or of a bourgeois class, Mosley prefers to talk about the 'Producer', which represents anyone who contributes to the process of production. As he states, 'The producer, whether by hand or brain or capital will be the basis of the nation. The forces which assist him in his work of rebuilding the nation will be encouraged; the forces which thwart and destroy productive enterprise will be met with the force of national authority'.[21] The concept of 'Consumer' is relevant as well and, to address the demands of this group, the Corporate State must create a Commodity Board to represent their interests. Since he writes mainly about economic issues when discussing how the Corporate State was to be organised, it is important to describe the actual proposals that he makes, even if it may seem unnecessary to go into much detail about such a topic. It is by describing such proposals that one may better understand how exactly Mosley envisioned the reorganisation of the economic life of the Nation.

Aiming at 'Class Conciliation', Mosley's programme includes the creation of a National Council with the function of representing several industrial corporations, each of them formed by organisations of employers and workers from different industries. It is with these corporations that conciliation shall be attained. 'Instead of being the general staff of opposing armies', Mosley says, 'they will be joint directors of national enterprises under the general guidance of corporative government'.[22] The corporations shall not deal only with the settlement of wages and hours of work but must also play a part in the direction of national economy. He compares the National Council to a machinery which is constantly working and 'interwoven with the whole industrial and commercial fabric of the nation'.

The function of this National Council is better understood when Mosley mentions 'Occupational Franchise'. This means that, in a fascist election, 'a steel worker will vote as a steel worker; a doctor as a doctor; a mother as a mother; within their appropriate corporation'.[23] With this system in place, so Mosley believes, the population will have greater control over the government than it happens in liberal democracies, and the parliament will consist of people who actually know the tenets of the profession or occupation they represent. 'An engineer will vote as an engineer; and thus bring into play, not an amateur knowledge of foreigner and domestic policies, but a lifelong experience of the trade in which he is engaged', he adds.[24] This is the only way to have a Parliament composed of people who truly know the issues with which they have to deal, thus avoiding a House of Commons occupied by what Mosley calls 'sugar-brokers'; that is, politicians who know nothing of technical and administrative questions but conquer the electoral vote due to their affability towards the masses.

It is worth noticing that the Corporate State that Mosley conceives does not intend to eliminate industrial capitalism and private initiative, providing that they do not go against the interests of the Nation. He clearly says that, 'within these limits [the welfare of the nation] all activity is encouraged; individual enterprise, and the making of profit, are not only permitted, but encouraged so long as that enterprise enriches rather than damages by its activity the nation as a whole'.[25] The toleration for working class demands will also depend upon the extent to which Trade Unions imperil the wellbeing of Great Britain.

However, the main goal of the Corporate system, when it comes to economic issues, was to fight the unemployment that was caused by the impact of the Great Depression. Mosley strongly opposed the way the British government had tried to deal with such a crisis, which was trying to increase exports. This was unreasonable for (so he believed) exporting to other countries was no longer a valid option since underdeveloped nations, which used to buy manufactured products, were now industrialising themselves and feeling less necessity to purchase products from the British. Besides, the increasingly fierce competition in foreign markets invalidated this choice as a reasonable one.

According to Mosley, the economic crisis originated not from an inability to produce (as it happened in past centuries) but rather from something current State mechanisms were not prepared to deal yet: a very efficient production that is not met by the capacity of the masses to buy what is produced.[26] There was thus a crisis of under-consumption that was triggered by the inadequate demand to the higher levels of production. To solve this problem, it is necessary to raise standards of living and also have higher wages, so that effective demand and higher levels of employment can be achieved. In this context, one problem must be solved: 'How to raise wages, salaries and the standards of life to that point, without the dislocation of industry which such a process would involve under the present system'.[27]

This cannot be done within the limits of the political system defended by the old parties for, in this context of anarchy and individualist competition, a possible increase in wages would lead to an increase in prices as well, thus leaving the poor in a condition similar to the previous one. The task of the Corporate machinery is to take hold of this anarchy and find a proper way to conduct it. It is necessary to create a home market that is self-sufficient and makes Britain less dependent on foreign markets. Britain must produce most of its goods and sell them within its own country, rather than relying on exports to flow products. Then, within the limits of this home market, it will be easier for Corporate institutions to solve social problems and control the economic system. It will be possible, for instance, to raise wages while guaranteeing that these will not be followed by a raise in prices for there will be agreements between all the intervenient in the economic process.

Note also that the goal of increasing national production does not include only the industrial but also agricultural production. The latter is necessary for Britain to become self-sufficient and be capable of producing the food and the raw materials that at the present moment can only be obtained in the international market. Mosley is confident that, when the necessary conditions are created, agricultural production will increase in due proportion: 'We will deliberately create the conditions in which British Agriculture can increase its production by 200 million per anum, if necessary, at the expense of the Foreign Investor'.[28] Undercutting foreign competition (with taxes and quotas), Britain will be able to obtain the main condition for creating a reliable market freed from foreigner influence in which farmers encounter the economic prices that they need. This will be possible if the purchasing power of the people in the cities is enhanced and if the Corporate State eliminates the intermediates that intervene between the agricultural producer and the buyers: 'the salvation of Agriculture can only be achieved by a clear-cut policy of exclusion', he says.

\*

In the configuration that is present in GB, Corporatism is given a bigger priority than in the generic configuration of fascism. This is explained by the political trajectory of the British leader and by the issues that had occupied his mind in the years immediately before he formed the BUF.[29] After all, disagreements about the social policies destined to tackle unemployment were the main reason he moved away from the Labour party, and these questions remained at the core of his political reflections in the years to follow. It is thus natural that his ideological configuration gives such relevance to these issues. This becomes even more understandable if one thinks that he wrote his text when the effects of the Great Depression were being felt in Great Britain (even if with less severity than in other countries) and many members of the political class were preoccupied with this problem.

It is worth noticing the close interlinkage between Corporatism and Nation, which takes place mainly due to the adjacent concept of 'Organicism'. Such an interlinkage shows that the Corporate State should not only serve to solve economic problems (even though this is an important function), but also represent the most appropriate form of organisation of a Nation that is seen as a kind of living entity.[30] To this leader, Corporatism was not just a theory, it was something necessary for the Nation to express itself in its organicist nature and in solving the crisis that ravaged it.

Finally, after analysing these three concepts, one must note that the concept of 'Holism' is in the vicinity of all of them and that it is mainly expressed through the use of the word 'Synthesis'. Mosley seemed to make a constant effort to unite opposites, aiming at the creation of a new synthetic whole that encompasses contradictory features both in the realm of ideas (of which more will be said in one of the next sections) and in the material world, as it becomes evident with the discussion of the conciliatory Corporatist measures that he defends. The Nation that Mosley envisions is thus a 'synthetic' Nation and it is in the Corporate State that all the opposite parts within the community should be synthetised to form a single holistic unity.

*The new revolutionary era*

Mosley rejects the idea that fascism is the 'white guard of reaction' (as many of its opponents were keen to point) and states that, on the contrary, 'fascism is the greatest constructive and revolutionary creed in the world'.[31] He also points out that 'in all countries, Fascism has been led by men who came from the Left, and the rank and file has combined the Conservative and patriotic elements of the nation with ex-Socialists, ex-Communists, and revolutionaries who have forsaken their various illusions of progress for the new and orderly reality of progress'. This supposed left-wing origins of the leaders was a further proof that fascism was not a reactionary but rather a revolutionary movement.

This Revolution shouldhave a spiritual dimension, for 'Fascism is a thing of the spirit'.[32] This does not mean that the changes that Mosley wanted to enact in society do not have a material component (the contrary becameevident in the section about corporatism) but rather, the spiritual transformation is a necessary precursor for the material transformations to occur. As he says, 'Before we can really begin that task [of saving the British nation] we must create a new spirit' and 'the supreme mission of fascism in the world [is] to create a revival in the spirit of man which is prerequisite to a revival in material environment'.[33] Mosley seems to have reasons for contentment for, as he says, 'In the brief space of eighteen months that spirit has been created in Britain'.

As to interlinkages, Revolution is close to the concept of Corporatism because the construction of a State according to corporatist lines should be an important step in the creation of a new society. Besides, the adjacent concept of 'Palingenesis' is noticeable when the leader of the BUF says that 'the task before us is nothing less than the creation of a new civilisation'.[34] Such civilisation represents the creation of a new era with 'new values and of a new morality in a higher and nobler conception of the universe'. This would also include the creation of a 'New Man', a 'Personality' that consists of an 'individual in his fusion with the ideal of service'.[35] At this point, it is worth noting that, contrary to some conservative and reactionary ideologues, Mosley does not reject the technological transformations and the developments of modern society. In one passage of his book, he describes the technological advancements of the last decades, stating that they can be considered as revolutionary. 'The intervening century has seen the invention of telegraph, telephone, and wireless', he says, and then adds many other recent changes in society: railways, the development of mass production, the progress of social justice, the financial system, and so on.[36] His acceptance of technological progress does not mean, however, that he does not see a fundamental problem with modern society: the decadence of spirituality.

For this reason, the adjacent concept of 'Palingenesis' was accompanied by the idea that the national community faces a state of 'Crisis' (a word often used by Mosley).[37] As was said in the last section, this crisis has a material side that has to do with poverty and unemployment, but in reality the BUF's conception of crisis is two-fold for it did not relate only to economic strife but also to a spiritual decadence that corrupts the Nation. Mosley's main concern is that such decadenceis affecting the greatness of his country in such a way that, in the future, it could lose its status as a great power and 'sink, almost in her sleep, to the position of a Spain', thus declining 'to the status of a second-rate power'.[38]

However, Mosley does not conceive Revolutionary change as an anarchic or disordered event, because the fascist Revolution does not intend to call into question the very fundamentals upon which the social order is based. Even if that seems contradictory, the concept of 'Order' is also in the vicinity of Revolution. Fascism 'seeks to achieve its aim legally and constitutionally, by methods of law and order; but in objective it is revolutionary or it is nothing', Mosley says, this way summarising the apparent contradiction between the call for a Revolution and the desire to maintain order in society.[39] Fascism seems to be an alternative type of Revolution, which is not to be confused with that of Communism, and that must be carried out with respect to the principles on which society is traditionally based.

Lastly, the 'Cult of Youth' is also present in the vicinity of Revolution, just like in the generic configuration. 'The real political division of past decade', Mosley believes, 'has not been a division of parties, but a division of generations'.[40] In this context of generational struggle, youths represent the age in which one has the vitalism that is necessary to put the fascist Revolution in motion. As the leader affirms, 'Our hope is centred in vital and determined youth, dedicated to the resurrection of a nation's greatness and shrinking from no effort and no sacrifice to secure that mighty end'.[41]

*Authority and violence*

As it is already known, it is common for the concepts of Authority and State to interlink in fascist configurations, since the fascist cult of State power implies the existence of a strengthened apparatus. In the case of Mosley, this interlinkage is noticeable, for instance, when he calls for a reinforcement of the executive powers of a future fascist government. However, in fascist ideology, this core concept does not relate only to State power and represents a principle that is necessary in society and, more importantly, for achieving the goals of the fascist Revolution. Thus, Mosley praises discipline as 'the essence of the Modern Movement.' And he continues saying that 'its leadership may be an individual, or preferably, in the case of the British character, a team with clearly allocated functions and responsibility'. In either case, 'The only effective instrument of revolutionary change is absolute authority'.[42]

However, Mosley supposedly believed that this obedience and discipline should be achieved voluntarily and not by force, because 'voluntary discipline is the essence of the modern movement'.[43] This apparent ambiguity is also displayed in the concept of 'Leader', about whom Mosley is quick to ensure that he must not be a Tyrant. Mosley does use the word 'Dictatorship', but explains that 'by dictatorship we mean leadership' and not tyranny. The modern dictatorship that Mosley envisions is one that is not implemented against the will of the people but rather with their consent: with the legitimacy of popular will by their side, the fascist leader shall use his power to enforce this will instead of oppressing the people. Mosley believes that 'fascism is leadership of the people with their willing consent along the pact of action which they have long desired'.

Authority and Violence seem to interlink due to the adjacent concept of 'Virility', which is particularly evident when Mosley says that 'we want men, not eunuchs, in our ranks, but men with a singleness of purpose which they order their lives to serve'.[44] The cult of virility is followed by contempt for the values associated with femininity, as we can see when Mosley states that to fight for the fascist cause, 'No ordinary party of the past, resting on organisations of old women, tea fight and committees can survive in such a struggle'.[45] While the female figure is associated with passivity and cowardice, the male is associated with adventure and strength. Even if admitting that women do have a role to play in his organisation, it is different from that of men, since 'we want men who are men and women who are women'.[46]

When it comes to the importance of Violence, Mosley sometimes seems to deny that he praises it for its sake and rejects the idea that the promotion of athletic activities by his party represents in any way a form of preparing his militants to fight. He says that 'we shall certainly meet force with force; but this is not the motive of these activities'.[47] However, in other passages, the leader of the BUF seems to be less shy in admitting that the victory of the fascist ideal demands the employment of Violence: 'in such a situation, new ideas will not come peacefully; they will come violently, as they have come elsewhere'.[48] After all, in spite of all his denials, Mosley does see Violence as inevitable in times of crisis: it is an inevitability that the study of the history of other European countries only seems to confirm. Such a study, he defends, shows that, in epochs of decay, the usual governmental instruments are useless and new and more violent means are required to save the Nation.

Likewise, the concept of 'Eliminationism' becomes more prominent each time Mosley writes about the necessity of combating the enemies of the Nation, especially communists: 'If, therefore, such a situation arises in Britain, we shall prepare to meet the anarchy of communism with the organised force of fascism' he says.[49] Even if reasserting that the BUF does not wish violent fights, Mosley assures his readers that Violence will be used in the future if that becomes necessary to avoid the victory of communism, which would have results that would supposedly be more dangerous than the consequences of the use of fascist violence.

Lastly, let us briefly mention his ambivalence towards 'Pacifism', which is not as thoroughly rejected as in other fascist permutations. Mosley, on the one hand, condemns the folly of the parties of the old liberal order that seem prone to adopt unilateral measures of disarmament that only contribute to place the Nation and the Empire in a position of weakness. He also shows a will to 'radically overhaul our present system of defence' and use the most modern naval and air armament in order to guarantee the security of the Empire.[50] However, on the other hand, Mosley seems to contemplate the hypothesis that, in some cases, an international pacifist policy could be useful if adopted by all major countries. He says that 'disarmament, if universal, is a step towards Peace and we should strenuously strive to secure it both as a contribution to Peace and as a relief from a heavy and unproductive burden'.[51] However, one should not make much of such a usage of the concept of 'Pacifism', for such rhetoric does not take away from Mosley's ideology his praise for virile and tough actions as a necessary component of the fascist Revolution. The concept of Violence is always somehow at the core of his conceptual configuration, even if he does not dedicate as much space as Hitler to explain why Violence is a basis on which the new society must be founded.

## *The autarchic empire*

The concept of Empire interlinks with the concepts of Nation and Revolution, even if his goal is not to conquer new territory. In the absence of an expansionist goal, Mosley even declares that 'our very preoccupation with internal reconstruction is some guarantee that at least we shall never pursue the folly of an aggressive imperialism'.[52] However, it is rather towards the maintenance of the already existing empire that fascist police must turn: 'we should be less prone to anxious interference in everybody else's affairs, and more concentrated on the resources of our own country and Empire'.[53] In this context, Mosley aims at guaranteeing the existence of the Empire that Britain already possesses, since he sees it as a portion of territory that contains the resources that the Nation needs in order to survive.

According to Mosley, Great Britain and its dominions should form an economic and political bond to construct 'a permanently functioning machinery of economic consultation and planning'.[54] The Empire is seen as a 'great economic entity, the largest and most economically self-contained area in the world, bound together as it is by a common loyalty to the crown'.[55] The adjacent concept of 'Autarchy' appears in the vicinity of Empire because Mosley aims at an Autarchic Empire. He wants it to be self-contained and promote economic relations between its members rather than with the outside world.

When talking about India, Mosley's ultra-nationalist credentials become unquestionable for he clearly states that 'Fascist policy is clear cut. We have a right to stay in India and we intend to stay there. We have more than a right; we have a duty to stay there. We have a right because modern India owes everything to British rule'.[56] Rather than a complete break with the British colonial past, Mosley proposes to carry out some changes in the Empire, as long as it is guaranteed that Britain remains as the guiding nation. This fascist leader is convinced that, when it comes to the exercise of power in colonial relations, 'we have used that power for the purposes of humanity and construction and not or the purposes of oppression and destruction'.[57] And that is one of the reasons why 'we claim the same historic right to be in India as those Indians who denounce us, with a difference that our right is fortified by the human spirit and constructive achievement of the modern world'.[58]

It is difficult not to note a reminiscence of old Victorian views about the 'civilising mission' of Britain in India and the role of the British as the educators of the natives. This educational goal and the fact that India was divided in several ethnic groups (which would supposedly fight between each other if left alone without a ruler) legitimates the right of the British to continue in this country: 'any withdrawal of British authority can only result in wide-spread destruction of life accompanied by unthinkable atrocities and ending in a relapse into barbarism'.[59]

In spite of this colonialist vision, Mosley is quick to defend a political system that 'include the vast masses of the Indian population' so that it becomes possible to 'build successive tiers of Indian representation until the voice of India is heard in the inner councils of government'.[60] This way, even the humblest members of the Indian working class will somehow be capable of participating in the political decisions that are taken within the Empire. The other colonies besides India are also supposed to participate in a planning that secures economic and political unity for the benefit of both the colonial potency and the native peoples that inhabit in different regions of the globe. The colonies of the British Empire will help Great Britain by contributing with trade concessions, but that does not mean that they should be mere servants in their relation with the metropolis. 'On the contrary, the regulation and planning of a Corporate Empire would prevent the exploitation of these populations which at present is in process', he says.[61] This

86  *Oswald Mosley and the British Union of Fascists*

supposed concern for the rights of the natives does not erase, however, the main chauvinist tenets of Mosley's ideological configuration.

## Other important features of the configuration

### Peripheral concepts

Just like in the case of Hitler, 'Liberty' appears as a marginal concept, mainly because Mosley does not seem to conceive the existence of freedom in a liberal society where employment and well-being are not guaranteed. He writes that:

> The essence of liberty is freedom to enjoy some of the fruits of life, a decent house, good wages, reasonable hours of leisure after hours of work short enough not to leave a man exhausted, unmolested private happiness with wife, children and friends, and, finally, the hope of material success to set the seal on private ambition.[62]

Mosley seems to prioritise material well-being over the concept of 'Liberty', for only when the most basic material needs are met can freedom have some value. This fascist leader thus places this concept in a secondary place and subordinates it to the solving of the economic problems with which the Corporate State must deal.

As to the perimeter, we find in it several themes which derive from his preoccupation with the economic crisis and his description of how to put in place the Corporate State. These include 'tackling unemployment', 'raising wages', or 'achieving effective demand', to name but a few. The appearance of such perimeter concepts is thus one more sign of the relevance of the concept of Corporatism and economic thinking in Mosley's ideology.

### Permeability and rejections

Mosley seems to be aware that many of the concepts and ideas of his movement are also present in other parties and regimes, and that even Roosevelt in the United States had put forward economic measures that resemble those of fascism.[63] Thus, this leader explicitly states that the interlinkages and combinations of his political thoughtare formed through the use of concepts coming from other ideologies. That becomes evident when he mentions the concepts of 'Progress' (that comes from left-wing parties and is fundamental to enact changes in society) and 'Order' (which is connected to right-wing parties and is necessary for stability). His goal is to unite and synthetise in his fascist programme these two seemingly contradictory concepts and thus be better prepared to meet the problems faced by Britain: without order, it is not possible to have the necessary stability; and without progress, it is not possible to alter society. As he states, 'our Fascist

Movement seeks on the one hand Stability, which envisages order and authority as the basis of all solid achievement; we seek, on the other hand, Progress, which can be achieved only by the executive instrument that order, authority and decision alone can give'.[64] At this point, we can conclude that the synthetic goals of Mosley's political and economic Corporatism are in fact only part of a wider project of synthesis towards the creation of a synthetic Nation and a synthetic worldview. Corporatism is unquestionably a characteristic of such synthesis, but there are more. If we find similar features in other fascist leaders, this may lead us to completly review our core concept of Corporatism in the final chapter.

As to rejections, Mosley totally opposes communist ideology for, among many other aspects (including his rejection of 'Class Struggle'), he does not accept its revolutionary goals on the grounds that they are destructive. Leninist principles, according to him, want to destroy everything that has been made before, and that does not fit his idea of using the instruments of the State already in existence to carry out a Revolution. He, however, does not react only against the revolutionary versions of Socialism and Communism, but against reformist Socialism as well. According to Mosley, the evolutionary views held, for instance, by Sidney and Beatrice Webb, have 'long been rendered irrelevant and untenable by modern conditions'.[65] Apart from the fact that this peaceful evolution to a different productive system seemed to be no longer possible, reformist socialists, in Mosley's view, had never been able to satisfactorily present a way of transiting to this society. Their ideology was therefore one in which this fascist leader placed no hopes.

Apart from Communism and reformist Socialism, Mosley rejects the political and economic system of Liberalism. To him, the problem faced by Britain is not due to a specific government or party but to the parliamentary system itself. Mosley has no faith in what he calls 'The Old Gang', that is, the politicians who are part of such an inefficient system. According to this leader, 'Setting aside any complaint of the conduct or capacity of individual Governments, I believe that, under the existing system, Government cannot be efficiently conducted'.[66] Most importantly, Mosley rejects in Liberalism a whole set of organisations and institutions which are no longer capable of facing the challenges of the contemporary world. Parliament has become decadent and is no longer capable of carrying out the popular will. It should be 'the mouth-piece of the will of the people; but, as things stand at present, its time is mainly taken up with matters of which the nation neither knows nor cares'.[67] As to political parties, their 'whole constitution, composition, tradition, psychology and outlook' inhibits them 'from facing the problems of the modern age'.[68]

## Contradictions: *nationalism/internationalism and public/private*

The contradiction between 'Nationalism' and 'Internationalism' is the first among the many that can be noticed. In this context, the ultra-nationalism of the BUF seems to collide with the notion, acknowledged by Mosley himself, that fascism is a universal creed and movement. Furthermore, it may seem inexplicable that a nationalist movement chooses to describe itself with a word referring to an ideology that first appeared abroad. To solve this problem, Mosley believes that, in the modern era, just like in previous eras, there exists a universal and coherent creed which can appear in different nations, manifesting itself with different characteristics. Since this creed, which in the present epoch is fascism, usually manifests itself with the coming of an economic crisis, it was only by circumstance that it first appeared in Italy. He says that 'if our crisis had been among the first, instead of among the last, Fascism would have been a British invention. As it is our task is not to invent Fascism, but to find for it in Britain its highest expression and development'.[69] Even if fascism was not invented in Britain, it can be adapted to the country and be a part of a wider universal movement which is having a worldwide impact. The contradiction between 'Populism' and 'Elitism' is also present when Mosley writes about the role of the dictator and of the popular will, even though it is not as evident as in the case of Hitler.

There is also a tension (even if not a real contradiction) between the concepts of 'Public' and 'Private'. Its pertinence is manifest when Mosley talks about how a strong government can limit individual freedoms, something which Mosley seems less prone to eulogise than other fascists. The Authoritarian Corporate State, so he argues, must find a balance between the seemingly contradictory concepts of public and private, creating a Nation where private affairs are permitted (as long as they do not run against national interests) but where the State controls the main aspects of public life and the new fascist man is capable of fully commit itself to the public cause (even if in private he must have a degree of freedom that does not usually exist, for instance, in fundamentalist religious cults).

Solving this tension, Mosley states that the Fascist principle is 'Liberty in private life. Obligation in public life. In his public capacity a man must behave as befits a citizen and a member of the state [...] In private he may behave as he likes'.[70] Thus, the idea of liberty is associated the private sphere, and the idea of duty (obligation) is associated with the Public realm, that way finding a balance that maintains the coherence of Mosley's morphology. The fascist movement wants to create dedicated citizens who are fully committed to a public cause, but who have freedom to do as they please in private matters, as long as they do not fall into what would be termed a decadent behaviour or jeopardise other people's freedom. Mosley summarises this idea in the following way: 'every man shall be a member of the State, giving his public life to the State, but claiming in return his private life and liberty from the state'.[71] However, one should not give too much importance to this apparent concession to liberalism, much less think that Mosley discards 'Totalitarianism', for he is quick to add that 'Liberty' must be enjoyed 'within the corporate purposes of the state'.

## Concluding remarks

Mosley's fascist morphology was the product of a specific context and of a lifelong preoccupation felt by the leader even before he turned to fascism. *The Greater Britain* thus appears as the corollary of a political path which had led Mosley to join both the Conservative and the Labour party in the search for an ideology and a political programme capable of conciliating the contradictions of modern era, as well as adjusting the British political system to new realities and solving economic problems like unemployment.

As it was mentioned earlier, Mosley intended to perform changes in three main areas of society. In order to finalise this chapter, the changes in each of these areas will be summarised:

> – *politics*: in this sphere, Mosley totally rejects the current parliamentary system, seeing it as a bureaucratic machinery that divides the people and blocks the decision making process. It is not just a problem of a specific government, but rather a problem of the political system itself. Such a system was created in an era when technological development was not so intense and which is incapable of facing modern challenges. In order to put an end to this obstruction of a useless parliamentary, it is necessary to build a system with an executive government invested with power and authority and a leader who is capable of executing the people's will.
> – *economics*: in this realm, the main problem is related to the fact that modern technology has developed productivity in such a way that the levels of consumption are no longer enough to tackle it. In a competitive international market, where entrepreneurs compete between each other, it is not possible to increase wages and achieve the necessary standards of living. Thus, Mosley proposes to abandon the international market economic system and replace it for one where the interests of the Nation are of the utmost importance. In order to permit standards of living to raise and conciliate the different classes that are part of society, what is needed is an economic corporate system, within which all producers can negotiate and contribute to the economic growth of the Nation.
> – 'life': by which he means all the aspects of national life that are subject to political scrutiny. In that sense, his fascist movement aims at creating a legion of dedicated militants who are ready to sacrifice their comfort in the name of the Nation, resorting to violence if necessary. Most importantly, the BUF must permeate British life with a new spirit, a new sense of living that unites the community and makes it possible to

achieve the revolutionary situation that Mosley wishes. The fascist 'New Man' will then be a fighter who conciliates the liberty of his private life with the dedication and obligations of public life.

## Notes

1 In a book written in 1933, Marxist writer and former Labour MP John Strachey recalls his memories of Oswald Mosley, with whom he tried to form a New Party with the aim of solving the problem of unemployment in Great Britain. He even evokes the moment when Mosley, 'sitting silent and alone, brooding with an indescribable bitterness', faced the rejection of his Labour comrades in a way that reminded him of Mussolini's faith when falling from grace with the 'Italian social-democrats' (sic). John Strachey, *The Menace of Fascism* (London, Victor Gollancz LTD., 1934), 156.
2 When trying to explain the failure of this New Party, Matthew Worley claims that 'The New Party was an organisation riddled with contradictions, paradoxes and tensions. Some of these were apparent from the outset and no doubt contributed to the party's failure to register beyond the margins of British politics. Its programme seemed to pull in conflicting directions; its early supporters appeared to commit to a marriage of convenience rather than conviction'. Matthew Worley, *Oswald Mosley and the New Party* (Basingstoke, Palgrave Macmillan, 2010), 164.
3 This and other events of confrontation between the BUF and their left-wing opponents entered the mythology of British anti-fascism. To read more about British anti-fascism, see Nigel Copsey, *Anti-Fascism in Britain* (London, Routledge, 2017).
4 Martin Pugh, *"Hurrah for the Blackshirts"* (London, Pimlico, 2006), 6.
5 Jakub Drábik, 'Historiographical Essay: British Union of Fascists', *Contemporary British History* (2015), 3.
6 Martin Pugh, *"Hurrah for the Blackshirts"*, 6.
7 Oswald Mosley, *The Greater Britain* (London, BUF, 1934), 184.
8 Ibid., 19.
9 Ibid., 34–35.
10 Ibid., 19.
11 Ibid., 36.
12 Ibid., 17.
13 Ibid., 28.
14 Ibid., 40.
15 Ibid., 42.
16 Ibid., 39.
17 The fact that Mosley, in spite all his desires for social change, still pays respect to the British monarchy shall not surprise us if we bear in mind that, to the BUF, the monarchic system that existed before Parliamentarianism was behind the ancient greatness of the British Empire. 'In particular, it was the vital spirit of endeavour that so characterised the Elizabethan age which the BUF tried to emulate. They believed that the Tudor nation-state concept which had produced the basis of British world supremacy had been undermined during the 17th century by the victory of parliament over the centralised authority of monarchy' Richard Thurlow, *Fascism in Britain: A History 1918–1998* (London, I.B.Tauris Publishers, 1998), 120.
18 Oswald Mosley, *The Greater Britain*, 35.

19 Mosley's call for an interventionist State have led some authors to notice the influence of Keynesian ideas on his thought, which was the case of Robert Skidelsky. This author even went as far as to argue that 'Mosley was a disciple of Keynes in the 1920's; and Keynesianism was his great contribution to fascism. It was Keynesianism which in the last resort made Mosley's fascism distinctively English'. Although we reject the idea that Keynesianism was the main defining feature of Mosley's ideology and of its uniqueness, this assertion by Skidelsky clearly indicates the importance of economic matters in Mosley's political movement. Robert Skidelsky, *Oswald Mosley* (New York, Holt, Rinehart and Winston, 1975), 302.
20 Oswald Mosley, *The Greater Britain*, 34.
21 Ibid., 35–36.
22 Ibid., 37.
23 Ibid., 42.
24 Ibid., 43.
25 Ibid., 35.
26 In Mosley's view, 'Unemployment was caused by a failure of demand to meet the productive potential of industry, and there was therefore an immediate need to institute consumer credits amongst the low paid in order to raise purchasing power' Richard Thurlow, *Fascism in Britain*, 122.
27 Oswald Mosley, *The Greater Britain*, 35.
28 Ibid., 98.
29 According to Thurlow, 'Mosley's fascist economic programme derived from the main ideas of his socialist and radical synthesis of the 1920s transposed into an ultra-national context'. Richard Thurlow, *Fascism in Britain*, 122.
30 As noted by Gary Love, 'for Mosley, corporatism was not just economic theory; it was an organic way of life, a method of organisation that could be applied to the whole of British society'. Gary Love, '"What's the Big Idea?": Oswald Mosley, the British Union of Fascists and Generic Fascism', *Journal of Contemporary History*, 42 (3), 2007, 450.
31 Oswald Mosley, *The Greater Britain*, 21.
32 Ibid., v.
33 Ibid., iii.
34 Ibid., iv.
35 Ibid., vi.
36 Ibid., 17.
37 As stressed by Thomas Linehan, 'The British fascist imagination during the interwar period was racked by a morbid dread of impending national dissolution. There was a perception that Britain was being assailed by destructive forces which the threatened very survival of authentic culture'. Thomas Linehan, *British Fascism, 1918–39: Parties, Ideology and Culture*. (Manchester, Manchester University Press, 2000), 222.
38 Oswald Mosley, *The Greater Britain*, 190.
39 Ibid., 22.
40 Ibid., 183.
41 Ibid., 33.
42 Ibid., 31.
43 Ibid., 33.
44 Ibid., 53.
45 Ibid., 33.
46 Ibid., 54.
47 Ibid., 53.
48 Ibid., 181.

49 Ibid., 182.
50 Ibid., 155.
51 Ibid., 155.
52 Ibid., 157.
53 Ibid., 152.
54 Ibid., 37.
55 Ibid., 148.
56 Ibid., 140.
57 Ibid., 140.
58 Ibid., 148.
59 Ibid., 141.
60 Ibid., 144.
61 Ibid., 45.
62 Ibid., 29.
63 At times, Mosley seems to be aware of some similarities between his programme and Roosevelt's New Deal. However, we do not support the idea that Roosevelt's policy, apart from some similarities in economic matters, is linked to fascist ideology.
64 Ibid., 26.
65 Ibid., 93.
66 Ibid., 17.
67 Ibid., 27.
68 Ibid., 182.
69 Ibid., 20.
70 Ibid., 51.
71 Ibid., 53–54.

## List of references

Brewer, John, 'The British Union of Fascists, Sir Oswald Mosley and Birmingham: An Analysis of the Content and Context of an Ideology', M.Soc.Sci Thesis, 1975, 1–171.

Carpenter, L. P., 'Corporatism in Britain, 1930–45', Journal of Contemporary History, 11/1, 1976, 2–25.

Copsey, Nigel, Anti-Fascism in Britain (London, Routledge, 2017).

Dorril, Stephen, Blackshirt: Sir Oswald Mosley and British Fascism (New York, Viking Publishing, 2006).

Drábik, Jakub, 'Historiographical Essay: British Union of Fascists', Contemporary British History, 30 (1), 2015, 1–19.

Eatwell, Roger, Fascism: A History (London, Penguin Books, 1997).

Griffiths, Richard, Fellow Travellers of the Right: British Enthusiasts for Nazi Germany, 1933–39 (Oxford, Oxford University Press, 1983).

Howell, David, Mosley and British Politics 1918–32 (London, Palgrave Macmillan, 2015).

Lewis, David Stephen, Illusions of Grandeur: Mosley, Fascism and British Society, 1931–1981 (Manchester, Manchester University Press, 1987).

Linehan, Thomas, British Fascism, 1918–39: Parties, Ideology and Culture (Manchester, Manchester University Press, 2000).

Love, Gary, '"What's the Big Idea?": Oswald Mosley, the British Union of Fascists and Generic Fascism', Journal of Contemporary History, 42 (3), 2007, 447–468.

Lunn, Kenneth and Richard Thurlow, British Fascism: Essays on the Radical Right in Inter-War Britain (New York, St. Martin's Press, 1980).

Mosley, Nicholas, *Beyond the Pale: Sir Oswald Mosley and Family 1933–1980* (London, Secker & Warburg, 1983).
Mosley, Oswald, *The Greater Britain* (London, BUF, 1934).
Mosley, Oswald, *My Life* (London, Black House Publishing, 2012 [1968]).
Muldoon, Andrew. *Empire, Politics and the Creation of the 1935 India Act: Last Act of the Raj* (Farnham, Ashgate, 2009).
Pugh, Martin, *"Hurrah for the Blackshirts": Fascists and Fascism in Britain between the Wars* (London, Pimlico, 2006).
Roberts, Martin, *Britain, 1846–1964: The Challenge of Change* (Oxford, Oxford University Press, 2001).
Skidelsky, Robert, *Oswald Mosley* (New York, Holt, Rinehart and Winston, 1975).
Strachey, John, *The Menace of Fascism* (London, Victor Gollancz LTD., 1934).
Thurlow, Richard, *Fascism in Britain: A History 1918–1998* (London, I.B.Tauris Publishers, 1998).
Worley, Matthew, *Oswald Mosley and the New Party* (Basingstoke, Palgrave Macmillan, 2010).

# 4 Francisco Rolão Preto and Portuguese National Syndicalism

Corporatism and the construction of an alternative modernity

Francisco Rolão Preto and his National Syndicalist Movement (*Nacional Sindicalismo* – NS) can be seen as the most important example of fascist ideology in Portugal, even if this political organisation was never able to take firm roots in the country. However, NS was not the only organisation which had tried to develop a portuguese variant of fascism, as the first attempts to do so go back to the 20s.[1] Nevertheless, none of those were successful enough to consolidate its implementation, and fascism did not become a relevant competitor in Portugal either with Lusitan Nationalism (*Nacionalismo Lusitano* – NL) or with *Cruzada Nuno Álvares Pereira*.[2] Interestingly enough, during the 1918 presidency of Sidónio Pais, which only lasted for a few months due to his assassination, one already finds some of the traits of proto-fascist discourse and style.[3] This places Portugal on the map of proto-fascism, but does not deprive the NS of its place as the most important subject of study when it comes to fascism in the country.

## Rolão Preto and NS

Francisco Rolão Preto was born on 12 February 1893 in the Portuguese region known as Alentejo. Being a monarchist, he was involved in the first attempts led by General Henrique de Paiva Couceiro to overthrow the so-called First Republic, which was installed in 1910 after the fall of the monarchy. He would later live in Belgium and France, but that would not stop him from continuing developing his political thought. After returning to Portugal, he would join the ranks of a political group called the Lusitan Integralism (*Integralismo Lusitano* – IL), a Radical Right organisation at the time known for its opposition to the Republic and for its reactionary ideas.[4] At this time, Rolão Preto's writings revolved around the themes of nationalism, the 'Social Question' and Organic Syndicalism. This political path seems to be unsurprisingly in tune with his fascist career during the 30s, but not so much with the evolution of his thought after World War II, when he rejected anti-democratic ideas.

According to José de Melo Alexandrino, it is possible to recognise two different phases in Rolão Preto's political trajectory.[5] The first phase went from 1915 to 1935 and was characterised by the predominance of themes like Nationalism, Anti-Parliamentarianism, the favoring of direct action and the concern with social questions. The second phase, which began after a decade of transition, went from 1946 to 1977 and witnessed Rolão Preto rejecting former Maurrassian notions of state power and defending the principles of humanism, freedom, and representative democracy. Preto's path is a complex one, but we shall not deal with the second phase of his political career, for that is outside of our scope.

The focus of this chapter shall more precisely be the period that goes from 1932 to 1934 when, after abandoning the IL, Preto became the indisputable leader of NS. This movement was the result of the activity of several radical ideologues who were influenced by Italian Fascism and were trying to form an organisation that should be guided by the ideas of revolutionary nationalism. In 1932, people like António Pedro, Dutra Faria, António Lepierre Tinoco and Alberto Monsaraz gathered around the newspaper *The Revolution* (*A Revolução*), having in mind the formation of a revolutionary nationalist group that could reunite members of former fascist and pre-fascist organisations (which included the most radical wings in the IL). All these rightist activists were greatly influenced by a text written by Preto during the 20s, before he became fascinated with fascism: *The Twelve Principles of Production* (*Os Doze Princípios da Produção* – DPP).

At this point, it is important to note that, when NS came to life, Portugal was no longer living under the democratic Republican regime, for this had been overthrown on 28 May 1926 by a military coup led by General Gomes da Costa. After this, a reactionary military dictatorship was established, following an uncertain course until the Minister of Finance, former professor António de Oliveira Salazar, gained such prominence that it became clear he would be the person leading the new regime. Thus, after becoming President of the Council of Ministers, Salazar proclaimed the instalment of the so-called New State in 1933. Appearing during this seminal phase of the new regime, the NS was mostly concerned with exerting influence on its course and guaranteeing that it was established along the lines of revolutionary nationalism.

Not much later after the creation of *The Revolution*, António Pedro invited Preto to join their group and conduct it. In the months that followed, in a context of political disorganisation and lack of leadership, he would progressively become the dominant figure of NS. The banquet that celebrated the first anniversary of *The Revolution*, taking place on 18 February in the Eduardo VII Park in Lisbon, occurred when it had already become manifest that Rolão Preto was the sole indisputable leader of the movement. The history of NS was nevertheless a short one for the frequent rallies and the increasing opposition to Salazar and his regime by Preto and its most radical members led the Portuguese dictator to outlaw it on 4 July 1934, even if leaving the door opened for the more 'moderate' members to join the party of the regime, the National Union (*União Nacional* – UN).

Rolão Preto was forced to exile in Spain, where he established ties with the Spanish leader Primo de Rivera, and came back to Portugal in 1935 only to be exiled again after trying to overthrow Salazar by instigating a rebellion that involved taking over the warship *Bartolomeo Dias*. As earlier mentioned, after World War II, Rolão Preto lost his faith in fascism and began opposing Salazar from a democratic point of view, even joining left-wing organisations like Movement of Democratic Unity (*Movimento de Unidade Democrática* – MUD). He died in 1977, three years after the Carnation Revolution of 1974 overthrew the regime that he had opposed his whole life (even if not always proposing the same alternatives), and seven years after the death of his major rival of the 30s: António Salazar.

## Rolão Preto amid the ideological struggles of his time

The conceptual configuration of Rolão Preto's fascist years emerged in a period in which a process of ideological reconfiguration among the political Right was about to come to an end. Its roots date back to the 10s, when the reactionary Right began to search for new alternatives with which to oppose the Republic. One of the most notable rightist groups of the time was the IL, which was already mentioned.[6] It was founded in 1914 and included in its ranks important personalities such as António Sardinha. This was a traditionalist organisation which supported a return to the monarchy and already dwelled in the concept of Corporatism as an alternative to the liberal Republic. The IL also praised Violence and espoused Elitism, interlinking this concept with Nationalism and Organicism.[7]

However, when Preto's Portuguese variety of fascism emerged, it was inserted in a context in which the fiercest ideological disputes concerned mostly the type of regime best suited for the country. This 'Regime Question' came in the wake of the political struggles that had been already fought in the 20s and was about to reach a climax due to the rivalry between Salazar and Preto, who, in 1934, represented the only opposition to the embryonic regime from a right wing perspective. Besides, the 'Social Question' was also a main preoccupation of some among the Right, including, as we shall see, Preto himself. This could involve an ideological dispute with the Left to take hold of their themes and reinsert them in a right wing configuration. This happened at a time when some right-wing circles thought it necessary to address the problems of the poorer classes, thus trying to guarantee their support for the nationalist cause. This explains the importance of the concept of Corporatism.

Preto's configuration was then the sole coherent political ideology of the right that was capable of providing an alternative to the course taken by the regime under the influence of Salazar. His conceptual configuration proves to be interesting both as the best example of a fully formed variant of fascist ideology in Portuguese territory and as the product of an ideological dispute between an authoritarian conservative regime and a more radical fascist movement. To study Preto's ideology, and since he did not write a definitive book like *Mein Kampf*, we chose to include in this analysis three important texts written between 1932 and 1933, each of them containing important insights into the political thought of the NS leader. These texts, which appear in the anthology of his complete works edited by José de Melo Alexandrino, are the following:

–*Beacons_Guidelines_Soul* (*Balizas_Directrizes_Alma*), published in 1932 and containing the most important features and goals of this fascist movement.
–*Beyond Communism* (*Para Além do Comunismo*), written in 1932 and dealing with the reasons why Preto rejects communist ideology and the alternatives that he purposes.
–*Salazar and his Epoch – Remarks on the Interviews between the current Head of Government with António Ferro* (*Salazar e a sua Época – Comentário às Entrevistas do Actual Chefe do Governo com o Jornalista António Ferro*), which was published in 1933. In this text, the leader of the NS discusses a book that had been recently published and that consisted in a series of conversations between the Portuguese dictator and António Ferro.[8] This text can be particularly useful in order to understand how Preto's ideology permeates with the official conservative ideology of the regime, where exactly do the two resemble each other, and which aspects are rejected by Preto.

While this choice may at first seem to depart from the previous chapters, this is the best option to allow for the disentangling of the morphological configuration of Rolão Preto's ideology in as much detail as possible. It shall also be mentioned that the *Twelve Principle of Production* will sometimes be quoted, for even though this small set of principles was written before the leader of the NS had developed a fully-formed fascist configuration, it still summarises some of the core concepts and features that are relevant in the fascist phase of his political path. Thus, many of the components of Preto's ideology as the leader of NS were already present when he wrote this text, which is reason enough not to neglect it.

## The conceptual core of Rolão Preto's texts

### The national corporate state

In Preto's ideology, as it happens with other fascist configurations, the core concepts of Nation, State and Corporatism interlink in such a way that it is wiser to analyse them together. It is clear that he (just like the other leaders) places nationalism at the core of his ideology and subordinates all the goals of NS to national interests. As he states, 'The National Syndicalist Revolution must develop within the cadres of the Nation, focusing decisively at the level of Portuguese society'.[9] Years before he became a fascist, Preto already asserted the importance of the Nation when he wrote in DPP that 'we proclaim the eternal Nation, the prime reason for our social existence', at the same time that he conceived the Family as the primary cell upon which the national community must be based.[10]

Nevertheless, and in spite of his organicist conception of the Nation, such view does not seem to imply a racist worldview, at least in a first impression. As Preto states, 'the National Syndicalist state will not have prejudices of race and will respect everyone's religious creed'.[11] Judging from what is written in these texts, the concept of 'Race' seems to be absent in Preto's morphology, or at least not to have the same preponderancy that one finds, for instance, in Adolf Hitler. However, this does not mean that we do not find racist notions in Preto's words, especially when the author describes the situation in Russia and mentions the Asian traits that are supposedly evident in Bolsheviks like Lenin himself (who is described as having mysterious 'eastern eyes'). Nevertheless, these slightly racist comments (common in his time) are not enough for us to consider explicit racism as a relevant concept in Preto's texts.

As for the State, which is compared to an 'arbiter' and a 'supreme judge', it must be a conciliator standing above the Nation and have the function of orienting and 'in a certain way conduct[ing] the gears of the national life'.[12] If the Nation, in this organicist view, is like a machine composed of several different pieces, the State is the mechanism that keeps all the pieces working in a harmonious way. The first main adjacent concept that we find in the vicinity of this core concept is 'Sovereignty', for 'the concept of state sovereignty must recapture its traditional sense, presiding and orienting superiorly over the economic and social masses of the country'.[13] This concept thus refers to the reconquering of the power that the National State has supposedly lost in the previous century.

Besides, there is also the adjacent concept of 'Integralism', which has a meaning that resembles that of 'Organicism' and which also closely interlinks with the core concept of Corporatism. According to Preto, the Integral State is not only the 'soul but also the natural organiser' of the Corporate State, which means that the Integral State exhibits the ideals of unity and harmony that only the Corporate State can materialise and concretise. The Integral State holds the promise of national harmony, while the Corporate State is the mechanism that can put this into practice. If the Integral State has to do with the realm of ideas and principles, the Corporate State refers to the actual material concretisation that allows for these principles to be applied in real life.

Still according to the leader, the principles of the Integral State must make themselves felt in at least three different areas of national life:

1. It must represent civic life and for that reason it must be a Representative State.
2. It must be a decentralised State in order to enable regionalism and municipalism.

3. It must be a Syndicalist State for its function is to work with the different stakeholders in the economic process.[14]

It is this third function of the Syndicalist State that allows us to better understand the function of the concept of Corporatism and to discern how exactly the Corporate State puts into practice the ideas of the Integral State. Once again, there is the concept of 'Class Conciliation', for Preto (like all fascists) sees class struggle as harmful to the Nation. He, therefore, wants the Corporate State to create a form of 'solidarity between capital and work' and all producers, be they reach or poor. He does not wish private property nor the search for profits to disappear, although he quickly assures that the unproductive capital (be it land or companies) will not be permitted and usury 'will be relentlessly punished'. As for the working classes, they too shall have their share of benefits and rights in the realm of the Corporate State (we shall later in this chapter return to Preto's proposals towards the needs of the workers).

However, Corporatism must not be limited to any of these two classes, for the middle classes, so Preto argues, are 'the basic elements of social balance' and their 'death' must be avoided. The number of this class has been increasing in the last decades with the improvement of living conditions. Members of the former working class are now ascending to a status that can be seen as middle class. Furthermore, there has been an increase in the number of professions associated with these sectors of society: directors, engineers, foremen, administration employees, etc. However, now, due to the menace of economic crisis, they face a dangerous challenge and may impoverish. For this reason, aware of the necessity of protecting the ones in the middle, he states, when talking about the goals of the Corporate State, 'in order to deliver them from the consequences of the crisis that is impoverishing them, the middle classes will be defended by special measures: long-term credits; housing, etc'.[15] This conception of the middle classes must not be overlooked, for it represents a clear departure from other ideologies which are also concerned with social matters but focus more on the working class.

This praise of the middle sectors of society fits perfectly in Preto's configuration. By focusing on the supposed struggle that led these classes to ascend in society, Preto is able to demonstrate his concerns about social justice, without at the same time reaching the conclusion that private property in itself and the search for profit are a form of exploitation (as Marxists think). Some of the characteristics of capitalist society (which the Left wanted to abolish) shall therefore remain under this new State envisioned by the fascist leader; after all, these characteristics do allow for some sectors of society to obtain gains and are in line with the more general fascist notion of human societies based on constant struggle.

With the goal of making his reader fully aware of the role that the future National State shall play in the productive process, Preto dedicates many pages to describe the future Corporate State and its functions. Such State is primarly defined as 'the representation of the solidary interests of all the branches of production'.[16] In the vicinity of this core concept of Corporatism, there are adjacent concepts such as 'Economic Traditionalism' and 'Economic Group'. The former refers to a notion of economy in which its elements are not seen as individuals competing between each other but grouped together. This is the concept that Preto believes to have once guided economic production but has since then been substituted by individualism.

As to the concept of 'Economic Group', it refers to the basic unity upon which the economic system must be based and is, according to Preto, the best way to organise the elements of production and defend their interests. The organic view of economy holds that the most important elements of production in want of being harmonised are: capital, labour and technic. One cannot construct a system that dispenses any of these for the simple reason that they are equally responsible for the good functioning of the economy.

Capital is 'the initial basis of a company and the indispensable reserve for the years in which revenue does not balance the expense'.[17] In the modern era, there are two forms of Capital: private capital (which an individual or group of individuals gather for themselves throughout the years) and state capital (when the collective capital of the Nation is owned by the State, an option that the experience of URSS has proven to be a failure). Technic is the science of directing production and it includes both administrative technic and industrial technic. As to Labour, 'it is the element of production that executes the plans made by industrial technic and by mutual accord with the possibilities of capital'.[18] These three elements must each play their part and cooperate in order to give production a social function.

In order to create harmony between all these elements, Preto introduces a discussion about two important institutions that must make part of the new State: Syndicates and Corporations (which must be the most important economic groups in the new State). The Syndicates are social-economic groups formed by groups of workers of the same element of production. Even though Preto admits the existence of mixed Syndicates, which are formed by workers from different branches, he warns that experience has shown that they are often inefficient. In the Syndicates that he wants to create, production must be organised by hierarchies (for in the productive activity there must be leaders and followers) and categories (for production must be organised according to its specific function). A production divided by categories shall imply that the productive process is not taken as a whole but rather organised according to a specific branch, be it bread, wine, cork, graphical arts, tissues, transports, etc. Preto also states that the Syndicates must have legal personality and be allowed to own property.

He defends Syndicalism, that is, the organisation of production on the basis of the Syndicate, by introducing the notion of 'Organic Revolutionary Syndicalism', which is a type of syndicalism in which the syndicates represent the different elements according to an established plan. This form of syndicalism promotes solidarity among the elements of production 'from the root to the fruit, from the creation of the product to its delivery to the consumer'.[19] For instance, the production of bread must be organised in a way that coordinates all the elements that sow and reap the cereals and also bakery services, for they share solidary interests.

As to the Corporations, they are organs that unite the Syndicates within the State. They result from the agreements between different elements of production and shall be formed by delegations of Capital Syndicates and Labour Syndicates. In the Corporation, the elements representing the Syndicates must have equal rights and equal representation: the Corporation has a horizontal and not vertical organisation (thus contrasting to the Syndicates). Its function is to draw up regulations, collective bargaining agreements, solve conflicts, organise production, etc. The State should intervene as an arbiter when the Corporation is incapable of reaching a peaceful agreement on a certain matter. Preto summarises the role that the Corporation shall play in the new state:

> The corporation is the essential organ; it is the organ of the Corporative State in a National Syndicalist Regime. Through it, one does not aim at maintaining the current position of producers: the rich in one side and the poor in the opposite side, connected only by the compromises that come out of collective bargaining. On the contrary, one tries to reinforce with the possibilities of capital (industrial company and land) the effort of the worker in order for him to attain a medium level of wealth and moral and material welfare, which is indispensable to its personality as Man.[20]

The main concept associated with the Syndicate is that of 'Solidarity', for this is the sentiment that must be inculcated among the productive forces. Corporations are associated with the idea of 'Unity', for they gather the different Syndicates within the Nation. These two institutions, when working together in harmony, can fulfil the main goals of the Integral State, being such State also associated with the concept of 'Justice'. Social solidarity and social justice towards the poorer and the working class can include measures such as: assistance in cases of sickness, unemployment, disability and old age; replacement of the individual wage by family wage for this is the best form to ensure the future of children; workers' participation in the profits of the companies; measures for fighting unemployment, and others.

Going further, one can verify that Preto envisions a country in which productivity is divided between different 'Economic Regions' (be they industrial or agricultural), where the Syndicates are reunited in Corporations that represent the interests of those regions.[21] The regions shall be represented in the Provincial Council of Corporations, and each province shall belong to a cluster of similar economic interests known as a Federations. According to Preto, the country shall be divided into three Federations (North, Centre and South), each of them containing three or more provinces. In another passage, Preto also defends the existence of a National Economic Council, capable of maintaining the contact between the Integral State and the agricultural and industrial production, as well as helping them to face possible crisis. This National Economic Council is fundamental for the organisation of production and can coexist with a National Assembly. Preto rejects, however, an Economic Parliament, for it would only represent particular interests and would not have a national scope.

Lastly, it is important to understand the historical role that, according to this leader, the Corporate State must fulfil. In his words, 'The corporate state is not an intellectual hypothesis borne out of mere cabinet ruminations erected to the height of a saving political-social fiction. The corporate state is a historical necessity: it is a social regime succeeds an individualist regime'.[22] Corporatism is not born out of intellectual wanderings but out of the historical necessities of the age. It is the only solution after the failure of both liberalism and communism, and it is the sole form of restoring the greatness of the Nation and create a whole new era. As will be seen in the next section, this core concept also interlinks with that of Revolution.

The concept of Corporatism seems to have a greater preponderancy than the one that is found in the configuration of generic fascism. This happens perhaps because the main goal of the texts chosen in this chapter (with the exception of the one about Salazar) is to present a coherent version of an economic system revolving around an organicist and integralist conception of society. This is the feature of the NS ideology that Preto intends to explain in further detail, and this partially explains the attention that Corporatism receives. Furthermore, it is worth remembering that, as previously mentioned, the discussion about the 'Social Question' and the borrowings from leftist ideas were a preoccupation of some that, on the political right, tried to reconquer the masses to nationalism. It is perfectly reasonable that, writing in such background, Rolão Preto chooses to place a great focus on corporatist ideas and on an adjacent concept which has not been much talked about until now: that of 'Social Justice'.

## *The alternative modernity and the national revolution*

Preto states that he sees his doctrine as a Revolutionary one when he writes that 'the Integral State can only triumph by revolutionary method'.[23] And he also says that this Revolution must concern all productive classes, for 'today the Social Revolution is not just reclaimed by the so called working class. In the folds of its flag are now all those who work, whatever may their profession and category be'.[24] Besides, the core concept of Revolution interlinks with Corporatism since the new society constructed by the National Revolution must aim at the fulfilment of the material necessities of those in need. As he says, 'the Revolution is the growing uneasiness, the eagerness for new forms in which it translates the movement of incessant transformation of the world searching for bread, searching for justice'.[25] Once again, there is the adjacent concept of 'Social Justice'.

Other adjacent concepts include, unsurprisingly 'The Cult of Youth'. His praise for the young is evident when he asks: 'Modern Men, when will we make the Modern State? Young Men, when will we get definitely rid of the old prejudices, the old formulas, the old illusions, the old words?'.[26] Preto favourably opposes the 'New' to the 'Old' and nowhere else does this appear so evident as when he compares age groups. According to him, the young are best suited to radically alter society for their spirit is not conditioned by party interests, and they are willing to fight for the national reconstruction. In some passages, the author has no qualms in saying that the National Syndicalist State must give 'all power to the young', even if he adds that does not mean that all functionaries of the old State will be fired. In the new State, old age will no longer be considered a sign of wisdom, for history shows that young people are the ones prone to do great deeds: that was the case of Nuno Álvares Pereira and Vasco da Gama, and it is now the case of Ataturk and Mussolini. Even Sidónio Pais, so Preto says, had 'surrounded himself with the young'.

Like in the configuration of generic fascism, we also find the adjacent concept of 'Palingenesis', since in Preto's view a spiritual rebirth is necessary to confront the present state of decay and 'abatimento' (a Portuguese word which can be translated as something like 'prostration') which is caused, not by the moral weakness of the Portuguese people, but rather by the internal divisiveness that have destroyed the Nation in the last decades. The leader of NS goes as far as saying that Portugal has fought a Civil War that lasted for a hundred years and it is still dealing with the impact and damages of internal strife.[27] To this state of decay Preto contrasts the 'Ideal', which represents the main transcendental force that drives revolutionary change: what drives Fascism onwards is an 'absorbent eagerness for Ideal', a higher force that is superior to materialism and guides spiritual change. Provided with this 'Ideal', the Revolution acquires a higher dimension that 'neither discusses nor contemporises. Either you accept it or you reject it. Revolution is a force that is superior to the will of the individual, something you cannot stop'.[28]

In the same vein, the Revolution also implies the creation of a new 'Personality', which is the word used by Preto that most resemble the concept of 'New Man' in generic fascism. According to him, 'the National Syndicalist Revolution has the goal of guaranteeing to the Human Personality the possession of all its rights for full compliance of its social duties'[29]. This 'Personality' is not an abstract notion (like the liberal 'individual') but the concrete human reality that is inserted in the community and other important social groups, enjoying in it a set of social and economic liberties that are the first condition for all other liberties. Since the family (the fundamental cell of society) is crucial to the development of the 'Personality', the Corporate State shall accordingly dedicate much of its efforts to promote the welfare of the familiar nucleus.

Lastly, one of the most important adjacent concepts surrounding Revolution is 'Progress', which is conceived by Preto as a march towards the new era of the Corporate State. According to the leader of NS, 'Progress' means the resuming of a path towards the construction of a new type of modernity which shall be based on 'Economic Traditionalism'. Such a path had been abandoned since the coming of Liberalism with its focus on the individual, and this fact was responsible for making modern society abandon ancient principles coming from the Middle Ages. For this reason, Preto believes that it is necessary to find once again 'the long avenue of the future, which is where we continue the interrupted march of the past'.[30] And he adds that 'it suffices to go back to the interrupted line of past teachings in order to find the true meaning of the present and the future'.[31] In other words, it is necessary to construct a new society which is based on principles that sink their roots in the 'the slandered land of the Middle ages'.[32]

Preto does not perceive 'Progress' as a simple march towards a better (and eventually more equalitarian) future, as it happens in Liberal ideologies, nor as a revolutionary change guided by the working class, as it is the case of Marxist ideology. This leader thus holds an alternative view of 'Progress' and, at least on the surface, his conception does not fit in the dichotomy presented, among others, by Norberto Bobbio. Such dichotomy simply divides ideologies in Left and Right according to whether they defend the march towards a better future (either through revolutionary or reformist means) or the end of this progressive march (and in some cases even its reversal). The NS leader's view is a more complex one, for he does not defend the return to the past but he also looks suspiciously to the changes brought by modernity.

Therefore, what he aims is an alternative future, one in which the values of the past are recuperated, not to return to ancient times, but to build a new society that is influenced by those values from yore. To Preto, the arrival of Liberalism did not mean 'Progress' but rather the interruption of a march towards a better future and the desertion of 'Economic Traditionalism'. Liberal society, instead of progressing, is becoming ever more decadent due to this interruption of a 'truer' form of 'Progress' based on the forms of societal organisation that were common in the Middle Ages.

This conceptualisation of 'Progress' and historical evolution, even if it seems more traditionalist than fascist actually puts him in tune with other varieties of fascism.[33] Independently of his admiration for the past, the Portuguese fascist leader does not seek to return to ancient societies, but rather to find in them the inspiration for the construction of a new era. The traditionalist features of his configuration are not due to the notion that the past was necessarily better than the future that he envisions but that the march towards the future was lost due to the decadence of liberal individualism. His goal is to resume this path towards the future and build a new era that contains in it a modernised reconfiguration of some principles that liberalism rejected, but that he still sees as a valuable political inspiration. Preto does see history as something that goes through a process of evolution, even if such process seems to have been interrupted by the course that modern age had been taking in the previous centuries.

*Authoritarianism and violence*

Apart from interlinking with the concept of State due to the defence of a strong executive government, the concept of Authority also interlinks with the adjacent concept of 'Hierarchy', for this is a principle to be respected in society in order for the Corporate system to be successful (let us remember, for instance, that even in the productive process there must be the leaders and the led). Also making use of the concept of 'Leader', Preto says that 'the soul of the machine, however perfect and strong it may be, is in the driver'.[34] If the Corporate State is the machine, then its driver is the chief, the leader of the State. Such a conductor must stand above private interests and his authority and legitimacy must not be questioned, for 'only the chief whose authority one does not discuss has in itself the true, complete and efficient social virtue. This is why the institution headed by a chief of this nature can be the social regime par excellence'.[35]

Furthermore, when criticising Salazar for his lack of capacity to move the masses in a revolutionary direction, Preto says that, 'the supreme virtue that distinguishes the Chief is in his power to assemble the imponderables, creating the moral and material conditions that are propitious to him'.[36] The chief must be someone who knows how to read the will of the masses and instill in them the necessary revolutionary spirit, even if that implies wearing a combat uniform, like fascist leaders throughout Europe were then doing. The importance of the leader becomes more evident when Preto, comparing modern times to the epoch of the French Revolution, writes about Mussolini,

> The French Revolution finds its creative expression in the revolutionary and restless soul of Napoleon. The Fascist Revolution finds it in the virile and burning soul of Mussolini – all the fevers that in this world mark the great étapes of its revolutionary march are born from man's disturbed heart in his absorbent eagerness for Ideal.[37]

The Italian dictator is presented as one of the most important symbols of the fascist Revolution. He was the man who could guide the process of social and spiritual transformation and be a source of inspiration.

When referring to the recent history of Portugal, the leader of the NS does not forget to mention the example of Sidónio Pais to show how authority and leadership can help perform social change: this Portuguese president was able to create a political force encompassing the whole Nation. His followers were no longer identified for political creeds that they once had (like monarchism or republicanism) but for their allegiance to the new leader: all of them became

Sidonists sharing a common mission. 'Sidónio Pais had thus done and from the four corners of the horizon of the country had the loud and enthusiastic mass of Sidonism had been summoned', he says.[38]

As to the concept of Violence, of which Preto does not seem to make an extensive use, it is still nevertheless discernable if one pays attention to some adjacent concepts. For instance, he mentions 'Virility' and dedicates the last pages of *Beyond Communism* to an ardent call for direct action in which he praises the 'virile and untamed cadence of the Nationalist Revolution on the march'.[39] Warning that the 28th May of 1926 had brought the conditions for Revolutionary change (conditions that had previously been destroyed in 1910 with the end of the monarchy), the leader of the NS mentions other European countries (Austria, Hungary, Italy) where fervent militants are already in the streets like 'anxious ferments of life, of struggle, of the future' and with 'flags that are pennants of battle'. They aim at restoring the greatness of the Nation and are fighting their enemies, among whom are the communists. This is what he encourages his readers to do in Portugal as well.

Furthermore, his views about Violence becomes more evident in a passage in which he criticises Salazar for his supposed moderation and inability to fight internal and external enemies. To him, the goal of national defence seems to justify the use of Violence, even if that must always occur in a way that does not disturb the order of society. As he says, 'organising the nation means, in the first place, to provide for its defence'.[40] In the case of internal defence, a stronger role must be played by the police, the press and even the enthusiast Portuguese patriots; while in the case of external defence, the role must be played by a modernised diplomatic representation and the power of public forces. With its spirit of vigilance, the army must also play an important role in fighting against the enemies: it shall be an 'elite body' prepared for war, and it shall preferably be led by a chief with martial convictions. What one finds here is therefore a call for tough methods of national defence that resemble those of an authoritarian and repressive regime.

## Other important features of the configuration

### *Imperialism: an absent concept?*

Preto does not seem to make use of the concept of Empire, for this seem practically absent from the texts that were here chosen. As it is already known, it is common for leader of countries with an Empire already in existence not to defend an unnecessary expansionism. However, in Preto's texts, one does not even find many references to the revalorisation of the Empire, as it happened with Oswald Mosley. However, one shall not jump to the conclusion that this concept was totally irrelevant to Preto, for the focus on economic and social questions of these texts may be one of the explanations for this absence.

Even though this is not the goal of this study, we can briefly mention that some references about the Empire do appear in some other texts. For instance, in his book *Justice*, written some years after the period that is here in analysis, he wrote that, 'only a national policy capable of considering the overseas provinces as an integrant part of the Portuguese nation, materialising the convergence of its elements in the same spiritual unity, can really interpret the aspirations of the country and its future'.[41] However, the simple fact that these important texts do not deal directly with 'Expansionism' or 'Empire' seems to be a first clear indication that, after all, it is possible to exhibit a fully formed fascist configuration without the prescence of this concept. The implications that this has for our conceptual configuration will be adressed later.

### Peripheral concepts

As it happens with other leaders, the concept of 'Liberty' is a marginal one for, though it does appear, it is always in the periphery and is seen as something that can only be attained within the scope of national union and collectivity. The recurrent marginality of this concept in other configurations makes it unnecessary to describe it with much detail in this chapter.

### Permeability and rejections

At the time of Preto's writing, since the Republic had been already defeated in 1926 and Liberalism was not a problem anymore, one of the main concerns of the NS and other Right Wing organisations was to meet the needs of the working class and thus prevent the growing of the communist menace. For this reason, the right had to deal with concepts that could resemble those of a left wing ideology like that of 'Social Justice'. This helps to explain why Rolão Preto's ideology seems to display a certain permeability with ideologies coming from the Left, including some forms of non-Marxism socialist. This is noticeable, for instance, when he mentions the example of the Belgian socialist Henrik de Mann, who was also searching for an alternative socialist path.

However, this does not mean that Preto does not reject vehemently the ideologies with which his thought permeates. The two main ideologies that the leader rejects are Liberalism (on the basis of its concept of 'Individual' and its notion of individual economy) and Communism (on the basis of the concept of 'Class struggle' and the notion of collective economy). As it is already known, instead of these systems of production, Preto proposes the 'Organic Economy', which is based on economic traditionalism and on the economic group rather than on the individual or on social class.

Liberal economy had been adopted for the last centuries and its base was 'free competition, the triumph of the individual over the organisation of the economic group'.[42] One of the main consequences of this economic system was the subjugation of the State to the interests of capitalism, "the intervention of capitalism in the governments of the people, which led to the tyranny of capitalism over parliaments".[43] Other consequences included the creation of a state of anarchy, which brought chaos to the economy, and the emergence of big trusts, which destroyed small and medium business. Economic liberalism, in sum, centred on the individual and for that reason it created disunity, at the same time that it placed a great deal of power in the hands of big business (a power of which the business owners made further use through the manipulation of the press). Note that Preto seems to refer to this conception of economics as a component of a past era, which had already been defeated in the society where he presently lives.

His rejection of Communism is also very clear in the pages that he dedicates to the description of the misery that befell on Russia after the instalment of the Bolshevik regime. The working class, so he says, had been one of the major victims of this regime, and its condition did not improve. The failures of communism in Russia, according to Preto, include the takeover of the state by the party bureaucratic elite, the inefficiency of cooperatives and trade unions, the terrible working conditions (for even women and children are exploited), low wages, lack of medical assistance, too much hours of work, and so on.

In Preto's view, the collectivist economy behind communism and Marxism, focusing on the working class, first appeared as a possible solution to the real problems of liberalism. According to the Portuguese leader:

> Industrial revolution, creating large agglomerations of workers in the interests of powerful companies, has revived the associative sense of the working masses, forcing governments here and beyond to accept trade unions in their legislation. The spirit with which liberal democratic power faces the official formations was always one of distrust, if not hostility.[44]

Therefore, there was an actual reason that explained and to a certain extent justified the emergency of socialist ideas. However, Preto believes that the defence of the working class by Marx is an excessive one, even if it has some fundamentals of truth. Promising impossibilities to the working class, Marxism imperils the unity of the Nation by fomenting class struggle and leading to a new economic system that can be even worse than the liberal one. Furthermore, Marx's theory of surplus value does not stand up to scrutiny, so Preto seems to think, for the value of a commodity is not only dependent on manual work but also onthe capital that was invested in it. Preto also rejects Marx's notion that capital accumulation is based solely on the greed of the bourgeoisie and on the exploitation of workers, for he rather sees profit as a necessary component of any economic system.

Preto's configuration has also the idiosyncrasy of having emerged not only in reaction to liberalism and Marxism but also in open dispute against a regime and a dictator whom he deemed too conservative. To Preto and his most radical colleagues, the elite supporting the dictatorship was not seizing the opportunity offered by the 1926 military coup to construct a truly

Revolutionary State. Thus, the most important feature of his ideological competition with Salazar revolves around the concept of Revolution, and to some extent the concept of Authority, for he does not see in the Portuguese dictator the will to lead the energy of the masses. Preto states that 'all will be useless and vain if before attempting to give a new feature to the national soul one does not seek first to raise it to the rediscovery of nationalist revolutionary enthusiasm'.[45] Revolutionary enthusiasm is something that Salazar does not seem willing to instill, at least not in the same way as other warlike European leaders in comparison to whom the Portuguese dictator distinguished himself due to his academic past.

In spite of some admiration for Salazar and his financial achievements, Preto has no doubts in admitting that, when it comes to the 'Social Question' and to Revolution, the chief of government is not on the side of fascism, even if he admires Mussolini and is inspired by him in some aspects. Even when acknowledging that Salazar takes into account the Revolutionary method, Preto asks rhetorically: 'with an anti-revolutionary temperament, how could the Finance Dictator actually consider up-and-coming a means which he analyses through his method of cold empiricism?'.[46] The Finance Dictator (as he calls him) is thus seen as a leader incapable of wearing the combat uniform of fascist leaders since he is too concerned with equilibrium and moderation. His cold temperament, so Preto argues, owes more to academic wisdom than to faith in Revolution. The party that he created, that is, the National Union, is not an organisation ready for revolutionary change but it represents instead 'a group of values, a General Staff from certain sectors of the Dictatorship', having Salazar drifted away from the European Revolution.[47]

## Contradictions: revolution/traditionalism

Some of the contradictions in Preto's configuration are also present in other varieties of fascist ideology, such as the contradiction between 'Individual' and 'Collectivity' (which is solved through the use of the concept of 'Personality') and the contradiction between 'Elitism' and 'Populism' (which is begining to seem to be a recurrent in fascist ideology). Furthermore, there seems to be also a contradiction between 'Idealism' (the higher truth that guides revolutions) and 'Materialism (focus on the material conditions and on social justice for the poor classes). This contradiction seems to be solved when Preto states that 'facts are indestructible and clear beacons that mark the path through which the Idea moves, contacting reality, scrubbing its glorious tunic'.[48] The Ideal is thus seen not as a force that can alter reality, but rather as one that operates within the limits that the material world offers, making its influence being felt in it.

Besides, there seems to be another contradiction that opposes 'Traditionalism' to 'Revolution' for, in spite of his adoption of revolutionary discourse, it is nonetheless evident his use of the concept of 'Economic

Traditionalism' and the praise forthe Middle Ages. However, as already said, such apparent contradiction is solved through the use of the concept of 'Progress' and its conception as non-linear process that needs to gain inspiration from the past in order to build a new future. Such rearrangement of concepts ensures that Preto's ideology holds some coherence, even while allowing for the coexistence of traditionalist and revolutionary conceptions.

## Concluding remarks

As we have discussed, Preto's configuration emerged in a time where the fiercest contestation taking place was against Salazar and the official view of the regime that he was constructing. His opposition to Salazar's authoritarian conservatism concerned both the weakness of his non-revolutionary ideology and the insufficiencies of the National Union as a political organisation. For this reason, he wants to present two alternatives: an alternative ideology that he terms 'Organic Revolutionary Syndicalism' and analternative political movement, which is National Syndicalism. It was precisely the core of this organic revolutionary syndicalist ideology that was here disentangled. In spite of the absence of one of the core concepts of our preliminary configuration, that of Empire, we can for now and without further ado conclude that Rolão Preto's ideology represents a permutation of fascism. The implications of the absence of 'Empire' will be later discussed.

The conceptual configuration that was disentangled was the final result of a political career that had begun several years before the writing of the texts and which already had some features that resembled fascism. The main difference between Preto and his integralist years was the use that he makes of the adjacent concept of 'Leader' during his fascist phase. The main rearrangement in Preto's ideology, therefore, was the substitution of his monarchist principles for the cult of the fascist leader. In relation to this, Cazetta reminds us that 'the figure of the chief as the conductor of the nation, overriding the king, only became definitive for him in the mid 1930s. Until then, Preto defended the project of a syndical monarchy, just like most integralists'.[49] When an integralist, this leader had indeed written that 'we proclaim the King as the Chief of National Production".[50] Altering the way how he saw the leader of the Nation, Preto thus arrived at a configuration that makes him closer to fascism than he was during the 10 s. However, the concepts of 'Social Justice' and 'Syndicalism' were already present in this thought well before he became a fascist. According António Costa Pinto,

> Between 1918 and 1934, when NS was banned, he attempted to 'nationalise' the working class, leading them towards 'organic syndicalism' and away from socialism and communism. In 1918 he did so by attempting to reconcile syndicalism with monarchism. Thus, in the 1930s, he supported 'integral corporatism' and replaced the monarch with a charismatic, fascistic leader.[51]

His defence of Corporatism in the fascist years thus resulted from a political path that always had at its core the concern with the working class and the necessity of bringing them back to nationalism. That is one feature of Preto's ideology that must be properly noted, since it is at the core of all his preocupations.

## Notes

1 According to António Costa Pinto, 'the most salient characteristics of the emergence of fascism in Portuguese post-war society were the precocious adoption of the paradigm of Italian Fascism, on the one hand, and its weak and fragmented party political expression, on the other'. António Costa Pinto, *The Blue Shirts: Portuguese Fascism and the New State* (New York, Columbia University Press, 2000), 32.
2 Cruzada Nuno Álvares Pereira displayed some authoritarian features that resembled Italian Fascism, even though it was not totally fascist. According to Pinto, 'the CNAP cannot be considered a truly fascist party because of its social base and organisational structure. Nonetheless, in the final years of the liberal regime it carried out pro-authoritarian propaganda with important fascist references'. Pinto, *The Blue Shirts*, 32.
3 'Sidónio Pais's political discourse was anti-plutocratic during the period of war shortages, directed against the party oligarchies, and espousing a messianic nationalism. He managed to unite monarchists and conservative republicans. In all this, he made full use of his charismatic strengths'. Pinto, *The Blue Shirts*, 32To read more about this charismatic Portuguese President, who was murdered in 1918, see also António Malheiro da Silva, *Sidónio e Sidonismo* (Coimbra, Imprensa da Universidade de Coimbra, 2006).
4 The militancy of Preto in the IL and the way he abandoned it to join more radical organisations rather resembles that of Georges Valois, the former AF member who left this organisation to form the first French fascist movement, *Le Faisceau*. This similitude between Preto and Valois has already been noted by authors who wrote about the history of the NS such as João Medina, *Salazar e Os Fascistas: Salazarismo e Nacional-Sindicalismo, a História de Um Conflito, 1932–1935* (Lisboa, Livraria Bertrand, 1978).
5 José Melo Alexandrino, 'Rolão Preto: Um Intérprete Do Século XX' in Francisco Rolão Preto, *Obras Completas*. Vol. I (Lisboa, Edições Colibri, 2015), xvi–xvii.
6 As stated by Pinto, 'Corporatism was presented as the alternative to liberalism and as the basis for the restoration of the monarchy. Historical legitimisation and reinforcing the theory of corporatism was much more important than any other anti-liberal elements in the ideology of IL, as shown by studies and texts published by the leaders of the movement'. Pinto, *The Blue Shirts*, 7.
7 As stated by Pinto, 'Corporatism was presented as the alternative to liberalism and as the basis for the restoration of the monarchy. Historical legitimisation and reinforcing the theory of corporatism was much more important than any other anti-liberal elements in the ideology of IL, as shown by studies and texts published by the leaders of the movement'. Pinto, *The Blue Shirts*, 7.
8 António Ferro was a Portuguese writer connected to the modernist movement, having befriended writers like Fernando Pessoa and Mário de Sá Carneiro. He later became fascinated by fascism and authoritarian regimes and would become the first Secretary of National Propaganda in Salazar's regime. To read more

about Ferro see Orlando Raimundo, *António Ferro: O Inventor do Salazarismo* (Alfragide, Dom Quixote, 2015).

9 Translated by the author from the original in Portuguese: 'A Revolução Nacional-Sindicalista desenvolver-se-á dentro dos quadros da Nação, incidindo decisivamente no plano da Sociedade Portuguesa'. Francisco Rolão Preto, 'Balizas_Directrizes_Alma' In José de Melo Alexandrino, Ed., *Obras Completas* (Lisboa, Edições Colibri, 2015 [1932]), 160. All the other translation in this chapter are translated by the author, and for this reason there is no need to mention this again.

10 'Proclamamos a Nação Eterna, razão primeira da nossa existência social' Francisco Rolão Preto, 'Os Doze Princípios da Produção' In José de Melo Alexandrino, Ed., *Obras Completas* (Lisboa, Edições Colibri, 2015 [1932]), 113.

11 'O Estado Nacional-Sindicalista não terá preconceitos de raça e respeitará as crenças religiosas de cada um'. Preto, 'Balizas_Directrizes_Alma', 158.

12 'Orientar e de certo modo conduzir as engrenagens da vida da nação'. Francisco Rolão Preto, 'Para além do Comunismo' In José de Melo Alexandrino, Ed., *Obras Completas* (Lisboa, Edições Colibri, 2015 [1932]), 208.

13 'Conceito de soberania do Estado retoma o seu sentido tradicional, presidindo e orientando superiormente as massas económicas e sociais do país'. Preto, 'Para além do Comunismo', 206.

14 Preto, 'Balizas_Directrizes_Alma', 160.

15 'Para as libertar das consequências da crise que as está proletarizando, serão as classes médias defendidas por medidas especiais: créditos a longos prazos, moratórias, etc.' Preto, 'Balizas_Directrizes_Alma', 159.

16 'O Estado Corporativo é a representação dos interesses solidários de todos os ramos da produção'. Preto, 'Para além do Comunismo', 199.

17 'O capital é a base inicial da empresa e a reserva indispensável para os anos em que a receita não equilibra a despesa'. Preto, 'Balizas_Directrizes_Alma', 150.

18 'O 'elemento' da Produção que executa os planos da empresa elaborados pela técnica industrial e de comum acordo com as possibilidades do capital'. Ibid., p51.

19 'Desde a raiz ao fruto, desde a criação do produto até à sua entrega ao consumidor''. Ibid., 203.

20 'A corporação é o órgão essencial, é o órgão do Estado Corporativo em Regime Nacional-Sindicalista. Através dela não se pretende, como a Itália e outros países poderiam fazer crer, manter a posição actual dos produtores: ricos a um lado e pobres a outro, ligados apenas pelos compromissos que resultassem dos contratos colectivos de trabalho – ao contrário –, procura-se reforçar com as possibilidades do capital (Empresa industrial e Terra) o esforço do trabalhador de forma a ele atingir um nível médio de riqueza e bem-estar moral e material indispensável à sua personalidade de Homem'. Ibid., 155.

21 Conceiving the Nation as an organism composed by different interlinked parts, Preto had already stated in *DPP* that the national community is divided in Provinces, Regions and Economic Groups.

22 'O estado corporativo não é uma hipótese intelectual nascida de meras congeminações de gabinete erguidas à altura de uma ficção político-social salvadora. O estado corporativo é uma necessidade histórica: é um regime social que sucede a um regime individualista'. Ibid., 197.

23 'O Estado Integral só pode, pois, triunfar pelo método revolucionário'. Preto, 'Para além do Comunismo', 209.

24 'Hoje, a Revolução Social não é apenas reclamada pela chamada "classe operária". Nas dobras da sua bandeira envolvem-se agora todos os que trabalham, seja qual for a sua profissão e categoria'. Francisco Rolão Preto,

'Salazar e a sua Época', In José de Melo Alexandrino, Ed., *Obras Completas* (Lisboa, Edições Colibri, 2015 [1932]), 216.

25 'A Revolução é a inquietação crescente; a ânsia de novas formas em que traduz o movimento de incessante transformação do mundo à procura de pão, à procura de justiça'. Ibid., 227.

26 'Homens modernos, quando fazemos o Estado Moderno? Homens Novos, quando nos desembaraçamos definitivamente dos velhos preconceitos, das velhas fórmulas, das velhas ilusões, das velhas palavras?'. Preto, 'Para além do Comunismo', 211.

27 This reference to a hundred years of conflicts sends us to the beginning of the Civil War that took place between 1828 and 1834 opposing liberal constitutionalists against absolutist defenders of the old regime. It seems evident that, according to Preto, the divisions and conflicts brought by Liberalism did not cease with the end of the war. The entirety of the liberal era can be seen as a Civil War in which conflicts between individuals and parties are constantly triggered.

28 'O seu triunfo depende do seu aspecto de bloco sem brecha, de unidade clara, total, dogmática. A Revolução não discute nem contemporiza. Ou se aceita ou se rejeita'. Preto, 'Salazar e a sua Época', 229.

29 'A Revolução Nacional-Sindicalista tem por fim garantir à Personalidade Humana a posse de todos os seus direitos para cumprimento integral dos seus deveres sociais'. Preto, 'Balizas_Directrizes_Alma', 158.

30 'A longa avenida do futuro, que é por onde se continua a marcha interrompida do passado'. Preto, 'Para além do Comunismo', 196.

31 'Basta voltar à linha interrompida dos ensinamentos do passado para encontrar o verdadeiro sentido do presente e do futuro'. Ibid., 198.

32 'O Estado Corporativo realiza assim uma etapa do tradicionalismo económico cujas raízes se afundam na terra caluniada da Idade Média'. Ibid., 196.

33 This praise for the so called 'Economic Traditionalism' in Preto's ideology has led some to conclude that he departs from the more purely fascistic defence of Revolution. As Pinto writes, 'Unlike other fascists, however, his syndicalist beliefs did not make him a believer in technological progress or modernisation. Indeed, Preto believed that by adopting these ideals, he was taking a strategic stance against such developments. This traditionalism was always present in his writings and activities even after he adopted the 'revolutionary' language of Fascism in the 1930s'.However, we argue that, even if it is true that Preto never fully adhered to technological progress as other fascists did, his conceptualisation of 'Progress' and historical evolution puts him in tune with other varieties of fascism.

34 'A alma da máquina, por mais perfeita e mais forte que seja, está no maquinista.' Preto, 'Para além do Comunismo', 206

35 'Só o chefe cuja legitimidade se não discute tem na verdade em si toda a virtude social eficiente e completa. Eis porque a instituição que tem à cabeça um chefe desta natureza é o regime social por excelência'. Ibid., 205.

36 'Eis porque a virtude suprema que distingue o Chefe está no seu poder de congregar os imponderáveis, criando as condições morais e materiais que lhe sejam propícias'. Preto, 'Salazar e a sua Época', 221.

37 'A Revolução Francesa encontra a sua expressão criadora na alma revolucionária e inquieta de Napoleão. A revolução fascista encontra-a na alma viril e ardente de Mussolini – todas as febres que marcam no mundo as grandes *étapes* da sua marcha revolucionária, nascem do coração perturbado do homem na sua ânsia absorvente de Ideal'. Ibid., 220.

38 'Sidónio Pais assim fizera e dos quatro cantos do horizonte do país tinha acorrido a massa fremente e entusiasta do sidonismo'. Ibid., 228.

39 'cadência viril e indomável da Revolução Nacionalista em marcha. sidonismo'. Ibid., 211.
40 'Organizar a nação é, em primeiro lugar, prover à sua defesa'. Ibid.,216.
41 'Só uma política nacional que saiba considerar as províncias de além-mar como parte integrante da nação portuguesa, realizando a convergência dos seus elementos na mesma unidade espiritual, pode, em verdade interpretar as aspirações do país e assegurar o seu futuro'. Francisco Rolão Preto, 'Justiça', In José de Melo Alexandrino, Ed., *Obras Completas* (Lisboa, Edições Colibri, 2015 [1932]), 330.
42 'A livre concorrência, o triunfo do individuo sobre a organização do grupo económico'. Preto, 'Balizas_Directrizes_Alma', 148.
43 'Intervenção do capitalismo no governo dos povos, a qual se traduziu pela tirania do capitalismo sobre os parlamentos'. Ibid., 147.
44 'A revolução industrial, criando grandes aglomerados operários para as necessidades das empresas poderosas, fez renascer o sentido associativo das massas operárias, obrigando aqui e além os governos a aceitar na sua legislação os sindicatos. O espírito com que o poder liberal democrata encarou as formações oficiais foi sempre o da desconfiança, quando não o da hostilidade'. Ibid., 148.
45 'Tudo será inútil e vão se antes de tentar dar nova feição à alma nacional se não procurar erguê-la primeiro ao rubro do entusiasmo revolucionário nacionalista'. Preto, 'Salazar e a sua Época', 216.
46 'Temperamento antirrevolucionário, como podia em verdade o Ditador das Finanças considerar com esperança um meio que ele analisa através do seu método de frio empirismo?'. Ibid., 220.
47 'Um grupo de valores, a um Estado-Maior saído de certos sectores da Ditadura'. Ibid., 229.
48 'Os factos são balizas indestrutíveis e claras que marcam o caminho por onde a Ideia, ao contacto da realidade, vai esfarrapando a sua túnica gloriosa'. Preto, 'Para além do Comunismo', 202.
49 'A Figura do chefe como condutor da nação, sobrepondo-se ao rei, só se tornou definitiva em meados dos anos 1930. Até então, Preto defendia o projecto da monarquia sindical, tal como os demais integralistas'. Felipe Cazetta, 'Do Integralismo Lusitano ao Nacional Sindicalismo: Tensões e Conflitos', *Passagens. Revista Internacional de História Política e Cultura Jurídica*, 9 (3), Setembro-Dezembro, 2017. 490.
50 'Proclamamos o Rei chefe da Produção nacional'. Preto, 'Os Doze Princípios da Produção', 113.
51 Pinto, *The Blue Shirts*, 22.

## List of References

Adinolfi, Goffredo, '*Le Destre Radicali e Il Liberalismo Portoghese: Alle Radici Di Una Dittatura*', Memoria e Ricerca, 30, 2009, 109–128.

Alexandrino, José Melo, 'Rolão Preto: Um Intérprete Do Século XX' in Francisco Rolão Preto, Ed., *Obras Completas*. Vol. I (Lisboa, Edições Colibri, 2015).

Bobbio, Norberto, *Teoria Geral da Política* (Rio de Janeiro, Editora Campus, 2000).

Cazetta, Felipe. 'Do Integralismo Lusitano ao Nacional Sindicalismo: Tensões e Conflitos', *Passagens. Revista Internacional de História Política e Cultura Jurídica*, 9 (3), Setembro-Dezembro, 2017, 483–500.

Medina, João, *Salazar e Os Fascistas: Salazarismo e Nacional-Sindicalismo, a História de Um Conflito, 1932-1935* (Lisboa, Livraria Bertrand, 1978).

Pinto, António Costa, *The Blue Shirts: Portuguese Fascism and the New State* (New York, Columbia University Press, 2000), 32.

Pinto, António Costa and Goffredo Adinolfi, 'Salazar's 'New State': The Paradoxes of Hybridization in the Fascist Era' in António Costa Pinto and Aristotle Kallis, Eds., *Rethinking Fascism and Dictatorship in Europe* (London, Palgrave Macmillan, 2014), 154–175.

Preto, Francisco Rolão, 'Balizas_Directrizes_Alma' in José de Melo Alexandrino, Ed., *Obras Completas* (Lisboa, Edições Colibri, 2015 [1932]).

Preto, Francisco Rolão, 'Para além do Comunismo' in José de Melo Alexandrino, Ed., *Obras Completas* (Lisboa, Edições Colibri, 2015 [1932]).

Rens, Ivo (ed.), *Sur l'Oeuvre de Henri de Man* (Geneva, Librairie Droz SA, 1974).

Silva, António Malheiro da, *Sidónio e Sidonismo* (Coimbra, Imprensa da Universidade de Coimbra, 2006).

Torgal, Luís Rei, *Estados Novos, Estado Novo: Ensaios de História e Política Cultural* (Coimbra, Imprensa da Universidade de Coimbra, 2009).

# 5 José António Primo de Rivera and the Spanish Falange

## The historical mission of the Spanish Nation

José Antonio Primo de Rivera became known as the leader of the Spanish Falange, the political movement that became the closest possible representative of a fascist configuration in this country, even if the leader himself oftentimes repudiated such label. The Falangist movement, however, was far from achieving wide support or even an electoral success big enough to bring it closer to acquire actual political power. This and the fact that the definitive leader of Spanish nationalism ended up being Francisco Franco and not Primo de Rivera may at first seem to discredit the importance of focusing on an apparently irrelevant leader. However, as we shall see in this chapter, Primo de Rivera's configuration presents a very interesting set of rearrangements of fascist ideology that are worthy of a more detailed study.

### Primo de Rivera and the FE de las JONS

José António Primo de Rivera was born in Madrid on 20 November 1903. He was the son of General Miguel Primo de Rivera, who later became the leader of a dictatorial regime that would last from 1923 to 1930. Initially removed from politics, José António worked as a lawyer until he decided to dedicate himself to the cause of Spanish nationalism in the beginning of the 30s. This only happened after the death of his father in Paris on 16 March 1930, a few months after the fall of the regime that he had led. With such decision, José António certainly intended to pay some kind of tribute to his father and continue his legacy. In this first years, he even collaborated in the so called 'Sanjurjada', a military coup led by General José Sanjurjo in 1932 that had the goal of overthrowing the government, in which it failed.

Some time later, José António formed the Spanish Falange (Falange Española – FE) in Madrid on 29 October 1933, when he led a convention at *Teatro de la Comedia* where he made a pivotal inauguration speech. This political movement clearly espoused a very extremist form of Spanish nationalism. Among its members were people like Ruiz de Alda and Alfonso García Valdecasas (these two also spoke at the inauguration) and, later, Matías Montero (who would become a martyr of Falangism after being murdered in 1934). The ideology of the movement was clearly influenced by Italian Fascism, although the influence of German National Socialism was also evident.[1]

Some months after its foundation, on 15 February 1934, the Falange merged with another movement formed three years earlier by Ramiro Ledesma Ramos and Onésimo Redondo: Councils of the National Syndicalist Offensive (*Juntas de Ofensiva Nacional-Sindicalista* – JONS). From that moment onwards, this movement was known as the Spanish Falange of the JONS (*Falange Española de las JONS* – FE de las JONS). This fusion took place not long after the elections of 1933, in which José António's party managed to elect only one deputy. Such electoral result is very representative of the marginal status of a political organisation that, during the years that the Republic lasted, was never able to conquer the same amount of popular support that characterised other European fascist parties. By 1936, in the last elections before the Civil War, the party had not significantly increased its base of support and its results were equally disappointing.

Nevertheless, the importance that the movement acquired after the beginning of the Spanish Civil War in 1936 cannot be left unnoticed. As it is generally known, this conflict opposed a Nationalist side against the left-wing Republicans and it started with a military uprising against the Republic that left Morocco on 18 July of that year. It is certain that the course of events was tragic for the Falangist leader. Imprisoned since March for illegal possession of weapons, Primo de Rivera was transferred from Madrid to Alicante and, in November 1936, was sentenced to death and shot two days after that. However, by that time, the Falange, which was unsurprisingly fighting on the side of the Nationalists was witnessing an extraordinary increase in its number of militants, becoming one of the most relevant political forces in the country.

After being led by the uncharismatic Manuel Hedilla for a few months, the FE de las JONS met a peculiar destiny in the history of fascism. The increasing relevance of the Falange did not go unnoticed by General Francisco Franco, who was then trying to consolidate his place as the leader of Spanish nationalists. Thus, Franco promulgated a Unification Decree on 19 April 1937, in which the Falange merged with the monarchists known as Carlists and other rightist groups. From that moment onwards, the party became known as the Traditionalist Spanish Phalanx of the Councils of the National Syndicalist Offensive (Falange Española Tradicionalista y de las Juntas de Ofensiva Nacional Sindicalista – FET de las JONS), and it can no longer be considered as a purely fascist due to the existence of conservative, monarchist, and catholic factions within it.

Nevertheless, Fascist ideology still played a relevant role in the first years of the dictatorial regime that would be established by Franco after he won the war in 1939, even if this regime, just like its party, cannot be considered a pure fascist one. The FET de las JONS was only dissolved in 1977, after the transition to democracy, having gone through a history that is too complex to be summarised here but about which it can be said that it always contained a fascist faction, which was more or less relevant in different periods. As for Primo de Rivera, he would continue to be revered by the most fervent Falangist militants. During the Francoist regime, he was referred to as 'The Absent' (*El Ausente*), which shows the importance of his legacy, at least among some sectors of Spanish fascism.

## Primo de Rivera amid the ideological struggles of his time

José António Primo de Rivera's conceptual morphology emerged during a time of great political turmoil and political battles that went beyond the realm of ideas, but from which they were not excluded. However, and even if the political Right did come to eventually dominate the politics of the country, at the beginning it did not seem to be able to present a well-defined political ideology of its own. For instance, Miguel Primo de Rivera's regime, which we already mentioned, was never able to put forward a full, cohesive ideology capable of legitimising it before the Spanish people. It is true that the regime was influenced by Italian fascism and it did dwell on the concept of 'Corporatism', but even in that regard its results were quite limited.[2] Ultimately, it can be said that the regime left a lasting influence among the Spanish Right, but only insofar as it helped to clarify which flaws a regime had to overcome to survive.

After Primo de Rivera's resignation in 1930 and the deposition of King Alfonso XIII in 1931, the Second Spanish Republic was proclaimed. During the first phase of this regime, the Right seemed not to have much prominence, since the main political forces were represented in Leftist parties like PSOE, PRR, and PRRS. However, the growing discontentment towards the new regime, even among the social groups who supported liberals and socialists, eventually allowed the Spanish Right to resurface and attempt to reconquer power. At this time, one of the main concepts that one finds in the ideological struggles among the right was 'Anti-Communism', being that the definition of Communism often conflated every other Left Wing ideology or party and eventually, thanks to the increasing bipolarisation, with the Republican regime itself. Therefore, many among the Right at the time tried to find an alternative political and economic organisation to substitute the regime then in existence, which is why the concept of 'Corporatism' also appears often in texts and speeches from that period.

Among the many factions and currents of thought in interwar Spain, there were the monarchists, who were divided between the Carlists and their rivals, the Alfonsists. The formers were anti-liberal ultranationalist Catholics who defended the return to the traditions of the Old Regime and were led by Manuel Fal Condé during the 30 s. They supported the restoration of the monarchy and the enthronement of Francisco Javier de Borbón. As to the Alfonsinists, they supported the restoration of King

Alfonso XIII, and became increasingly authoritarian due to the influence of Italian Fascism, mostly after the creation of the group Renovación Española in 1933, led by the Alfonist José Calvo Sotelo. Besides the monarchists, there were also groups like the Acción Española, formed in 1931, which was influenced by the Action Française and became a meeting group for the several factions within the Spanish ultraconservative right. More importantly, one must mention the Spanish Confederation of Autonomous Right (*Confederación Española de Derechas Autónomas*-CEDA), a political conservative party led by José Maria Gil-Robles, founded in 1933. Gathering several factions of the Spanish Conservative Right, this party began to include some formal features that resembled fascist organisations and adopted corporatist and authoritarian principles. As the Civil War approached, it abandoned legalist practices and started to support the seize of power through a violent coup.

Besides Corporatism and Anti-Communism, the concept of 'Nationalism' was particularly relevant since one of the main preoccupation of the several factions of the Right was to consolidate a nationalist ideology among the Spanish masses, something which apparently had been lacking in the country for a long time. Stanley Payne mentions that, according to Spanish nationalists, there was what was called 'el problema nacional', that is, an absence of nationalist feelings among the population of the country. Such was due to a set of factors that included the following: Spain's independence since the eleventh century; the pluralist character of the Spanish dynastic confederation; the exclusive mutual identity of Spanish catholic religion; the absence of foreign threat after the Napoleonic wars; the domination of classical liberalism for more than a century; the unique role of peripheral nationalism; neutrality in WWI; a slow pace of modernisation, etc.[3]

It was in this context that several rightist factions tried to put forward an ideological point of view capable of solving what they thought to be the most important problems of the country. With such fierce competition, the appeal of fascism seemed to be very limited, for many of the concerns that might be held by fascists were already at the core of the preoccupations of their many competitors. Such a picture is not altered by the fact that we find in Ernesto Giménez Caballero's thought a permutation of fascist ideology. This intellectual was one of the first to espouse fascism in Spain but he did not become the most influent fascist figure of his country. As we know, such status would belong to Primo de Rivera, even if the first years of the political movement that he created seemed to confirm the idea that there was not much space for fascism to thrive in Spain.

The relevance of Primo de Rivera's ideology to a study about fascism is rather found after the establishment of Franco's regime, in which the tributes to the Falangist leader were a constant, at least during the first years. For instance, it is possible to witness the impact of his legacy in the place that was given to his corpse in the monumental memorial built in a place known as Valle de los Caídos. Even after World War II, when several fascists came seeking for refuge in the Iberian Peninsula, the memory of the Falange leader was kept alive and several anthologies that gathered his main works were published. José António is, therefore, an inescapable figure in the history of the Spanish Right, and the importance of studying his ideology is easily justified if one thinks that, with it, one has a more thorough understanding of one of the main currents of thought of the dictatorship that ruled the country from 1939 to 1975.

However, the task of studying his ideology becomes quite difficult because he never published a fundamental work that summarised the main tenets of his political thought, something like a Spanish version of *Mein Kampf*. Thus, we argue that the best way to disentangle the conceptual core of José Antonio Primo de Rivera is by referring to one of the anthologies published during Franco's regime. For this reason, we decided to use a collection of quotes by the Falangist leader that was edited in 1939 by the novelist Gonzalo Torrente Ballester, a Spanish author who, in the earlier phases of his life, displayed nationalist sympathies and even adhered to the Falange.[4] We are aware that this option may be problematic, for Ballester's choices might have been influenced by his own interpretation of Jose Antonio's texts. We thus risk disentangling not the configuration of Primo de Rivera, but rather the configuration of the reading of his works by Ballester.

Nevertheless, we argue that in these excerpts of essays, speeches and articles, we shall find the main concepts that were part of this leader's worldview. After all, independently of Ballester's personal reading and of the possibility that some concepts may display a weight that is only due to the personal choices of the compiler, the core concepts and interlinkages will still be possible to discern. Meanwhile, acknowledging the limitations of using only this anthology, we will sometimes recur to other texts that are included in Primo de Rivera's complete works. This book is not a selected anthology but a collection that reunites everything that Primo de Rivera ever wrote, even before he became a fascist. However, we shall only resort to this in order to complement the information found in Ballester's anthology and not as our main textual source. After all, it would be difficult not to include, for instance, a complete reading of the text known as 'Initial Points' ('Puntos Iniciales'), which was written in 1933 and published in the official periodical of the movement, *F.E.*, or the Twenty-Seven Points of the Falangist programme, which were written in 1934.

## The conceptual core of Primo de Rivera

### *The historical mission of the nation and the empire*

The concept of Nation is unsurprisingly at the core of Primo de Rivera's ideology. Already in the 'Initial Points' of the Falange, he refers to it as a 'unity of destiny. A historical reality'.[5] Elsewhere, he decontests the concept more accurately as a 'unity in the universal, the dimension to which a people ascend when it fulfils a universal destiny in history'.[6] A Nation is therefore an entity that surpasses ethnic, linguistic, and geographic realities: it is a unity that acquires unique features that distinguishes it from every other Nation in the world. Its reality is bigger than the individual men and women who inhabit it. In this context, Spain exists as 'something distinct from each individual and class and group that integrate it' and 'as something superior to each of these individuals, classes and groups, and even the set of all of them'.[7]

In other passages, Primo de Rivera also uses the word 'Patria' (which can be better translated as 'Fatherland' rather than Nation) but the meaning of such term resembles that of Nation. Just like the Nation, the 'Patria' is:

> a total unity, in which are integrated all the individuals and all classes; the fatherland cannot be in the hands of a stronger class nor the best organised party. The fatherland is a transcendent synthesis, an indivisible synthesis, with proper goals to accomplish.[8]

The adjacent concept of 'Holism' is thus in the vicinity of this core concept, for the fascist leader envisions a homogenous national community that is indivisible. It is this for this reason that he favourably evokes moments in which several nationalists from different backgrounds seemed to have come together as one. For instance, he mentions a nationalist manifestation against the Republic, saying that, during it, 'There was neither socialists nor liberals, neither bourgeois nor workers. We all were the same: a hopeful mass of people, prone to be moulded by its best elements'.[9] In the same holistic vein, the People is defined as an 'integrity of destiny, of effort, and of sacrifice and struggle'.[10]

Furthermore, Primo de Rivera always mentions the 'Historical Mission', referring to a mission that the Nation was destined to fulfil. Even if not a political concept in itself, this 'Historical Mission' is a theme that always interlinks with the Nation. According to this leader, all the individuals within the Nation are a part of such mission and cannot repudiate it, for Nations are not contracts which one can revoke, but rather 'foundations with their own sustainability, not dependent on the will of a few or many'.[11] This view of the Nation moves Primo de Rivera away from what he himself calls 'Romantic' conceptions of nationalism, which are based on the cult of nature and on the 'spontaneous reality of peoples'. Primo de Rivera's nationalism is the 'Nationalism of the Mission' and not a nationalism simply based on shared traditions, languages or mores, nor even on 'racial characteristics'.

The repudiation of tradition as the basis of nationalism does not mean, however, that tradition does not play a role in his configuration, for he acknowledges the importance of the Catholic tradition in the history of Spain and is sure that the national historical mission must have a Catholic content. Primo de Rivera does not seem to find any contradiction between

Catholicism and the defence of a political movement that somehow resembled Italian Fascism. As he notes, in spite of still being seen in Spain as a form anti-clericalism, Fascism made peace with the Church thanks to the Latran Treaty and the regime was even responsible for bringing religion back to everyday life after decades of Liberalism: with Fascism, the crucifixes were once again used to adorn schools in Italy. The concept of 'Tradition' thus appears as well in the vicinity of the Nation, even if it can sometimes lead to some apparent contradictions, as it will later be mentioned again.

One last topic worth mentioning in relation to the Nation is the way Primo de Rivera conceived the perils that endangered its holistic unity. He specifically enumerates three most important menaces: the struggle between parties (caused by Liberalism); class struggle (fomented by Socialism); and local separatisms. This last point is particularly interesting for it relates to something that is specific to the situation in Spain and, therefore, acquires unique features in this fascist permutation. Separatists in regions like Catalonia and the Basque Country, so he believes, imperil the survival of his country by espousing a misguided form of nationalism that does not take into account the historical unity and mission of the Nation, for they are only concerned if 'they speak a different language, if they have specific racial characteristics, if in its region there is a different climate or a special topographic physiognomy'.[12] In other words, they perceive nationalism in the way that the Falangist leader precisely repudiates, and they run the risk of breaking the unity of Spain by aspiring to bring independence or at least more autonomy to regions which, in Primo de Rivera's view, are not true unities of destiny and have no historical mission to fulfil.

Nevertheless, Primo de Rivera does not deny the importance of regions like Catalonia or the Basque Country in Spanish history. His admiration for them, however, only exists to the extent that they are a part of Spain and play a role in its historical mission. Nevertheless, he still pays homage to a region like Catalonia (providing that it belongs to Spain) when he says 'all those who feel Spain say 'Long Live Catalonia' and long live the lands that belong to this admirable, indestructible and glorious mission, which bequeathed us several strenuous centuries with the name of Spain'.[13] Primo de Rivera thus asserts how fundamental Catalonia is to the Spanish Nation: it is a part of its history (just like the Basque Country) and cannot be separated from the common destiny of the country as a whole.

Just like in other fascist configurations, the core concept of Empire interlinks with the Nation, but their proximity is more evident, thanks to the theme of 'Historical Mission', and that is why the two concepts must be approached together. In Primo de Rivera's ideology, it is in the conquering of the Empire that one finds the main goal of the national mission. The greatness of the Nation was so dependent on the existence of an Empire that Falangist nationalism places the two concepts in close proximity and sees the very existence of the Spanish Nation as reason enough to propel an imperialist mindset.[14] Already in the Programme of 1934, containing Twenty-Seven points, it is said that 'we have the will to Empire. We affirm that the historical plenitude of Spain is the Empire'.[15]

The adjacent concept of 'Holism' also surrounds the Empire, because this Empire should be capable of uniting and synthetising in a same unity the most varied types of peoples and cultures. Such happens when Primo de Rivera says that 'Spain justifies itself through an imperial vocation to unite languages, to unite races, to unite peoples and unite costumes in a universal destiny'.[16] Furthermore, this holistic Empire must have a spiritual conception at its basis and not just a material one. In this context, the leader of the Falange eulogises the ancient Spanish Empire, the one that was conquered during the time of the Discoveries and was supposedly encouraged by the Catholic mission of bringing a universal truth to other peoples who did not know Christianity yet. According to him, 'Spain went to America not for silver, but to tell the Indians that we were all brothers, the same as whites and blacks, everyone, since centuries before, in faraway lands, a Martyr had shed his blood in sacrifice'.[17]

This mentioning of the ancient Empire does not happen merely by chance, since Primo de Rivera believes that it is still to the countries of the South American continent that nationalists must turn their eyes to in the present. Concerning such countries, Spain must 'tend to the unification of culture, economic interests and power'. Besides, 'Spain alleges its condition as the spiritual axes of the Hispanic world as a title of preeminence in universal enterprises'.[18] In this sense, Primo de Rivera aims at reconquering the greatness and prominence of Spain in South America by making the country acquire once again the status of a leader, a spiritual guide within the territory that encompasses its zones of influence.

Therefore, one finds in this fascist leader the goal of turning his country into a world power and putting it in a place of command once again, even if the actual materialisation of such a goal remains dubious in the entirety of Primo de Rivera's texts.[19] In this sense, it is debatable whether Rivera's vision of the new Empire implied only a role of spiritual leading in relation to Hispanic nations or if it would require actual conquest of territories, but there is no doubt that, whatever the case, the idea of altering the position and prestige of his country was one of the main goals of Falangism.[20]

## *The corporate state*

The State interlinks with the core concept of Nation for the latter should be a 'political society that is capable of finding in the state its operant machine'.[21] The existence of the Nation also presupposes the existence of a State since it is precisely in its ability to gather around a State that a Nation can exist. But the State must have a specific task to perform, because it shall be 'an instrument at the service of a historical destiny, at the service of a historical mission of unity'; it must be a 'synthesis of all fruitful activities' and the 'carrier of a mission, a fulfilling unity of a destiny'.[22] Primo de Rivera sees the State as a fundamental instrument for the fulfilment of the Spanish historical mission and for the achievement of national unity. It shall be guided by a permanent norm, a principle, and not by the circumstances of a specific context. Even if stating that he does not want the divinisation of the State or the instalment of a tyrannical State, this leader clearly asks for a strong State apparatus that 'serves a great destiny, when he is the executor of the great destiny of a people'.[23]

Apparently, such State must be a Corporate State, even if the true place of the concept of Corporatism in Primo de Rivera is difficult to assess. In spite of that, it is clear that, at least in some moments, this leader did defend the existence of something that we can call Corporatism. That is what happens when he writes that, 'we want everyone to feel a member of a complete and serious community; that means that the tasks to perform are many: some have manual work; others the work of the spirit; other still with a teaching of costumes and refinements'.[24] His configuration is also pretty much in tune with the other leaders that were already analysed when it comes to the main adjacent concepts surrounding Corporatism: 'Organicism', 'Holism' and 'Order'. Such concepts refer to the goal of reaching harmony within the national community and of redefining the role that the individual plays in a society organised according to organicist principles. As Primo de Rivera states, the construction of a new Corporate Order must include a re-integration of the individual within the community, as 'Western men, as Spanish men, and as Christians'. Most of all, it is necessary to reconnect the individual with the several 'Organic Unities' to which he belongs. With that in mind, it is possible to go from the man to the family, from the family to the municipality, from the municipality to the syndicate, until one reaches the most important of all the organic unities: the State, which 'will be the harmony of everything'.[25]

Furthermore, it should come as no surprise that Primo de Rivera also makes use of the adjacent concept of 'Class Conciliation', which is evident when he says that 'neither the workers nor the bosses realise this truth: both of them are cooperators in the collective work of the NATIONAL PRODUCTION'. For this reason, when they quarrel between each other, 'without thinking in the national production but only in the interest or ambition of one class, both workers and bosses end up ruined'.[26] The discussions about this concept are accompanied by several appeals to the working class that are destined to conquer it back to nationalist ideology. He seemingly believes that workers too are members of the Spanish Nation, even if they are presently influenced by communist ideology and are deluded into declare themselves as enemies of the Falange. As he says, 'workers are the blood and the soil of Spain, they are a part of us. Do not think that they are enemies, even if they cry against us. No, comrades; the ones who look at us with bad eyes when you show them our periodical or distribute our pamphlets are not our enemies'.[27] Thus, advising his followers not to be ill disposed against Spanish workers, he seems to have faith in the returning of this class to nationalist ideology, once the influence of Communism is annihilated. It is for this reason that he advises the members of the Falange to approach workers and peasants: 'we will go to those fields and to those peoples of Spain to convert their desperation in impulse. To incorporate them in an enterprise that belongs to everyone'.[28]

In the adjacency of Corporatism one also finds the concept of 'Social Justice', the achievement of which is one of the main goals of the social transformation that Spain must go through. 'Fatherland and justice for a suffered people' is thus a motto cherished by Primo de Rivera for, together with the lack of a historical mission, the insufficiency of social justice is one of the most severe problems faced by his country. In the same vein, he summarised his goals before the elections of 1936 in the following manner: 'Above all, we want a Spain that gives once again to its people the three things that we proclaim in our cry: fatherland, bread and justice'.[29] Apart from Rolão Preto's configuration, this study had not yet encountered a configuration that gave so much relevance to this 'Social Justice'.

One last important feature of the concept of Corporatism is that, due to its insertion in an ideological configuration that has at its core a holistic conception of the Nation, the economic system to be put in place will attain more justice without implying the instalment of a system based on collective propriety. Primo de Rivera does intend to substitute the private property such as it exists in a capitalist system but rather for the several different types of property that are connected to the organic unities of society, which means that, 'we will dismantle the economic apparatus of the capitalist property that absorbs all the benefits, and substitute it for individual property, family, property, communal property and syndical property'.[30]

However, to end this section about Corporatism, we must mention that Primo de Rivera, in spite of his admiration for Italy, criticises the way the Corporate system had already been built in other countries, including Fascist Italy. In a lecture in 1935, he criticises the Italian economic system for its insufficiency and says that:

> Until this moment, corporative organization is nothing else, approximately and in general terms than this: that the workers form a Great Federation; the bosses form another Great Federation (the givers of work, as they are called in Italy), and between these two great federations the state erects as if it were a sort of link piece.[31]

This state of affairs is not sufficient to please Primo de Rivera since, according to him, it has done nothing to change the economic system or alter the condition of workers, who still need to work for an employer to have a job. Thus, it seems that this leader was really hoping for a major social transformation that had not yet happened in Italy. This leads to the next core concept: Revolution.

## The elitist and violent revolution

As it will be shown in this section, the concept of Revolution in Primo de Rivera's configuration closely interlinks with Authority and Violence, more so than in the generic configuration, which is why these three concepts are discussed in the same section. As already mentioned, the theme of 'Historical Mission' and the adjacent concept of 'Social Justice' are in the vicinity of this core concept, since the two most important goals of the Falangist Revolution should be the achievement of national cohesion and economic justice for the poor. Besides, this concept also interlinks with the adjacent concepts of 'Order' and, once again, 'Tradition', which seem to cause some contradictions due to the apparent antithetical meaning of these two concepts and that of Revolution. However, Primo de Rivera appears not to think that it is so, for he sees Revolution as something that must be achieved with respect for the norms of society: the Falangist Revolution is an 'orderly revolution', he says. Even if he wants to destroy the 'old order', his goal is to build a 'new order', and not to annihilate the principle of 'Order' in itself.

He evidently sees the old order as a decadent one, 'Under which Spain endured international humiliation, internal disunity, the reluctance of large companies, neglect, dirt, the subhuman life of millions of beings'.[32] The factors responsible for such decadence are parliamentary democracy, socialist class struggle, and regional separatisms. To solve all these problems, it is necessary that the Nation rejuvenates, and it is here that one finds the adjacent concept of 'Palingenesis' once again. Already in the 'Initial Points' of the Falange it is said that, to revert the state of things and put an end to national divisions, it is necessary to instill the idea of Spain as a unity of destiny: 'If the struggles and decay come from the loss of the permanent idea of Spain, the remedy will be to restore that idea. We have to consider Spain once again as a reality that exists by itself'.[33]

The contrast between old greatness and present decay is also present in a passage that can help us understand how Primo de Rivera perceives time and historical evolution: in this passage, the author compares the old 'Hidalgos' (nobles) to the current 'Señoritos'. Contrary to his predecessors, 'Señoritos' in modern Spain form a social type that does not produce and is fully devoted to idleness: they represent the most unproductive parasitic members in society. In his own words, "Señoritismo' is the degeneration of the 'Señor', of the noble that wrote, until very recently, the best pages of our history'. In ancient times, 'The noble was noble for he was capable of abnegation, of his privileges, comforts, and pleasures in honour of a higher idea of service', which are characteristics that the decadent classes of Spain no longer exhibit.[34] The decadence of this noble class that was once great functions as a symbol of the decay of the Nation itself: Spain, like the 'Hidalgos', has gone through a process in which it has been losing its moral virtues is now corrupted and weak.

This passage seems to point to a conception of 'Progress' that is closer to that of Rolão Preto, one which sees the recent development of Liberal societies as a process of decline and departure from of greatness of yester. In another text, Primo de Rivera mentions the theories of Oswald Spengler about the decaying of civilisations. In a conference held in Santander in 1934, he draws from the German author to conclude that the evolution of history is not 'linear nor continuous' and that 'history marks a curve that goes from the classic ages to the middle ages'.[35] In this regard, the history of civilisations passes through two main ages: the Classic Ages, which are the ages of greatness and in which there is a 'constant direction' to go through; and the Middle Ages, which represent a decaying state when compared to the preceding age and which 'are not in conformity with themselves'.

During these Middle Ages, there is 'a constant desire for a norm for the future', which is lacking. The descent from the Classic Ages to the Middle Ages is not normal and only happens if there is a catastrophe: 'An invasion of the Barbarians'. The last time Spain reached something that could be seen as a Classic Age was in the 16th century, when the country had an Empire that 'fills the pride of us all'. During that time, the country was a 'constant unity' and was the 'arm of God'. However, decadence arrived in the 18th, when four factors made the ancient Spain start to descend into a Middle Age: a political system based on the ideas of Jean Jacques Rousseau about the Social Contract; an economic system based on materialist conceptions; the loss of faith; and the technological progress that took place in an age without faith. The present age of decaying is in even more danger now that Communism is a menace similar to that of an invasion of the barbarians. With it, there is the risk of Spain falling even further into a state of crisis and lose whatever legacy of the greatness that it once had.

In this context, Primo de Rivera's Palingenetic Revolution implies the finding of a 'new path of historical future', with which it will be possible to found 'the architecture of the new meaning of life'.[36] The creation of this new classical age will encompass both the saving of all the 'glorious remains' of old ages and all that is constructive in the future age to come. Thus, the Falangist leader aims at building a 'bridge' that is capable of uniting what was valuable in past ages with the greatness of the civilisation that is going to be built. This union of the past and the future in a new great age is at the core of Primo de Rivera's conceptualisation of Revolution and is necessary to bear it in mind in order to understand how Revolutionary and traditionalist themes coexist in this conceptual configuration.

As for the concept of Authority, one finds in its adjacency the concept of 'Leader'. The 'Chief' (the word that Primo de Rivera prefers to use) has the duty to 'conduct men', and must do the 'highest task' and be the 'guide of the course of the great ship of the nation'. However, the Falangist leader does not see the exercise of leadership as a tyrannical use of power, for the concept of 'Sacrifice' also interlinks with this adjacent concept. Thus, to him, the Chief must be capable of abnegation and of sacrificing himself to a higher purpose, since 'leadership is the supreme burden, the one that obliges all sacrifices'.[37] Most of all, the 'Leader' must be a server of the people and a 'server of the servers of God'.[51] He must always be aware of the necessities felt by the people and act according to them.

However, 'the chief must not obey the people, it must follow it', which is to say that he must keep his place of command and not simply obey the wishes of the masses, but at the same time he must take his decisions while keeping in mind the best interests of the people and not act against them.[38] As to the Falangist militants, they shall also bear in mind the principle of 'Authority', since they have to permanently obey the Chief. As Primo de Rivera says, 'a good Falangist militant must always trust that chiefs do not make mistakes. Leaders have many advices and weigh many facts that not everyone knows. For this reason, one must presume that chiefs are right'.[39]

The reason Authority closely interlinks with Revolution is the adjacent concept of 'Elite'. This becomes more evident if one thinks that, in Primo de Rivera's views, the Revolutionary acts are always the task of small 'Elite'. According to him, the Revolution is 'the task of a determined minority, unavailable to discouragement'.[40] Instead of a historical moment that will lead to the emancipation of society or a social class, the Revolution must always be an elitist process, in which only the wisest members of society have enough clairvoyance to act. Holding a very hierarchical view of society, Primo de Rivera believes that 'Elites' are always necessary and (even more importantly) that they are the only ones destined to perform radical changes in society. Only elites can be revolutionary.

Furthermore, to fulfil the historical mission of the Nation, the new elites must find a way to be accepted by the masses or, at least, of making them not to accuse the elites of treason, for it is common for the people to become disappointed with the same elites who try to save them (here we find Primo de Rivera's mistrust of the masses in a way that resembles that of Hitler). He says that 'the sole way for the revolution to save itself consists in finding someone the masses won't soon call a traitor. The masses, in their naïve insolvency, always consider lukewarm what their chiefs do: they always consider themselves betrayed', so he says.[41] The chief must gain the respect of the popular masses, since their constant mistrust for the leaders might endanger the Revolution.

The most important justification for an elitist Revolution is found in the passages where Primo de Rivera says that 'the mass of a people that needs a revolution cannot do the revolution'.[42] According to this leader, to possess the tools, capacity and vision to carry out a Revolution is itself a sign that the Revolution is not needed, for such revolutionary act only becomes necessary if the Nation has lost sign of its historical mission and does not know how to save itself. Paradoxically, if a Nation knows how to do a Revolution, that is a sign that it does not need one: its people already know how to fulfil the historical mission. It is in periods of degeneracy that the Revolution must occur and, since the masses are incapable of doing it, it becomes necessary for the elites to act.

Lastly, the concept of Violence plays a pervasive role in Primo de Rivera's configuration for, as it happens with other fascists, it is considered as a natural part of life in society. Even political activity in itself is perceived as a struggle, and the Falangist militant 'will consider life as a militia: discipline and danger, abnegation and renounce to all vanity, to envy, to sloth and slander'.[43] However, the reason this concept interlinks with Revolution is because Violent actions must be used whenever the Revolution requires them. Already, in the founding speech of the Falange, the leader states that if the Revolution 'will in some case be achieved through violence, we won't deter from it'. Thus, Violence is not 'systematically reprehensible' if employed in the name of the greater cause of the Nation.

In such a context, Violence cannot be discarded in the name of pacifist values, as it becomes obvious when Primo de Rivera asks: 'Who said that when some insults our feelings, before reacting as men, we must be kind?'[44] Falangist militants are legitimised to use Violence if retaliation is necessary. Furthermore, the concept of 'Eliminationism' makes its appearance when this leader praises its use against the supposed enemies of the Nation. After all, there is 'there is no more admissible dialectic than the dialectic of fists and pistols when someone offends justice or the Nation'.[59] For this reason, Violence is understandable if used against groups of people that 'deny national continuity' or are 'obedient to foreigner mottos'.

Together with this praise for Violence, there comes the cult of the fallen soldiers, the martyrs who gave their lives during a fight. This is the adjacent concept of 'Sacrifice', which becomes evident, for instance, when Primo de Rivera writes about Matias Montero, murdered in February 1934 to become a martyr in the Falange's mythology. According to the leader, martyrdom must be endured by Falangists with conviction and honour, and not with the goal of protesting, since that is the 'liberal fashion'. Falangists 'do not complain' when they praise their dead, for that would be a sign of weakness, something to which Liberals are prone, but not the militants of the FE de las JONS. This last point also relates to the adjacent concept of 'Virility', which appears whenever Primo de Rivera shows his contempt for the supposed weakness and cowardice of those who are influenced by the manners of democratic societies.

## Other important features of the configuration

### *Personality*

It is here argued that, in the case of Primo de Rivera's configuration, the concept of 'Personality', due to its relevance, is placed closer to the core than in the generic configuration. Primo de Rivera perceives 'Personality' as something different from the individual, which is a concept used by liberal ideologues. 'Personality' is linked to the creation of the 'New Man' of fascist Revolution and represents the man who knows his place in the world and acknowledges that he belongs to certain social groups: to a family, a municipality, and a Nation. It represents the man that is reconciled with the Nation in which he lives and is therefore ready to fulfil its destiny and be a part of its historical mission. Furthermore, 'Personality' can only be determined by the relations that take place in society, since,

> One is only a person when one is 'other'; that is, one in front of others, possible creditor or debtor with respect to others, holder of positions that are not those of others. Personality, therefore, is not determined from the inside, for being an aggregate of cells, but from the outside, for being the bearer of relationships.[45]

The Person is the individual that ceases to be just an individual and becomes a carrier of eternal values. It is in that condition of carrying values that a Person is able to relate to his peers, since 'what makes us Persons is not our individual physical equipment, but it is with the existence of others that being a "person" differentiates us'.[46] It is by relating with the other members of the Nation that the Person is formed, and it is in unity with the Nation that one's mission in the community can be fulfilled.[47] In this sense, the concept of 'Personality' is crucial to understand how the synthesis and unification of the Nation should take place. Just like in the case of Rolão Preto (and, in a different way, Hitler), it is once again possible to see in 'Personality' the solution for the contradiction between 'Individualism' and 'Collectivism'. Furthermore, just like in the case of Mosley, one sees that the goal of creating a new synthesis of the national community went beyond the integration of the working class in the corporate system. We shall resume this point when the time comes to rethink about the core concept of Corporatism.

### Peripheral concepts

As expected, the concept of 'Liberty' is in the margins of Primo de Rivera's ideology. This concept is a secondary one and relates to a state of affairs that shall only be achieved after individuals resume their ties with the organic unities to which they belong. As he says, 'only when man is considered in this way, it is possible to say that his liberty is truly respected'.[48] As to the perimeter, the main phrases that one finds are related to the specific conditions with which Spain was dealing and the specific problems that Primo de Rivera wants to solve. Thus, since he aims at creating a new form of nationalist ideology that reintegrates the regions where separatist goals exist, one of the main perimeter concepts is 'reinsertion of Catalonia and Basque Country in the national community'. Other perimeter phrases are, for instance, 'leadership of the Hispanic American world' and 'rediscover the greatness of the Age of Discoveries'.

## Permeability and rejections

Permeability in Primo de Rivera's ideology seems to happen both in relation to Socialism and other variants of Right Wing Conservative ideologies. The pseudo-socialising components of his configuration come from the use of the adjacent concept of 'Social Justice', while the strive for the unity of the Nation and the fight against Communism bring him closer to Right Wing ideologies. The proximity between Rivera and other nationalist thinkers becomes more obvious, for instance, when he quotes intellectuals like Ortega y Gasset. However, Rivera ends up rejecting conservative ideology as a whole for he does not accept the absence of the concept of Revolution in its configuration. As he states, when writing about the dictatorship of his father Miguel Primo de Rivera, 'the dictatorship grandly and tragically failed because it did not know how to concretise its revolutionary task'.[49] Rivera's rejection of existing Right-Wing ideologies is thus based on the idea that they lack what is necessary to unite Spain on the basis of a new type of nationalism.

Most importantly, Rivera explicitly rejects Marxist Communism (due to the concept of 'Class Struggle', which endangers the Nation), and Liberalism (due to the concept of 'Individualism' and 'Parliamentarianism' as well). When rejecting Marxism, he states that 'the Russian regime would be hell' if it ever came to Spain'. And he also adds that 'the class struggle ignores the unity of the fatherland, for it breaks with the idea of national production as a whole'.[50] As to Liberalism, his hatred for it is perceptible already in the founding speech of the Falange, when he speaks against Jean Jacques Rousseau (whom he sees as a main figure in the history of democracy) and the ideology on which the liberal State and the universal suffrage found their legitimacy. As the leader says,

> Jean Jacques Rousseau supposed that the group of those who live in a same people has a soul [...] capable of defining in all moments the just and the unjust, good and evil. And since this collective will, this sovereign will, only expresses itself through suffrage [...] it came to result that suffrage, that farce of ballot papers entering a Chrystal urn, had the virtue of telling us at every moment if God existed, if truth was or not true, if Fatherland should remain or if it was better that, at some moment it committed suicide.[51]

Besides, as Rivera explicitly states, there is a rejection of other variants of nationalism which do not have at its core the idea of 'Mission', that is, forms of nationalism that are propelled by 'spontaneity' and 'instinctiveness'. The 'Patriotism of the Mission', so he argues, is distinct from such examples of 'elemental patriotism'. The Falangist leader rejects 'romantic' versions of Nationalism, since, according to him, romanticism is a school of thought without a coherent line of thought, which conceived the Nation as an entity that was close to nature. The Nation, in this way, is seen as a set of ethnic, linguistic and geographical traditions, which is everything that Primo de Rivera rejects. According to him, 'the most dangerous forms of nationalism, because they disintegrate, are the ones who have understood the nation in this fashion'.[52] Even if he sometimes acknowledges the relevance of such type of nationalism (mostly because this instinctive feeling can create a true love for the national community), he still believes that what truly matters to determine if a people constitute a Nation is its role in the historical destiny, its missionary character.

### *Contradictions: tradition/revolution and elitism/populism*

There are two important tensions in Primo de Rivera, the first opposing the 'Individual' to the 'Collectivity': as it was already mentioned, this contradiction is solved with the concept of 'Personality'. The other one is the contradiction between 'Revolution' and 'Tradition', which was also mentioned during the preceeding analysis. The tension between these two concepts exists because the will to create a new society does not exclude a praise for traditions and for past heritages. This contradiction is solved thanks to the way the concept of 'Progress' is used and how the leader of the Falange envisioned the coming of a new era that would contain some of the best features of the times when Spain held an Empire. The maintenance of past values and the creation of a new society are not, therefore, contradictory goals in Primo de Rivera's variety of fascism because he aims to build a 'bridge' that unites the past with the future.

Finally, the tension between 'Elitism' and 'Populism' seems to be less proeminent than in other leaders due to the extremely elitist features of Primo de Rivera's revolutionary goals. When writing about the last texts by Primo de Rivera before his death, Stanley Payne says that 'these final essays would tend to confirm Ledesma's contention that Jose Antonio's rightist, aristocratic, elitist, and neotraditionalist proclivities were too deep-seated to be completely overcome by his (ultimately superficial) fascist political choices'.[53] Nevertheless, at times, this contradiction does come into the fore, mainly when the Falaginst leader idealises the people as an entity that acquires strength through its unity. Perhaps, the best example of Primo de Rivera's conception is in the phrase 'We all were the same: a hopeful mass of people, prone to be molded moulded by its best elements'. Thus, like in many other fascists, the praising of a unified 'People' and its strength (a populist idea) coexists in Primo de Rivera with the elitist notion that the best elements of the 'People' shall rise above the masses and guide them.

## Concluding remarks

In spite of the flaws of our method (due to the lack of a single work by Primo de Rivera) we nevertheless managed to disentangle a configuration that is a variant of fascist ideology. In the absence of a single work by this fascist leader, the option to analyse an anthology of texts and complement it with some passages from his *Obras Completas* was the best feasible. We can conclude this chapter by quoting the following passage from Primo de Rivera:

> because Spain, which is to say a real nation, when the Basque officers traveled the world in the ships of Castile, when the Catalonian admirals conquered united the Mediterranean in ships of Aragon, because we understand it that way, we want all the peoples of Spain to feel, not the elemental patriotism with which the land casts us, but the patriotism of the mission, the patriotism of the transcendental, the patriotism of Great Spain.[54]

In this quote, we find the main tenets of Primo de Rivera's ideology, namely his constant focus on the 'patriotism of the mission', which is one of the distinctive features of his configuration. To Primo de Rivera, Spain needed to resume a national unity (or 'Synthesis') that it had supposedly had in the past, when the whole territory of the country was not divided by separatisms and was therefore capable of completing its mission of conquering the American continent and spreading the message of Catholicism. The ideology of the Falange was all about recuperating such unity and updating the national historical mission in order for it to fit in modern times.

## Notes

1. Ledesma Ramos would deserve a study wholly dedicated to him, for he also contributed to the emergence of Spanish fascism, even if his variant of the ideology had a rather radical anti-capitalist tone that was less present in Primo de Rivera's ideology. To read more about Ledesma Ramos see José Maria Sanchéz Diana, *Ramiro Ledesma Ramos* (Madrid, Editora Nacional, 1975).
2. The regime's experiments with corporatism took place with the reforms introduced by the Minister of Labour Eduardo Aunós, a profound admirer of Italian fascism, and the creation of the National Corporate Organisation in 1926.
3. Stanley Payne, *Fascism in Spain, 1923–1977* (Maddison, Wisconsin University Press, 2000), 13.
4. Ballester was a Spanish novelist associated with the so called 'Generation of '36', that is, the generation of writers that were active during the period of the Civil War. His first novel, *Javier Mariño*, was published in 1943 and from then onwards his notoriety as a writer would increasingly grow.
5. Just like the previous chapters, all the translations are made by the author. In this case, the original in Spanish is: 'Una unidad de destino. Una realidad histórica'. José Antonio Primo de Rivera, *Obras Completas* (Madrid, Ed. Instituto de Estudios Políticos, 1976), 179.The text of *Obras Completas* that we used was found in the following site: http://www.maalla.es/Libros/Obras%20completas%20de%20JA.pdf. All the page numbers refer to the document that is available in this site.
6. 'Una unidad en lo universal, es el grado a que se remonta un pueblo cuando cumple un destino universal en la Historia'. José Antonio Primo de Rivera, in

Gonzalo Torrente Ballester, Ed., *Antologia* (Madrid, Ediciones FE, 1940), 20. The text of *Antologia* that we used was found in the following site: http://www.fundacionjoseantonio.es/doc/Antologia_en_espanol.pdf. All the page numbers refer to the document that is available in this site.

7 'Como algo DISTINTO a cada uno de los individuos y de las clases y de los grupos que la integran' and 'Como algo SUPERIOR a cada uno de esos individuos, clases y grupos, y aun al conjunto de todos ellos'. Primo de Rivera, *Obras Completas,* 179.

8 'La Patria es una unidad total, en que se integran todos los individuos y todas las clases; la Patria no puede estar en manos de la clase más fuerte ni del partido mejor organizado. La Patria es una síntesis trascendente, una síntesis indivisible, con fines proprios que cumplir'. Primo de Rivera, *Antologia,* 18.

9 'No había socialistas ni liberales, obreros ni burgueses. Todos éramos unos: masa esperanzada y propicia a que nos modelaran nuestros mejores. ¿Qué pasaba para que nos hubiéramos confundido en una emoción sola'. Ibid., 53.

10 'una integridad de destino, de esfuerzo, de sacrificio y de lucha, que ha de mirarse entera y que entera avanza en la Historia y entera ha de servirse'. Ibid., 16.

11 'Fondaciones, con sustantividad propia, no dependiente de la voluntad de pocos ni de muchos'. Ibid., 16.

12 'Los separatistas se fijan en si hablan lengua propia, en si tienen características raciales propias, en si su comarca presenta clima propio o especial fisonomía topográfico'. Primo de Rivera, *Obras Completas,* 180.

13 'Todos los que sienten a España dicen viva Cataluña y vivan todas las tierras hermanas en esta admirable misión, indestructible y gloriosa, que nos legaron varios siglos de esfuerzo con el nombre de *España*'. Primo de Rivera, *Antologia,* 20.

14 As Payne reminds us, 'All Spanish nationalists were aware that Spain had achieved world greatness as empire. The palingenesis of Spain required the revival of empire'. Payne, *Fascism in Spain,* 152

15 'Tenemos voluntad de Imperio. Afirmamos que la plenitud histórica de España es el Imperio'. Primo de Rivera, *Obras Completas,* 359.

16 'España se justifica por una vocación imperial para unir lenguas, para unir razas, para unir pueblos y para unir costumbres en un destino universal'. Primo de Rivera, *Antologia,* 19.

17 'España fue a América, no por plata, sino a decirles a los indios que todos eran hermanos, lo mismo los blancos que los negros, todos, puesto que siglos antes, en otras tierras lejanas, un Mártir había derramado su sangre en el sacrificio para que esa sangre estableciera el amor y la hermandad entre los hombres de la tierra'. Primo de Rivera, *Obras Completas,* 232.

18 'Respecto de los países de Hispanoamérica, tendemos a la unificación de cultura, de intereses económicos y de Poder. España alega su condición de eje espiritual del mundo hispánico como título de preeminencia en las empresas universales'. Ibid., 359.

19 Payne quotes the following words by Primo de Rivera: 'But in international affairs the democratic idea promoted by the League of Nations is in decline. The world is once more tending to be led by three or four racial entities. Spain can be one of those three or four. It is situated in an extremely important geographic keypoint, and has the spiritual strength to enable it to aspire to one of those places of command. That is what may be proposed. Not to be a mediocre country, because either it becomes an immense country that fulfils a universal mission or it is a degraded country without significance. The ambition to be a leading country in the world must be restored to Spain'. Payne, *Fascism in Spain,* 153.

## José António Primo de Rivera and the Spanish Falange    135

20  Stanley Payne summarises the several conceptions of Empire held by more moderate Falangists like Onésimo Redondo, and concludes that Primo de Rivera would agree with his vision of spiritual guidance, but would certainly go beyond that goal. Payne, *Fascism in Spain,* 152–154.
21  'La sociedad política capaz de hallar en el estado su maquina operante'. Primo de Rivera, *Antologia,* 21.
22  'Instrumento al servicio de un destino histórico, al servicio de una misión histórica de unidad', 'síntesis de tantas atividades fecundas', "portador de una misión, unidad cumplidora de un destino'. Primo de Rivera, *Antologia,* 22.
23  'Cuando sirva un gran destino, cuando se sienta ejecutor del gran destino de un Pueblo'. Primo de Rivera, *Antologia,* 23.
24  'Queremos que todos se sientan miembros de una comunidad seria y completa; es decir, que las funciones a realizar son muchas: unos, con el trabajo manual; otros, con el trabajo del espíritu; algunos, con un magisterio de costumbres y refinamientos'. Primo de Rivera, *Antologia,* 88.
25  'La construcción de un orden nuevo la tenemos que empezar por el hombre, por el individuo, como occidentales, como españoles y como cristianos; tenemos que empezar por el hombre y pasar por sus unidades orgánicas, y así subiremos del hombre a la familia, y de la familia al Municipio y, por otra parte, al Sindicato, y culminaremos en el Estado, que será la armonía de todo'. Primo de Rivera, *Antologia,* 87.
26  'Ni los obreros ni los patronos se dan cuenta de esta verdad: Unos y otros son cooperadores en la obra conjunta de la PRODUCCION NACIONAL. No pensando en la producción nacional, sino en el interés o en la ambición de cada clase, acaban por destruirse y arruinarse patronos y obreros. El nuevo Estado, por ser de todos, considerará como fines propios los fines de cada uno de los grupos que lo integren y velará como por sí mismo por los intereses de todos'. Primo de Rivera, *Obras Completas,* 180.
27  'Los obreros son sangre y suelo de España, son parte de los nuestros. No les creáis enemigos aunque griten contra nosotros. No, camaradas; no son enemigos todos los que os miran con malos ojos cuando voceáis nuestro periódico, cuando repartís nuestras hojas'. Primo de Rivera, *Antologia,* 90.
28  'Nosotros iremos a esos campos y a esos pueblos de España para convertir en impulso su desesperación. Para incorporarlos a una empresa de todos'. Ibid., 92.
29  'Por arriba queremos que se escape una España que dé enteras, otra vez, a su pueblo las tres cosas que pregonamos en nuestro grito: la Patria, el pan y la justicia'. Ibid., 88.
30  'Desmontaremos el aparato económico de la propiedad capitalista que absorbe todos los beneficios, para sustituirlo por la propiedad individual, por la propiedad familiar, por la propiedad comunal y por la propiedad sindical'. Ibid., 90.
31  'La organización corporativa, hasta este instante, no es otra cosa, aproximadamente, en líneas generales, que esto: los obreros forman una gran Federación; los patronos forman otra gran Federación (los dadores del trabajo, como se los llama en Italia), y entre estas dos grandes Federaciones monta el Estado como una especie de pieza de enlace'. Ibid., p.48.
32  'Bajo él España soportaba la humillación internacional, la desunión interna, la desgana de las empresas grandes, la incuria, la suciedad, la vida infrahumana de millones de seres'. Ibid., 79.
33  'Si las luchas y la decadencia nos vienen de que se ha perdido la idea permanente de España, el remedio estará en restaurar esa idea. Hay que volver a concebir a España como realidad existente por sí misma.' Primo de Rivera, *Obras Completas,* 221.

34 'El "señoritismo" es la degeneración del "señor", del "hidalgo" que escribió, y hasta hace bien poco, las mejores páginas de nuestra historia. El señor era tal señor porque era capaz de "renunciar", esto es, dimitir privilegios, comodidades y placeres en homenaje a una alta idea de "servicio'. Ibid., 219.
35 'No es una ni continua la secuencia; la Historia marca una curva que va de las edades clásicas a las edades medias'. Ibid., 318
36 'Así, pues, si nos adelantamos a lo que va a ser el nuevo camino del futuro histórico, podemos tender un puente para empalmar los restos de una civilización en plena decadencia con los principios de la nueva, construyendo la arquitectura del nuevo sentido de la vida. Este es el esfuerzo inmenso que tiene que acometer la Humanidad, recogiendo de la edad futura lo que traiga de constructivo y salvando de la antigua todos los restos gloriosos'. Ibid., 220.
37 'La jefatura es la suprema carga, la que obliga a todos los sacrificios, incluso a la pérdida de la intimidad'.Primo de Rivera, *Antologia*, 30.
38 'Y como el jefe es el que tiene encomendada la tarea más alta, es él el que más sirve. Coordinador de los múltiples destinos particulares, rector del rumbo de la gran nave de la Patria, es el primer servidor; es como quien encarna la más alta magistratura de la tierra, "siervo de los siervos de Dios".' Ibid., 26.
39 'El jefe no debe obedecer al pueblo, debe servirlo, que es cosa distinta'. José Antonio, Ibid., 26.
40 'Un buen militante de la Falange debe confiar siempre en que los jefes no se equivocan. La jefatura dispone de muchos asesoramientos y pesa muchos datos que no conocen todos. Por eso hay que presumir que los jefes tienen razón, aunque, desde fuera cueste, en algún caso, adivinar sus antecedentes o sus móviles'. Primo de Rivera, *Obras Completas*, 211.
41 'La tarea de una resuelta minoría, inasequible al desaliento'. Primo de Rivera, *Antologia*, 29.
42 'La única manera de que la revolución se salve consiste en que encuentre lo que las masas no tardarán en llamar un traidor. Las masas, en su ingenua insolvencia, siempre consideran tibio lo que hacen sus jefes: siempre te consideran traicionadas'. Ibid., 29.
43 'La masa de un pueblo que necesita una revolución no puede hacer la revolución'. Ibid., 28.
44 'Habrán de considerar la vida como milicia: disciplina y peligro, abnegación y renuncia a toda vanidad, a la envidia, a la pereza y a la maledicencia. Y al mismo tiempo servirán ese espíritu de una manera alegre y deportiva económico'. Primo de Rivera, *Obras Completas*,185.
45 'Y queremos, por último, que si esto ha de lograrse en algún caso por la violencia, no nos detengamos ante la violencia. Porque, ¿quién ha dicho –al hablar de "todo menos la violencia"– que la suprema jerarquía de los valores morales reside en la amabilidad? ¿Quién ha dicho que cuando insultan nuestros sentimientos, antes que reaccionar como hombres, estamos obligados a ser amables?' Primo de Rivera, *Antologia*, 79.
46 'No es nuestra interna armadura física lo que nos hace ser *personas,* sino la existencia de otros de los que el ser *personas* nos diferencia'. Ibid., 13.
47 'No se es persona sino en cuanto se es otro; es decir: uno frente a los otros, posible acreedor o deudor respecto de otros, titular de posiciones que no son las de los otros. La personalidad, pues, no se determina desde dentro, por ser agregado de células, sino desde fuera, por ser portador de relaciones'. Ibid., 13.
48 'Sólo cuando al hombre se le considera así, se puede decir que se respeta de veras su libertad...' Ibid., 13.
49 'La Dictadura... fracasó trágica y grandemente porque no supo realizar su obra revolucionaria». Ditadura'. Ibid., 51.

50 'La lucha de clases ignora la unidad de la Patria, porque rompe la idea de la *producción nacional* como conjunto'. Primo de Rivera, *Obras Completas*, 180.
51 'Juan Jacobo Rousseau suponía que el conjunto de los que vivimos en un pueblo tiene un alma superior, de jerarquía diferente a cada una de nuestras almas, y que ese yo superior está dotado de una voluntad infalible, capaz de definir en cada instante lo justo y lo injusto, el bien y el mal. Y como esa voluntad colectiva, esa voluntad soberana, sólo se expresa por medio del sufragio –conjetura de los más que triunfa sobre la de los menos en la adivinación de la voluntad superior–, venía a resultar que el sufragio, esa farsa de las papeletas entradas en una urna de cristal, tenía la virtud de decirnos en cada instante si Dios existía o no existía, si la verdad era la verdad o no era la verdad, si la Patria debía permanecer o si era mejor que, en un momento, se suicidase'. Primo de Rivera, *Antologia*, 163.
52 'Los nacionalismos más peligrosos, por lo disgregadores, son los que han entendido la nación de esta manera '. Ibid., 21.
53 Payne, *Fascism in Spain*, 222.
54 'Porque España fue nación hacia fuera, que es como se es de veras nación, cuando los almirantes vascos recorrían los mares del mundo en las naves de Castilla, cuando los catalanes admirables conquistaban el Mediterráneo unidos en naves de Aragón, porque nosotros entendemos eso así, queremos que todos los pueblos de España sientan, no ya el patriotismo elemental con que nos tira la tierra, sino el patriotismo' de la misión, el patriotismo de lo trascendental, el patriotismo de la gran España'. Primo de Rivera, *Obras Completas*, 195.

## List of References

Beevor, Anthony, *The Spanish Civil War 1936–1939* (London, Penguin, 2001).
Ben-Ami, Shlomo, *Fascism from Above: The Dictatorship of Primo de Rivera, 1923–1930* (Oxford, Oxford University Press, 1983).
Blinkhorn, Martin, *Carlism and Crisis in Spain 1931–1939* (Cambridge, Cambridge University Press, 1975).
Blinkhorn, Martin (ed.), *Fascists and Conservatives: The Radical Right and the Establishment in Twentieth-Century Europe* (London, Psychology Press, 1990).
Diana, Jose Maria Sanchez, *Ramiro Ledesma Ramos* (Madrid, Editora Nacional, 1975).
Garrido, Belén Moreno. '*El Valle de Los Caídos: Una Nueva Aproximación*', Revista de Historia Actual, 8 (8), 2010, 31–44.
Mainer, José-Carlos, 'Ernesto Giménez Caballero o la inoportunidade' in Ernesto Giménez Caballero, Ed., *Casticismo, Nacionalismo y Vanguardia* (Fundacion Santander Central Hispano, 2005), pp. ix–lxviii.
Maurel, Marcos, 'Un asunto de fe. Fascismo en España (1933–1936)' in Ferran Gallego and Francisco Morente, Eds., *Fascismo en España: ensayos sobre los orígenes sociales y culturales del franquismo* (Madrid, El Viejo Topo, 2005), 133–162.
Payne, Stanley, 'Spain', in Eugen Weber and Hans Rogger, Eds., *The European Right: A Historical Profile* (Berkeley, University of California Press, 1965), 168–207.
Payne, Stanley, *Spain's First Democracy: The Second Republic, 1931–1936* (Maddison, University of Wisconsin Press, 1993).
Payne, Stanley, *Fascism in Spain, 1923–1977* (Maddison, Wisconsin University Press, 2000).

Pecharromán, Julio Gil, *José Antonio Primo de Rivera: Retrato de un Visionario* (Barcelona, Temas de Hoy, 2003).
Preston, Paul, *The Coming of the Spanish Civil War: Reform, Reaction and Revolution in the Second Republic 1931–1936* (London, Macmillan, 1978).
Primo de Rivera, José António, in Gonzalo Torrente Ballester, Ed., *Antologia* (Madrid, Ediciones FE, 1940). http://www.fundacionjoseantonio.es/doc/Antologia_en_espanol.pdf.
Primo de Rivera, José António, *Obras Completas* (Madrid, Ed. Instituto de Estudios Políticos, 1976). http://www.maalla.es/Libros/Obras%20completas%20de%20JA.pdf.
Quiroja, Alessandro, *Making Spaniards: Primo de Rivera and the Nationalization of the Masses, 1923–30* (Basingstoke, Palgrave Macmillan, 2007).
Seixas, Xosé Manoel Ñúnez. 'Falangismo, Nacionalsocialismo y El Mito de Hitler En España (1931–1945)', *Revista de Estudios Políticos*, 169, 2015, 13–43.
Tardio, Manuel Álvarez, *Jose Maria Gil-Robles: Leader of the Catholic Right During the Spanish Second Republic* (Eastbourne, Sussex Academic Press, 2019).
Thomás, Joan Maria, *The Reality and Myth of a Spanish Fascist Leader* (Oxford, Berghan, 2017).

# 6 Corneliu Codreanu and the iron guard

The Manichean Battle between good and evil

Nationalism has been a pervasive phenomenon in Romanian politics throughout the last decades and, even after the end of the Soviet Block, former quasi-fascist dictator Ion Antonescu was praised in the Parliament of Bucharest as a national hero. Also during the communist years, Ceausescu's regime fomented a kind of nationalism which mixed elements coming from Marxism-Leninism with a cult of the Romanian Dacian past. However, since the present goal is to focus on the fascist epoch, it is impossible not to note that the utmost expression of ultra-nationalist ideology in interwar years was an organisation that became known as the Iron Guard (*Garda de Fier* – GF). This was led by Corneliu Codreanu, known among his followers as 'The Captain' (*Căpitanul*). In the ideology of this leader, we will find a particularly interesting permutation of fascist ideology that is worthy of a detailed study.

## Corneliu Codreanu and the GF

Corneliu Codreanu was born on 13 September 1899 in the Romanian city of Huşi. His father, Ion Zelea Codreanu, was a teacher who was also an active member of Romanian nationalist movements, a fact that helps to explain why this future fascist leader was influenced by nationalist ideas since his childhood. After being prevented from fighting in World War I due to his young age and having spent some years in a military school, Codreanu moved to the city of Iaşi in order to proceed with his studies.[1] It was in this city that Codreanu began his political career by joining a movement named Guard of National Conscience (*Garda Conştiinţei Naţionale* – GCN), which was led by the electrician Constantin Pancu. Years later, in 1923, he also became one of the founders of the far-right party National-Christian Defense League (*Liga Apărării Naţional Creştine* – LANC).

It is important to note that, at the time, Codreanu's tendency for political violence was already noticeable, because he was pressuring the LANC to create a paramilitary section of its own. Besides, in 1924, he murdered a police prefect named Constantin Manciu as revenge for having been previously arrested by him during a nationalist meeting. Due to the influence he had already acquired as a nationalist figure, Codreanu faced trial that caught the attention of the country and in which he would be acquitted by the members of a jury that was clearly not neutral. After traveling to France, Codreanu came back to Romania to form the Legion of the Archangel Michael (*Legiunea Arhanghelului Mihail* – LAM) on 24 June 1927. This was the original name of the movement that came to be known as the Iron Guard, even though this was actually the name of its paramilitary faction, which was only created in 1930. This would turn out to be the most notorious example of a fascist organisation in Romania, and it would also include famous members like Ion Moţa and Vasile Marin, both of whom would die in the Spanish Civil War and become martyrs in the mythology of the Legion.[2]

According to Traian Sandu, it is possible to point out several phases in the development of the movement. In the first years, Codreanu proved unable to achieve a noteworthy following, but the adhesion of the peasantry began to grow in 1929. The years between 1933 and 1938 were, according to Sandu, a period of maturation, in which the GF developed its political organisation and methods of mass mobilisation to the point of frightening the elites of the country. Thus, after several electoral acts in which Codreanu's organisation was unable to elect a significant numer of deputies, it obtained 66 seats in the Chamber of Deputies and 4 seats in the Senate in the elections of 1937. During the election, the Legion was using as its official name Everything for the Country (*Totul pentru Ţară* – TPT), a nomenclature that was adopted a few years earlier.

It is worth noticing, however, that this apparent acceptance of legal principles did not prevent the party from engaging in violent actions against several figures of the Romanian state. Actually, few fascist movements became so famous for resorting to terrorist acts, which were usually carried out by some of the most fanatic militants and were many times destined to target important politicians like Ion Duca of the National Liberal Party (*Partidul Naţional Liberal* – PNL). This prime minister was assassinated in 1933, when he was trying to suppress the GF, and the act became particularly infamous as it was the first political murder in Romania since the 19th century. It was carried out by a group of three fanatical legionaries who became known as the *Nicadori*. This cult of violence was accompanied by a constant carrying out of rituals and mystical celebrations, which included events where Codreanu's followers drank each other's' blood, among other exquisite practices. The fusion of ritual and violence was present, for instance, in the revenge assassination of the former comrade Mihae Stelescu, who was killed by ten legionaries in his hospital bed. After shooting him, the murderers performed a ritualist dance around the pieces of his body (which they had cut to pieces).

As the conflict between the Iron Guard and the authorities increased, legionaries became one of the prior targets of King Carol II, who ruled the country since 1930 and by 1938 was starting to take his first steps to turn its reign into a personal dictatorship. The King banned political parties and created his own government party: the National Renaissance Force (*Frontul Renașterii Naționale* – FRN). Furthermore, the dictatorship that was under construction began to adopt increasingly more violent methods to deal with its opponents (many times resembling those espoused by the GF). Many legionaries, and Corneliu Codreanu himself, became victims of this institutional violence, with the fascist leader being imprisoned and killed on 30 November 1938 in what was officially called an attempt of escaping. After his death, the Legion began to be led by Horia Sima, who lacked the charismatic appeal of his predecessor. Nevertheless, the Legion did not stop its activities and it soon carried out another political assassination as a revenge for Codreanu's death: that of Prime Minister Armand Călinescu in 1939.

Later, when Carol II abdicated in favour of his son Michael I in 1940, General Ion Antonescu, asympathiser of the Legion, became Prime Minister, soon leading the country into another dictatorship. In the first phase of his regime, Antonescu established an alliance with the GF in order to create the so called 'National Legionary State' (being this the only case apart from Germany and Italy in which a fascist party came to power without the help of a foreigner country). However, the uneasy relationship between Antonescu and the Legion soon led to an attempt of rebellion by the GF, in which the fascist movement was defeated and officially extinguished. This happened on 21 January 1941. However, the ideology of this fascist movement left a trace of death and destruction behind it, mostly due to the participation of the legionaries in massacres that victimised a large proportion of the Romanian Jewish population.

## Corneliu Codreanu amid the ideological struggles of his time

The emergence of Codreanu's configuration falls within a context of ultranationalist ideological debates that had begun in the previous century. Thus, going from the 19th to the 20th century, one comes across ideological struggles that encompassed reconfigurations and redefinitions of concepts usually connected to conservative nationalist thought and radical ultranationalist ideologies. One thus finds important concepts such as 'Anti-Semitism', 'Palingenesis' and 'Messianic leader'.

Anti-Jewish sentiment was a part of Romanian elitist thought, something which is visible, for instance, in the writings of poet Mihai Eminescu, who attacked the Jews for supposedly wanting to get hold of the Romanian state. Even though Ioanid states that this anti-Semitism 'expressed itself in economy, social, religious, and political modes' and not in racist ones, Drace-Francis seems to disagree and notes that authors such as Eminescu did make use of the concept of 'Race' to attack the Jews, thus anticipating the most violent ideologies of following century.[3] As to 'Palingenesis', it is evident in the works by the poet Ion Heliade Radulescu, who interlinked this concept with themes of mystical Christian salvation.[4] One of the main features of Romanian nationalism was therefore its connection to eschatological religious conceptions which aimed at a spiritual awakening. The cult of Christ and of the Archangel Michael, commonly revered in Christian Orthodox tradition, was also recurrent in nationalist circles. Apart from this religious type of regeneration, there were also palingenetic trends based on historicist ideas and on the cult of a medieval past. The theme of the 'Messianic Leader' was mainly noticeable in the cult of past figures like Michael the Brave and Stephen the Great, who became symbols of national unity and greatness.

As one goes further into the 20th century, one sees that Romanian nationalism acquires more violent and authoritarian traits, and that political discourse also began to dwell with concepts like 'Corporatism' and 'Class Conciliation', which is evident in the works by Mihail Manoilescu. In organisations like the People's Party, created by Alexandru Averescu in 1918, it is also possible to find a growing disenchantment with liberal institutions, even if not a radical one. The discussion about the 'Greater Romania' also became dominant due to the changes in the borders after World War I. This new Romania that came out of the conflict incorporated territories that were not part of the country before (Transylvania, Bukovina and Bessarabia), which seemed to be the materialisation of Pan-nationalist goals. However, many within the nationalist circles became disappointed with the 'Greater Romania' due to the difficulties of integrating the people of these regions in their new state and to the political divisions that still existed.

The definitive inclusion of racist notions in nationalist discourse occurred with personalities like A. C. Cuza, known for his virulent anti-Semitism and his calls for a regeneration of Romanian national life. In 1910, while a professor at the University of Iasi, he and his associate, historian Nicolae Iorga, created the PND, which espouse da form of corporate nationalism. Years later, Cuza's nationalism became even more radical as he founded the LANC, which, as we already know, was an organisation of which Codreanu initially was also part. Nevertheless, and however virulent his anti-Semitism may have been, Cuza still displayed a kind of ethnic conservative nationalism which did not have every characteristic of fascist ideology and still was too elitist.

For this reason, one must definitely turn to the GF to study fascism in Romania. Given its impactful legacy in the history of fascism, it is easy to argue that a thorough analysis of fascist ideology cannot ignore this Romanian permutation. Writing about its specific features, Payne noted that this movement was 'a mystical, kenotic form of semireligious fascism that represented the only notable movement of this kind in an Orthodox country'.[5] These semireligious components are among the features that make the GF's ideology an interesting case to include in this study. To disentangle Codreanu's configuration, the best text that one can use is *For My Legionaries* (*Pentru Legionari* – PL), which was written in 1936 (at the peak of the period of maturation that Sandu talks about), and is sometimes referred as kind of Romanian *Mein Kampf*.

Even though this was not the only important text written by the leader of the GF, one finds in it a mixing of autobiographical account and ideological manifestoes that justify its inclusion in this study. In many passages, Codreanu quotes extensively from other authors, mostly from articles in newspapers, both to approve or disapprove their words. This adds further interest to our study, since it can be a way to better understand the struggle for meaning and the permeability and ideological rejections occurring at the time. For this reason, we shall not deter from quoting the passages of the text that were not written by Codreanu himself but are still important to understand how he thought.

## The conceptual core of *Pentru Legionari*

### *Holist nationalism and the 'Greater Romania'*

In this section, we will see how the leader of the GF dwells with the concepts of Nation, State and Empire. In Codreanu's configuration, the Nation cannot be simply seen as individuals that live in the same territory and share common traditions. As this leader states, the Romanian Nation refers to 'all Romanians, alive and dead, who have lived on this land from the beginning of history and will live here also in the future'.[6] In the adjacency of this core concept, one finds the adjacent concept of 'Holism' and themes such as 'Spirituality', 'Transcendence' and 'Eternity'. The decontestation of this concept acquires a unique dimension due to Codreanu's conception of time, that is, due to the idea that the Romanian Nation encompasses all the people who have lived and will live in it. Past, present and future are thus a part of the Nation, which is a holistic entity not only in space but also through time.[7] In Codreanu's view, Romania acquires a metaphysical dimension that includes both the living, the dead and the ones who are not yet born: 'All our parents are here. All our memories, all our war-like glory, all our history here, in this land lies buried'.[8]

The spiritual dimension of the Nation also becomes evident when Codreanu writes that 'the Nation then is an entity which prolongs her existence even beyond this earth'.[9] In the wake of this spiritual conception, he also affirms that the Nation contains three types of patrimonies: physical (that is, her flesh and blood), material (the soil and the riches of the country), and a spiritual one. The latter type of patrimony is the most important one, 'for only it carries the stamp of eternity; it alone endures through all the centuries'.[10] It is thanks to the spiritual patrimony that the Nation acquires its holistic dimension, that is, the eternal dimension which has an everlasting quality. This patrimony is composed of three different components:

- God, for it is the capacity of the Nation to conceptualise the spiritual dimension of God that createsits greatness.
- Honor, 'which shines to the extent that the nation has conformed during her history to the norms stemming from her concept of God, the world and life'.[11]
- Culture, which is the result of efforts of expression through arts and thought, 'it is the expression of national genius, of the blood'.[12] While defending this national culture, Codreanu also rejects the notion of international culture, for 'culture is international as far as its luminescence may reach, but national in origin'.[13] The importance of culture is made clear when the leader states, referring to ancient nations, that 'the ancient Greeks are not remembered because of their physique – nothing but ashes is left of that – nor their material riches, had they had any, but because of their culture'.[14]

The worship of the spiritual past of the Nation has, nevertheless, a material core too, mirrored in the reverence of cultural achievements and of heroic and intellectual figures such as Michael the Brave and Stephan the Great. In this vein, there is also in PL a deep respect for figures such as Bogdan Petriceicu Hajdeu, Vasile Conta, Mihail Eminescu, Vasile Alecsandri, and even living people like Professor Cuza. Likewise, Codreanu displays a fervent adoration for places which were relevant to the development of Romanian cultural patrimony, such as the city of Iasi. There, as he narrates, Codreanu not only carried out his university studies, but he also became engaged in nationalist activity: 'I myself owe this Iasi an important share of gratitude for anything that I was able to do' he says. And continues, 'I have always felt the concern that this spirit of Iasi held for me, I have felt the ray of its love, I have felt its admonition, encouragement, urging, its call to the fight'.[15] Iasi is thus seen as a crucial place for the survival of the Nation due to its greatness and the nationalist struggle that occured in the city when he was a student there.

Besides, the more material side of the Nation is also evident in the adjacent concept of 'Race', which is in the vicinity of the concept of State as well. In this regard, it is said in the book that the same blood shall runthrough all the members of Romania, and that, that is the right way to be. We shall note that the mentions to racial matters that we are about to quote appear in a passage of the book that reproduces a speech delivered by Romanian writer and politician Vasile Conta in 1879. Nevertheless, the mere inclusion of such references can legitimately make us conclude that Codreanu approves of Conta's ideas. As it is said, 'bearing in mind that the same blood flows through the veins of all the members of a people, one understands that all these members will have through heredity, about the same feelings, about the same tendencies, and even about the same ideas'.[16] If there exists such a racially homogeneous community, all its members will be united by a 'general feeling of love' and 'what is called racial sympathy'.

The reason why 'Race' is also interlinked with the State is because the homogenous community is a necessary precondition for a State apparatus to exist. In this sense, it is also said in the book that 'it is a recognized fact, even by those attacking us today, that the first condition for a State to exist and prosper, is that the citizens of that State be of the same race, same blood, and this is easy to understand'.[17]

This passage probably suffices for concluding that, contrary to what is sometimes said, Codreanu did conceive the Nation in racial terms. At the very least, he evidently has no qualms in quoting approvingly other authors who make use of racist conceptions. Nevertheless, it is perhaps true that racism is not as important as they here as in Hitler's configuration because, as it is also said in the speech by Vasile Conta, 'it is possible for various races that would exist in some country to have sometimes a common interest, that the hereditary tendencies of one race be just as favored as those of another by the same circumstances'. In such a state of affairs, 'both indigenous and naturalized would certainly live peacefully' and can be a time when 'there is no distinction between these foreigners and ourselves, either as regard blood or love of country'.[18] However, this relatively ethnically tolerant view (which could even agree to intermarriage in order to fuse the blood of foreigners with that of Romanians) is quickly put aside when the author acknowledges that there are types of people that never assimilate and therefore represent a danger. Among them, there is a race that represents a particular peril: Jews (more of this will be said later).

As to the concept of State, it does not seem to be such a secondary feature of Codreanu's ideology, as it is sometimes said, for the reason that he does seem to see it as a crucial instrument for the preservation of the rights of a future national community (mostly defending Romanians against Jews). However, whatever the alterations to be carried out in the State apparatus, these do not include the abolition of the monarchy because this leader believes that this institution is in itself superior to that of the Republic, independently of the merits of an individual king. As he says:

> One has met some monarchs that were good, some very good, others weak or bad. Some enjoyed honors and the love of their people to the end of their lives, others were beheaded. Therefore, not all of the monarchs were good. Monarchy itself, however, has been always good. One must not confuse the man with the institution and draw false conclusions.[19]

As to the concepts of 'Empire' and 'Irredentism', they do not seem to appear in Codreanu's ideology (at least not in this particular book), and instead there is the concept of 'Greater Romania', which unfolds in 'Achieving unity within Greater Romania' and 'Defending the territory of Greater Romania'. His main preoccupation is not the conquering of new territories but rather the territory that was added to the country after World War I and the people that live in it but somehow are not yet a real part of the national community. For this reason, the several peoples and communities existing within the boundaries of Romanian territory, independently of the actual place where they live, are highly praised and valued by this leader. This is noticeable when he eulogises the Moti, a people from Central Transylvania who 'have lived for centuries the same existence always dominated by two characteristics: poverty [...] and the struggle for liberty'.[20] When referring to them, Codreanu demonstrates his belief that not all the communities living in Romania are given the right treatment they deserve, in spite of all the contributions that they can give to the country. The Nationalist ambitions of Codreanu thus include the idea of restoring the respect for these forgotten people living in the Romanian soil.

The plight of people like the Moti supposedly happens because what the 'Greater Romania' achieved after the war is not satisfactory and had not been able to create a true national unity. It had been materialised,

> with much sacrifice, but it seems that the alien domination and the old injustice had extended even this side of the Greater Romania's birth. Ten years of Romanian administrations had not succeeded in healing our painful wounds nor had they corrected the injustices of centuries.[21]

To people like the Moti, 'Greater Romania did not turn out to be an invigoration, a triumph, a coronation following a thousand years of suffering, with joyous reward for all their people'.[22] Thus, Codreanu sees the existing 'Greater Romania' as a failure because given the corruption of politicians and other weaknesses, this territorial extension after WWI was not successful when it came to the integration of its new people in the national community.

Note that Codreanu does not reject the existence of such a greater country. Quite the contrary, he praises it as the result of a struggle of the Romanians and says that it 'emerged from the sacrifice of our blood'. Nevertheless, even if the 'Greater Romania' 'had given us a semblance of unity', the truth is that the 'Romanian soul still was split into many pieces as there were political parties'.[23] As will be seen later, the presence of antisemitic feelings in Codreanu makes him attribute part of the blame for this failure on Jewish influence and on the Romanian politicians who supposedly sold out to them. Likewise, it is against the supposed Jewish invasion that the territory of 'Greater Romania' must be defended. For now, however, what is important to acknowledge is that the concept of 'Irredentism' is not used in PL in the same way as in other configurations, since this leader does not really aim to conquer new territories nor writes extensively about the redefinition of Romanian borders. His preoccupations when it comes to the concept of 'Greater Romania' is rather that of valuing what the country had already achieved and make it succeed.

## The 'New Man' of the palingenetic revolution and the concept of authority

The concept of 'Holism'is the first that one finds in the adjacency of Revolution. As Codreanu says, expressing a strong wish regarding the people of his country, 'let the Romanians open their eyes to see the disunity in present day Romanian public life; let them open their eyes and see well'.[24] In the first place, this Holistic Revolution has a spiritual dimension, since to be a revolutionary in the Legion's mythology means to be aware of the historical higher mission that God has given to the Romanian people and to act according to it, always having in mind the higher realities of the divine world that is beyond physical death. According to him, 'a people become conscious of itself when it attains the consciousness of this whole, not only of its own aims'.[25]

In this sense, the final goal of the Romanian Revolution has a transcendent dimension and cannot be attained in the material world. As the leader of the GF explicitly says, 'the final aim is not life but resurrection. The resurrection of peoples in the name of Jesus Christ'.[26] All the material things produced by the Nation are not in themselves the final aim, for 'Creation, culture, are but a means, not a purpose as it has been believed, of obtaining this resurrection'. In his view, 'peoples are realities even in the nether world, not only in this one', and there is a path that leads to God and to a supreme final moment in which the resurrection of the dead will take place. Codreanu strives for a national salvation with a spiritual and divine dimension.[27]

However, this salvation implied a purging of Romanian society and the destruction of some impure elements. This means, therefore, that there was also a materialistic dimension in the Holistic Revolution, or at least a dimension with more 'worldly' goals. Codreanu's main objective in relation to the materialistic side of the Revolution is the creation of a 'New Man'. As he himself says:

> from this legionary school a new man will have to emerge, a man with heroic qualities; a giant of our history to do battle and win over all the enemies of our Fatherland, his battle and victory having to extend even beyond the material world into the realm of invisible enemies, the powers of evil.[28]

This will be 'a man in whom all the possibilities of human grandeur that are implanted by God in the blood of our people be developed to the maximum'; he would fight against corruption and decay and would be capable of showing abnegation and the will to sacrifice himself.[29] In the creation of such man, youth will have a crucial function, for 'there are calls, urgings, mute comma which only the youth hear and grasp because they address themselves only to it'.[30] The development of such new type of human being represents such a primordial goal in Codreanu's politics that he said, when creating the LAM, that 'this country is dying of lack of men, not of lack of programs; at least this is our opinion. That, in other words, it is not programs that we must have, but men, new men'.[31]

The 'New Man', as it is here argued, is at the core of Codreanu's ideology, even more so than in other fascist configurations. It is Codreanu himself who says that, since the morals of Romanian men have been corrupted, 'the cornerstone on which the Legion stands is man, not the political program; man's reform, not that of the political programs'.[32] Rather than composing political programs or discussing political theory, this leader has one main practical goal: to alter the nature of the inhabitants of Romania. That is the fundamental aim at the basis of his political activity.[33] The adjacent concept of 'Palingenesis' also comes to the fore with the dichotomy that opposes the 'Old Man' and the 'New Man', the former representing materialism and corruption, while the other represents the 'Rebirth' of the Nation.

The core concept of Revolution also interlinks with Authority thanks to the adjacent concepts of 'Leader' and 'Elites', as it already happened with Primo de Rivera. In Codreanu's configurations, leaders are seen as clairvoyant individuals who are aware of the eternal laws of life and death that determine the survival of the Nation. As he states, 'Nations' leaders must reason and act, not only according to the physical or material interests of the people, but also by taking into account its historic honor, its eternal interests. In other words, not bread, but honor at any price'.[34] The 'Leader' must reject all personal interests and the interest of specific groups or classes, for 'he must avoid all these lines and follow that of his people'.[35] Listen and command are his most important tasks. According to the author, 'the Romanian nation has no need of a great politician as many wrongly believe, but of a great educator and leader who can defeat the powers of evil and crush the clique of evil-doers'.[36]

The cult of the chief explains why Codreanu oftentimes refers reverently to past national leaders who had led the Nation in times of ancient greatness. As is known, that is the case of Michael, the Brave, but there are also references to Stefan the Great, 'who has shone in history for 500 years and Romanians remember him because he identified himself perfectly with the destiny of his people'.[37] Another example of an ancient leader is that of King Ferdinand, who 'in spite of pressure from outside interests and influences, placed himself on the line of the nation's destiny; he suffered with her, sacrificed side by side with her, and won with her. It is by virtue of this that he is great and immortal'.[38]

As to the adjacent concept of 'Elite', it refers to 'that category of men born within its bosom who possess certain aptitudes and specialties'.[39] However, in spite of his elitism, Codreanu rejects the idea that any elite is eternal. As a former generation of elites disappears or becomes decadent, it becomes necessary to substitute it for another rejuvenated elite, through a process of renovation that is called 'social selection'. The leader of the GF rejects both heredity, that is, the renovation of elites based on blood ties, as well as the principles of election by the people, which was adopted by democracies as a way to solve the problems raised by heredity but only leads to the election of the worst elements in society. It is for this reason that a new elite must be formed by a process of natural selection: this process shall select the most important members of a community and make them conquer a new position of power due to their superior qualities. 'In other words', so he says, 'a category of people endowed with certain qualities which they then cultivate, is naturally selected from the nation's body, namely from the large healthy mass of peasantry and workingmen, which is permanently bound to the land and the country'.[40] Thus, even though holding an elitist view of society, Codreanu does not shy away from the idea that the new elite will arise from all the classes of society, including the humblest ones, like peasants and workers. That is because 'just as the bees raise their "queen" a people must raise its elite'.[41]

The mission and function of these elites, however, do not include only the guiding of the Nation, but also the creation of the future elites that shall emerge after the present ones disappear. It is their task to guarantee that the Nation is not left without elites, and that they will not be chosen neither by election or heredity. The elite is thus compared to a gardener that ensures that a substitute will still take care of the garden after he is gone. The characteristics of the elite must include, according to Codreanu: purity of soul; capacity of work and creativity; bravery; tough living and permanent warring against difficulties facing the nation; voluntary renunciation of amassing a fortune; Faith in God; Love.[42] This is why the concept of 'Elite' interlinks with Revolution:the selection of a new 'Elite' of 'New Men' is one of the main components of the renewal of the national community.

*Violence, racism and the cult of death*

In Codreanu's book, the praise for Violence reaches such an importance that it surpasses the apology found in other fascist leaders (perhaps with the exception of Adolf Hitler). Holding the view that all life is a merciless struggle between good and evil, this leader sees political activism as a battle in which violence against the enemies must be constantly used. Right in the beginning of PL, he says that 'I do not pay attention to any regulation imposed on book authors. I have no time. I write hastily on the battlefield, in the midst of attacks. At this hour we are surrounded on all sides. The enemies strike us treacherously and treason bites us'.[43]

This appraisal of a violent life is evident, for instance, when the author recollects his memories of WWI and the way this event helped him to start admiring those who fight for the nation. 'Here I learned to love the trench and to despise the drawing room', he says.[44] There is clearly a deep contempt for those who Codreanu deems to be cowards, those whose lives are spent mostly within the limits of the 'drawing room'. A legionary is supposed to be a militant who acts and is not afraid of physical confront with his enemies and not even of giving his life for the cause in which he believes. For this reason, it is as if the entire book consists of a call to arms and an incentive for the Legionaries to fight for their cause. In this context, Violence also interlinks with the concept of "New Man", for this adjacent concept seems to evoke the notions of virility and vitalism that were part of the Legion's activities and themes.

There are two dimensions in the concept of Violence, one of them connected to a material dimension and the other to a spiritual one. The first dimension is related to the struggle against enemies, among whom we find Jews and Bolsheviks. This Violence is justified by the idea that a worse type of Violence would befall the Nation if the legionaries did not fight back. As Codreanu acknowledges when talking about his first years of political activity, 'we provoked disorder ... but those disorders would stop the great disorder, the irreparable disorder'.[45] In other words, the momentary disorder of Legionary Violence was supposedly necessary in order to avoid a greater disorder, the one brought by the victory of Romania's enemies. The Violence of these enemies can only be fought with more violence, for 'a man who was beaten and did not retaliate is no longer a man. He feels ashamed, dishonored'.[46] The use of Violence by Codreanu himself is not concealed, for he narrates how he killed Constantin Manciu in an act of revenge.

In another dimension, Violence also acquires a transcendental component for it relates to aneternal fight between good and bad. The idea that there is a struggle between divine and satanic materalistic forces permeates the whole configuration of Corneliu Codreanu. It is a conflict that occurs within the individual as well. As Codreanu states, the 'New Man' will need 'to overcome the evil within himself and within his men'.[47] Thus, the fight between good and bad takes place at three different levels: the transcendental, the physical and the inner self. In all these dimensions, we find a Manichean view opposing goodness and purity to evilness, and Violence (even if sometimes considered a sin) is justified when used for the victory of the forces of good.

In relation to its material dimension, Violence has in its vicinity the concept 'Eliminationism' and also 'Anti-Semitism', since the hatred against Jews is a fundamental part of Codreanu's ideology. The eliminationist view is evident in the moments when he reminds his readers of the necessity of purging the Nation from the elements that imperil it. These includes the enemies (that is, the Jews) but also the traitors, that is, the ones who are not Jews but allow them to inhabit in Romania (for instance, corrupt politicians). As the author states, he has a greater hatred against these traitors than against the enemies:

> The Jews are our enemies and as such they hate, poison, and exterminate us. Romanian leaders who cross into their camp are worse than enemies: they are traitors. The first and fiercest punishment ought to fall first on the traitor, second on the enemy. If I had but one bullet and I were faced by both an enemy and a traitor, I would let the traitor have it.[48]

In this context, Codreanu believes that the Jews are the main enemies of Romania because they endeavour to destroy its unity and spiritual patrimony. The following description shows what this leader thinks about this group:

> The Jews use these plans like poison gas in a war, to be used against the enemy, not their own people. They propagate atheism for Romanians but they themselves are not atheistic, as they fanatically hold to respecting their most minute religious precepts. They want to detach Romanians from their love for the land, but they grab land. They rise up against the national idea, but they remain chauvinistically loyal to their own nation.[49]

Jews are thus the main responsible for decay, materialism and corruption. In order to achieve their goal, they use both parliamentarian democracy and bolshevism since 'the partner-in-crime of the Jew in exploiting the misery of thousands of peasants, was the Romanian politician who gorged himself on his portion of this fabulous profit'.[50] Codreanu is also convinced that the Jews have become a powerful class that endeavours to weaken and even colonise the Nation. 'What does the fact of the two million Jews settling on Romanian territory mean, if not colonization?', he asks.[51] In fact, the belief that Romania is being invaded by Jews, and that the Romanian people is being made a victim of an injustice, is one of the bases on which Codreanu justifies his 'Anti-Semitism'. As he says, Romania 'has never throughout its long history known an invader to reach such formidable numbers as those of the present day Jew.'[52]

In this context, Jews are a supposed menace to Romania, so this leader argues, firstly because they attack the moral values of the people, and 'systematically spread all sorts of moral sickness, thus to destroy any possibilities of reacting'.[53] Besided, they also imperil the racial purity of the Nation because 'the greatest national peril is the fact that they have deformed, disfigured our Daco-Romanic racial structure' and have given birth to a type of politician that 'has nothing in common with the nobility of our race anymore; who dishonors and kills us' (in this passage, the racist tenets of Codreanu's ideology come once again into the fore).[54]

Another main feature of Codreanu's anti-Semitism is the perception of the Jews as being both a race and a community with a set of laws codified in religious texts, since 'all Jews over the entire world form a great collectivity bound together by blood and by the Talmudic religion'.[55] They form a very restricted community with a law of their own and it is this entire community, and not some specific individual Jews, that Romania must fear: 'They are constituted into a very strict state, having laws, plans, and leaders making these plans. At the foundation, there is the Kabal. So, we do not face some isolated Jews but a constituted power, the Jewish community'.[56] The main problem posed by this community is the fact that they constitute an entirely different nationality within the Romanian territory, since 'in Romania, Jews not only constitute a different religious community; they constitute in the full sense of the word a nationality, foreign to Romanians by virtue of origin, language, dress, customs, and even sentiment'.[57]

In another passage, Codreanu approvingly quotes an essay by A.C. Cuza, published in the newspaper *Apararea Nationala*, which has as its main subject the difference between the various types of anti-Semitism. We can assume that Codreanu himself adopts the views held by his former professor. According to the theory espoused in this essay, there are three main stages of anti-Semitism:

> – the first is based on instinct, which is felt mostly by the crowds who instinctively react against Jewish parasitism, often with popular movements that use violence. This instinctive anti-Semitism is not based on thought or reflection, but rather on the most immediate material interests of the masses.
> – the second is based on consciousness and not on material interests. It has its origin in the educated classes and is then propagated through all the classes in the nation. In this stage of anti-Semitism, the masses become progressively aware of the Jewish danger in a more conscious way, thus preparing to fight it properly.
> – the highest stage in anti-Semitism is the one that is based on science and on accurate study. It involves 'studying Judaism as a social phenomenon, lifted out from the medium in which it seeks to hide, concluding that it is a human problem, in fact the biggest, whose solution must be found'.[58] Scientific anti-Semitism aims at studying Judaism as a social problem in order to find a solution to it.

The theory espoused by Cuza tries to give a rational and rigorous explanation for the hatred against Jewish people. According to this 'historian', all former sciences can help studying the 'Jewish problem' by adding some contributions to a scientific approach: with history, one learns that the Jews have always been a nomadic country and therefore a danger to national unity; with anthropology, one finds that the Jews are the result of a mixture of very different races, and therefore a threat to blood unity; theology teaches that their religion is a exclusivist one, separating the Jews from the ones who do not profess the same God; Politics makes one conclude that the Jews always form a state within the state and that part of their danger derives from this, etc. Codreanu does not forget to quote the conclusions at which this author arrives: 'the elimination of Jews from the midst of other people putting an end to their unnatural, parasitic existence that is due to an anachronistic concept opposed to the civilization and peace of all nations who can no longer tolerate it'.[59]

In sum, the concept of Violence displays a relevance that is proportionally greater than that of any other fascist leader that we have thus far analysed (with the exception of Hitler). This aspect has not been unnoticed by previous researchers. For instance, Walters has stated that 'a fairly unique aspect of the Iron Guard was its extreme cult of violence'.[60] Violence was a necessary instrument for the Legionaries to succeed in their fight and eliminate their enemies, but it was also something else: it was the essence of a worldview which conceived existence as a battle between good and bad. In this context, one cannot leave unnoticed the recurrence of the adjacent concept of 'Sacrifice' and even 'The Cult of Death', which is related to the spiritual dimension of the concept of Violence.

In this sense, all political violent activities are conceived by Codreanu as acts of sacrifice, to which the Romanians were supposedly intrinsically prone, for 'our people has never laid down its arms or deserted its mission, no matter how difficult or lengthy was its Golgotha way'.[61] The idea of becoming a martyr was essential to the Legionary conception of life and politics.[62] As to the 'Cult of Death', it is like an obsessive theme in the ideology of the LAM and even goes beyond the reverence for the ones that had fallen in combat, even though this is also present. According to Codreanu, all those who become martyrs in the fight for salvation, those who received 'the baptism of death', must be eternally revered, for 'when they die, the whole people lives from their death and is honored by their honor'.[63] As Codreanu states, legionaries 'do not die. Erect, immovable, invincible and immortal, they look forever victorious over the impotent convulsions of hatred'.[64] But apart from that, there is also a cult of death itself, and not just of the people who had previously died. The legionaries should learn to love death and see it as an act of supreme abnegation against materialism. The theme of death is always present in Codreanu's configuration and it permeates all the other concepts and interlinkages.[65] This is a consequence of the spiritual component of Codreanu's holism, which surpasses the limits of the material world and includes in the Nation also the people who have died and are not yet born but are still part of the transcendental national community. Thus, death becomes like a component the National Revolution, something that Legionaries must happily accept instead of rejecting.

## Other important features of the configuration

### *Corporatism as a less relevant concept*

The adjacent concept of 'Class conciliation' is present in this configuration, stemming from Codreanu's awareness about the plights of the industrial working class, whose sufferings he seems to acknowledge even when violently lamenting the manipulation that 'Jewish Bolshevists' practice upon workers. That social conflicts must be solved within the context of a national solution provided by a strong State becomes evident when Codreanu tells of the moment in his past life when he reaffirmed his believe 'in a State, supporter of social harmony through minimizing of class differences; and in addition to salaries, nationalizing factories (the property of all workers) and distributing the land among all the ploughmen'.[66] The goals of such a State should also include the distribution of benefits among workers and the assurance of rights and security, with the State using a 'risks fund' to provide storehouses for food and clothing. This 'Class Conciliation' and the formation of a unified national community or 'People' (uniting workers, peasants, students and other classes) are evident, for instance, when this leader praises group activities in which manual labour seems to blur class distinctions.

However, the concept of Corporatism does not seem to play a significant role in this configuration, at least not as much as in other fascists. We can, for now, depart momentarily from our close reading of Codreanu's book to quote Pinto:

> Corporatism was a minor ideological component for Codreanu's Iron Guard, despite Manoilescu's attempts to develop it. As the legionary leader Ion Mota stated, corporatism 'is entirely colourless from a folk point of view' and just after modification of the 'ethnic structure of the state' could be an option for Romania.[67]

Pinto thus remarks, by quoting Ion Mota, that Corporatism was in fact a marginal concept in the ideology of the GF and that it was secondary in relation to the goal of constructing a State which would focus on ethnic issues. This is a view which the reading of Codreanu's book seem to support. Some of the implications that this feature may have to our configuration of generic fascism will be discussed in the conclusive chapter.

*Peripheral concepts*

Due to the lesser relevance of the concept of Corporatism, it is possible to argue that the concept of 'Social Justice' is a marginal one in this configuration for, even if social concerns are not totally absent in Codreanu's text, they play a smaller role than in configurations such as the one from Primo de Rivera. As in other configurations, the concepts of 'Liberty' can also be seen as a marginal one. As to the perimeter, it is possible to highlight the 'Integration of the New Populations in the National Community', which derives from the problems raised by the failures of the 'Greater Romania' and the fact that a great number of people was still not truly integrated in the country that was formed after WWI.

*Permeability and rejections*

As it is known, Codreanu's configuration emerged in a context of fierce ideological competitiveness that revolved around concepts like 'Anti-Semitism' and Nationalism: it is therefore logical that this leader incorporated in his ideology elements and concepts coming from other ideologies and organisations with which he might somehow agree. This is the reason why Codreanu's book extensively quotes from articles in Rightist newspapers, most of them written by people with whom the Iron Guard's leader had something in common. For instance, the permeability with an authoritarian conservative party like Cuza's is mentioned by Sandu, when he states that 'few things separate Cuza from Codreanu on a purely ideological dimension: only the certainty of national transformation, the faith in the chief, the ideology of accomplished fact, the importance of organization and radical violence distinguish them'.[68]

In Codreanu, like in other fascist permutations, one finds a rejection of Communism and Liberalism on the basis of the concept of 'Anti-Semitism'. Codreanu does not reject Marxist Revolution by recurring to a profound reflection about its goals or social consequences: it is rather the obsessive fear of the Jews that prompts him to do it. He seems to be sure that, had the bolshevists been victorious, 'the next day we would have become the slaves of the dirtiest tyranny: the Talmudic, Jewish tyranny. Greater Romania, after less than a second of existence, would have collapsed. We, the Romanian people, would have been mercilessly exterminated, killed or deported'.[69] The rejection of liberal democracy is also related to the concept of 'Anti-Semitism', for parliamentarian politicians are supposed traitors who have let themselves be corrupted by the Jews, while democratic institutions are but a form of dividing the unity of the Romanian Nation.

## *Contradictions: populism/elitism and spirituality/materialism*

As to the contradictions of Codreanu's ideology, no differently from the configuration of generic fascism, one finds in it a tension between 'Populism' and 'Elitism'. On the one hand, there is a tendency to see the people as a group that is pure in comparison to the existing corrupt elites. On the other hand, there is once again the contempt for this same people, seen as a mass that needs to be educated by an elite of future heroes. In the words of Codreanu himself, 'a people is not capable of governing itself. It ought to be governed by its elite. Namely, through that category of men born within its bosom who possess certain aptitudes and specialties'.[70] However, it is possible to find at least some degree of esteem for the masses in the following passage:

> When can a multitude be consulted, and when must it be? It ought to be consulted before the great decisions that affect its future, in order to say its word whether it can or cannot, whether it is spiritually prepared or not to follow a certain path. It ought to be consulted on matters affecting its fate. This is what is meant by the consultation of the people; it does not mean the election of elite by the people.[71]

This quote can give us a hint about how this contradiction is solved: the people is consulted in certain matters (matters which concern them) but is ignored in others. Its will must be taken into account and respected, even if the role of leading the Nation is still left to Elites.

Ultimately, this tension between Populism and Elitism is never completely solved, for the Romanian people is conceived as having both the purity and wisdom to originate new elites and at the same time a tendency to be submissive and to show vassalage to leaders. The best elements to form a new elite can rise from workmen and peasants without this disturbing Codreanu's view (which would not happen in a purely aristocratic and elitist ideology), but the guidance by an elite nonetheless remains as one of the fundamental features of the ideology. To elements of humble origin won't be denied the ascent to a place of elite, if they are fit to the task, but the people as a whole still cannot dispense the guidance of the leader. In this way, Codreanu's conception of 'Elitism' and 'Populism' closely ressembles that of Hitler.

Also importantly, there is an apparent contradiction between Spirituality and Materialism. If Codreanu'sultimate goal is a transcendental one, there is still a preoccupation with biological and material questions such as the purity of blood and the creation of the 'New Man's. It is as if the spiritual and material dimensions, when interlinked with the concept of Revolution, lead to two ways of conceiving the historical mission of Romania: a spiritual salvation through resurrection and sacrifice; and the creation of said 'New Man'. It is here argued, however, that Codreanu endeavours to give a spiritual dimension even to the earthliest concepts of his configuration.[72] The material and 'earthly' goal arealways somehow subordinated to the spiritual ones. Ultimately, Codreanu is always trying to redefine all the aspects of his ideology, even the ones related to biological themes, in a metaphysical way, valuing the purity of blood if that means that the purity of soul will also be attained.

The idea of subordinating practical action to spirituality becomes evident in the following passage:

> During those first beginnings we found the only moral strength in the unshaken faith alone, that placing ourselves in life's original harmony, matter's subordination to the spirit, we could subdue the adversities and be victorious over the satanic forces coalesced with the purpose of destroying us.[73]

## Concluding remarks

It is common to look to the ideology of the GF as a form of political religion that had at its core a faith rather than a political conceptual core. This idea is held by Codreanu himself, who states that:

> This was a signal that the statue of another Goddess – Reason – was to be smashed; that which mankind raised against God, we – not intending

to throw away or despise – should put in her proper place, in the service of God and of life's meaning. if then we had neither money nor a program, we had, instead, God in our souls and He inspired us with the invincible power of faith.[74]

In this view, the GF had no real political program and consisted rather in set of believes about the Manichean struggle between good and evil, a struggle in which the Legionaries had a fundamental role to play by subordinating their will to God and fighting for the victory of good. However, we argue that the content of this faith can also be analysed as a political ideology with a conceptual core, even if its political program seems to rest on simple and sometimes vague notions like the creation of a 'New Man'.

It is thus possible to come to the conclusion that Codreanu's configuration has at its core an interlinkage between the concepts of Nation and Revolution and that such Revolution has both a material and a spiritual dimension, even if the former subordinates to the latter, thus pointing towards the main goal of spiritual salvation. The concept of 'Anti-Semitism' is an adjacent one but it is placed close to the core since the fight against Jewish materialism is necessary to attain the salvation of both the Nation and the soul. In this context, one must not leave side of the idea that the Nation is seen by Codreanu as a holistic and transcendental entity which encompasses all those who have been a part of it, even if already dead or not yet born. This definition of the Nation is the starting point of Codreanu's ideology and explains most of its interlinkages.

## Notes

1 This important city, second only to Bucharest, is mostly famous for the importance of its cultural patrimony and its university, the oldest in the country. To read more about the emergence of ultranationalist groups in Iasi, see Roland Clark, *Holy Legionary Youth: Fascist Activism in Interwar Romania* (London, Cornell University Press, 2015), 30.
2 Their bodies returned to Romania and were buried in an event of great solemnity in which was present many representatives of several countries somehow ideologically close to the fascist cause. This event captured the legionary cult of dead martyrs who gave their life for the cause of national revival. In order to read more about the lives of this famous legionaries see Philip Rees (ed.) *Biographical Dictionary of the Extreme Right Since 1890* (New York, Simon & Schuster, 1980).
3 To read more about the influential personalities of 20th century in Romania, see Lucian Boia, *History and Myth in Romanian Consciousness* (Budapest, Central European University Press, 2011); and Leon Volovici, *Nationalist Ideology and Antisemitism: The Case of Romanian Intellectuals in the 1930s* (Oxford, Pergamon Press, 1991).
4 According to Iordachi, 'the essence of Heliade's theory of palingenesis was evangelical Christianity, having at its forefront the figure of Christ. Heliade was convinced that the key to understanding the nature of the universe and the ideal organization of society was to be found in the Bible. The final goal of history was the accomplishment of the new "evangelical man" through salvation and the

158  *Corneliu Codreanu and the iron guard*

establishment of the Bible Republic'. Constantin Iordachi, 'God's Chosen Warriors: Romantic Palingenesis, Militarism and Fascism in Modern Romania' in Constantin Iordachi, Ed., *Comparative Fascist Studies: New Perspectives* (London, Routledge, 2010), 328.

5 Stanley Payne, *A History of Fascism: 1914–1945* (Madison, Wisconsin University Press), 466
6 Corneliu Codreanu, *For My Legionaries* (Madrid, Libertatea, 1976), 217.The text that we used was found in the following site:https://dinghal.com/bibliotheek/Corneliu_Zelea_Codreanu-For_My_Legionaries.pdf. All the page numbers refer to the document that is available in this site.
7 Writing about the ideology of this leader, Jackson notes that 'he links the present to an, essentially imagined, sense of connection to past national ancestors as well as to future generations, thereby generating a sense of time marked by a mythic sense of past and future that impacts on, informs and inspires the present'. Paul Jackson, 'A Case Study In Fascist Ideological Production: Corneliu Codreanu's For My Legionaries', *Anuarul Institutului de Istorie*, XLV: 154.
8 Codreanu, *For My Legionaries*, 54.
9 Ibid., 217.
10 Ibid., 217.
11 Ibid., 217.
12 Ibid., 217.
13 Ibid., 217.
14 Ibid., 217.
15 Ibid., 38.
16 Ibid., 74.
17 Ibid., 74.
18 Ibid., 75.
19 Ibid., 218.
20 Ibid., 183.
21 Ibid., 189.
22 Ibid., 183.
23 Ibid., 189.
24 Ibid., 84.
25 Ibid., 217.
26 Ibid., 216.
27 According to Iordachii, 'although the chosen ones enjoyed the assistance of God, through the support and guidance of the Archangel Michael, his highest messenger and minister, salvation was neither automatic nor inevitable; it was the result of gigantic struggle, a heroic crusade against materialism and atheism'. Iordachi, 'God's Chosen Warriors', 343.
28 Codreanu, *For My Legionaries*, 159.
29 Ibid., 159.
30 Ibid., 194.
31 Ibid., 159.
32 Ibid., 159.
33 We thus agree with Săndulescu and Haynes, when they assert the centrality of this concept to the GF, and do not accept the conclusions recently put forward by Clark, who sees the use of this concept as a pragmatic devise that could be highlighted or minimized according to circumstances. While acknowledging that social constraints could sometimes contribute to place this concept closer or further away from the core, we do not share Clark's view, for we see in this 'New Man' the core itself of Codreanu's ideology. It is through him that the goal of national salvation can be achieved and, besides, he also represents the principles

of vitalism and regenerations around which this fascist leader rearranges his conceptual core. If we downsize the concept of 'New Man', we cannot grasp the true meaning of the GF's program and its social implications.
34 Codreanu, *For My Legionaries*, 217.
35 Ibid., 218.
36 Ibid., 159.
37 Ibid., 47.
38 Ibid., 218.
39 Ibid., 215.
40 Ibid., 214.
41 Ibid., 212.
42 Ibid., 215.
43 Ibid., 11.
44 Ibid., 14.
45 Ibid., 32.
46 Ibid, 109.
47 Ibid., 159.
48 Ibid., 192.
49 Ibid., 84.
50 Ibid., 89.
51 Ibid., 54.
52 Ibid., 51.
53 Ibid., 159.
54 Ibid., 159.
55 Ibid., 82.
56 Ibid., 82.
57 Ibid., 76.
58 Ibid., 38.
59 Ibid., 39.
60 E. Garrison Walters, *The Other Europe: Eastern Europe to 1945* (New York, Syracuse University Press, 1988), 235.
61 Codreanu, *For My Legionaries*, 218.
62 According to Iordachi, 'the essence of the Legionary salvational formula was resurrection through the martyrdom of the chosen ones. The legionaries personal sacrifice was meant to redeem the Romanian nation [...] the resurrection of the nation followed the model of *imitation Christi*'. Iordachi, 'God's Chosen Warriors', 345.
63 Codreanu, *For My Legionaries*, 47.
64 Ibid., 10.
65 Once again according to Iordachi, 'Legionary ideologues also referred to the cult of the death practiced by the Dacians/Thracians, ancient inhabitants of the territory of Greater Romania, celebrated as ancestors of the Romanian people'. Iordachi, 'God's Chosen Warriors', 346.
66 Codreanu, *For My Legionaries*, 22.
67 António Costa Pinto, *Corporatism and Fascism: The Corporatist Wave in Europe* (London, Routledge, 2017), 23.
68 Traiu Sandu, *Un Fascisme Roumain* (Paris, Perrin, 2014), no page reference.
69 Codreanu, *For My Legionaries*, 18.
70 Ibid., 212.
71 Ibid., 214.
72 As stated by Jackson, 'Codreanu conflated spiritual and biological dimensions in his conception of the Romanian homeland.' Jackson, 'A Case Study In Fascist Ideological Production', 23.

73 Codreanu, *For My Legionaries*, 155.
74 Ibid., 156.

## List of References

Barbu, Zeev, 'Romania: The Iron Guard' in Aristotle Kallis, Ed., *The Fascism Reader* (London, Routledge, 2003), 195–200.

Boia, Lucian, *History and Myth in Romanian Consciousness* (Budapest, Central European University Press, 2011).

Clark, Roland, 'Regional Cooperation according to Interwar Romanian Nationalists' in Ivan Biliarsky, Ovidiu Cristea, and Anca Oroveanu, Eds., *The Balkans and Caucasus: Parallel Processes on the Opposite Sides of the Black Sea* (Newcastle Upon Tyne, Cambridge Scholars Publishing, 2012), 96–115.

Clark, Roland, *Holy Legionary Youth: Fascist Activism in Interwar Romania* (London, Cornell University Press, 2015).

Clark, Roland, 'The Salience of the New Man: Rethoric in Romanian Fascist Movements, 1922-1944' in Jorge Dagnino, Matthew Feldman, and Paul Stocker, Eds., *The New Man in Radical Right Ideology and Practice, 1919–1945* (London, Bloomsburry, 2018).

Codreanu, Corneliu, *For My Legionaries* (Madrid, Libertatea, 1976). https://dinghal.com/bibliotheek/Corneliu_Zelea_Codreanu-For_My_Legionaries.pdf.

Deletant, Dennis, *Hitler's Forgotten Ally: Ion Antonescu and His Regime, Romania, 1940–1944* (London, Palgrave Macmillan, 2006).

Drace-Francis, Alex, *The Traditions of Invention: Romanian Ethnic and Social Stereotypes in Historical Context* (Boston, Brill, 2013).

Haynes, Rebecca, 'Work Camps, Commerce, and the Education of the New Man in the Romanian Legionary Movement', *The Historical Journal*, 51 (4), 943–967.

Ioanid, Radu, *The Sword of the Archangel: Fascist Ideology in Romania* (New York, Columbia University Press, 1990).

Ioanid, Radu, *The Holocaust in Romania: The Destruction of Jews and Gypsies Under the Antonescu Regime, 1940–1944.* (Chicago, Ivan R. Dee, 2008).

Iordachi, Constantin, 'God's Chosen Warriors: Romantic Palingenesis, Militarism and Fascism in Modern Romania' in Constantin Iordachi, Ed., *Comparative Fascist Studies: New Perspectives* (London, Routledge, 2010).

Jackson, Paul, 'A Case Study In Fascist Ideological Production: Corneliu Codreanu's For My Legionaries', *Anuarul Institutului de Istorie*, XLV, 2006. 139–168.

Konrad, Hugo and Thomas Jarausch, (eds.), *Conflicted Memories: Europeanizing Contemporary Histories* (Oxford, Berghan Books, 2007).

Nagy-Talavera, Nicholas, *The Green Shirts and the Others: A History of Fascism in Hungary and Romania* (New York, Hoover Institution Press, 1970).

Payne, Stanley, *A History of Fascism: 1914–1945* (Madison, Wisconsin University Press, 1995).

Pinto, António Costa, *Corporatism and Fascism: The Corporatist Wave in Europe* (London, Routledge, 2017).

Rees, Philip (ed.), *Biographical Dictionary of the Extreme Right Since 1890* (New York, Simon & Schuster, 1980).

Sandu, Traiu, *Un Fascisme Roumain* (Paris, Perrin, 2014).

Săndulescu, Valentin, 'Fascism and its Quest for the "New Man": The Case of the Romanian Legionary Movement', *Studia Hebraica*, 4, 2004, 349–361.

Veiga, Francisco, *Istoria Gărzii de Fier, 1919–1941: Mistica Ultranaţionalismului* (Bucharest, Humanitas, 1993).

Volovici, Leon, *Nationalist Ideology and Antisemitism: The Case of Romanian Intellectuals in the 1930s* (Oxford, Pergamon Press, 1991).

Weber, Eugen, 'The Men of the Archangel', *Journal of Contemporary History*, 1, 1996, 101–126.

# 7 Marcel Déat and the French RNP
## The European Revolution and the new party

It is undeniable that at least some small fascist parties and organisations did exist in France during the interwar period. However, the extent of fascist influence in this country is a matter of controversial dispute among historians and researchers in general. Thus, if a researcher like Sternhell goes as far as proposing that the roots of fascist ideology are to be found in France and not in Italy (evoking, among others, the populist movement of Boulanger, the Radical Right *Action Française*, or the writings of George Sorel) others, like René Rémond, have stated that France was practically immune to fascism and that the only organisations that achieved some degree of recognition belonged to the Conservative Right (like Coronel de La Rocque's *Croix de Feu*).[1] Others still, like Burrin, note that several of these organisations, previously fitting in the Radical Reactionary Right or even the Left, went through a process of increasing fascization, later becoming supporters of the Nazi Regime and even collaborating with the German occupant.

To our current purposes, it is fundamental to assume that there were indeed some French organisations that can be classified as fascists and, based on such assumption, try to find a political party and a leader to be analysed in a manner similar to that of the previous chapters. However, if in the countries thus far included there was always a main example of a fascist leader that could be almost instinctively chosen, that is not so much the case with France. For this reason, we shall here dedicate some space to verify who were the fascists in France and who we shall choose. According to Payne's typology, which distinguishes between the authoritarian Conservative Right, the Radical Right and Fascism proper, the French groups and parties which fall into the category of fascism are the following:

1. *Le Faisceau*, the first French Fascist Party, formed by *Action Française* dissident Georges Valois in 1925.[4] Albeit its importance for the history of the epigones of the Italian regime, it met with political failure and was extinguished in 1928.
2. The Francist Movement (*Mouvement Franciste* – MF), founded in 1933 by Michel Bucard, after he split from the Gustave Hervé's *Milice*

*Socialiste Nationale.* Believing to be creating in France a correspondent to what Fascism was doing in Italy, Bucard led one of the few parties that could be unanimously classified as fascist around the time of the notorious manifestations of 6 February 1934 against the second *Cartel de Gauches.*

3. The French Popular Pary (*Parti Populaire Français* – PPF), founded in 1936 and led by ex-communist Jacques Doriot, who left the PCF because of disagreements about the policy of alliances then defended by the Comintern. After such turning point, his political path and slow transition to nationalism were mostly motivated by a vengeful desire against communism. Even if, in the beginning, the party was mainly influenced by a variant of reactionary nationalism (expressed, for instance, in the cult of Joan D'Arc), it ended up developing a favourable view of fascism and adopting many of its traits. During the Nazi Occupation, Doriot and his party became one of the main forces of collaborationism.

4. Popular National Rally (*Rassemblement National Populaire* – RNP), formed in 1941 by ex-socialist Marcel Déat, who had previously been a member of the Right wing of the SFIO.

In spite of their incapacity to achieve actual political power and (perhaps with the exception of Doriot's organisation), to attain a significant social base of support, we argue that these fascist parties constitute a fruitful subject of study and a valuable source of knowledge about the interactions and configurations of nationalist authoritarian ideologies in the 30s and 40s. We further argue that, in order to complete our study, it is interesting to turn to a fascist leader who configured his ideology in a context when World War II had already begun. This could render the study even more interesting and make us find new sets of interesting interlinkages. For this reason, we shall dedicate this chapter to one of the French fascist parties who collaborated with the Nazi occupier and had to construct an ideological configuration which conciliated ultra-nationalism with a call for collaborating with a foreigner invader.

Our choice, therefore, is Marcel Déat, leader of the RNP, for, even if his party never achieved the same degree of social support that Doriot was able to conquer, his prolific activity as a writer makes it easier to find a text or set of texts that can be analysed in the same way as the previous fascist leaders. Even if Doriot was, perhaps, the most obvious choice (and also the most paradigmatic case of a figure of the French left that later adhered to fascism), most of his texts rather deal with his obsessive fear of Stalinism and desire for revenge against his former comrades than with ideological thinking.[2] In Déat, on the contrary, one finds an interesting exposition of principles and ideas that also reveal the complexity of the path taken by this former socialist. That is the main reason why we choose to deal with this leader rather than with Doriot.

## Marcel Déat and the RNP

Born on 7 March 1894, Marcel Déat was initially a member of the French Section of the Workers International (*Section Française de l'Internationale Ouvrière* – SFIO), the main socialist party of France, which he joined in 1914. At the end of World War I, Déat still believed in Pacifism and Socialism, even if he always placed himself in the Right-Wing sectors of the party. However, at the beginning of the 30s he started to developed a rather heterodox view, which he first expressed in his book *Socialist Perspectives* (*Perspectives socialistes*). His revisionist version of socialism, which was called 'neosocialism', preached national corporatism, economic planning by a strong interventionist state and class collaboration rather than class struggle, which included an opening to the middle classes rather thant a focus on the working class. These views collided with those officially held by the party and for this reason he and other 'neosocialists' were expelled during a Congress on 5 November 1933.

After that, he joined two more socialist parties: the Socialist Party of France (*Parti socialiste de France*) and the Socialist Republican Union (*Union socialiste républicaine*). However, even if in 1936 he at first supported the government of the Popular Front, led by Léon Blum, by this time his anticommunist feelings were already sufficiently pronounced for him to fear soviet infiltration. For this reason, he participated in anti-communist manifestations at the same time that he was coming increasingly closer to espouse explicit Right-Wing and nationalist views. His admiration, or at least tolerance, for Adolf Hitler was already noticeable, and it was in this context that on 4 May 1939 he published a notorious article named 'Why die for Danzig?' ('Mourir pour Danzig?'). In this text, which at the time became quite influent among those who refused to participate in a new war, Déat argued that France should not enter into a conflict with Germany. even if the Nazi regime decided to annex the parts of Polish territory According to his view, this nation had the right to do it. Wishing to defend Pacifism and to avoid a new world war, Déat was already close to espouse some points of view that, back then, were generally held by the Far Right.

After the beginning of the war on 1 September 1939 and the defeat of France in 1940, Déat became a supporter of Marechal Pétain's Vichy regime. This new state came into being not much after World War I hero Philippe Petain, then Prime Minister of France, signed an Armistice with Germany 22 June 1940. After having been granted full powers by the Assembly on 10 July 1910, Pétain created his authoritarian government with its *de facto* capital in the city of Vichy. From then until 1942 (when the Germans invaded the territory of Vichy, but still left Pétain at the head of the state), the territory of this regime in Southeast France remained as the unoccupied zone of the country, while the rest of it, including Paris, was under German occupation. Déat initially moved to Vichy, but he soon became disappointed with the regime because of what he saw as a predominance of reactionary elements. Nevertheless, he still supported the nationalist and anti-communist policies of Vichy, even when criticizing its conservatism.

After the rejection of his proposal for the creation of a single party for the regime, Déat left Vichy for Paris, and it was in this city that he would create the RNP in the month of February of 1941 with the aim of turning this organisation into the instrument with which his revolutionary nationalist goals could be achieved. His political path in this years consisted of an increasing oblivion towards the leftist components that might still be remnant in his ideology and an increasing valorization of the nationalist component. Whatever he still lacked to become a full fascist, it would not be much longer before he acquired it . According to Burrin, 'his nazification was essentially complete at the end of the summer of 1942, and it is in that condition that the allied landing in Northern Africa found him'.[3]

After an ephemeral fusion with another Far Right political party, the Revolutionary Social Movement (*Mouvement Social Révolutionnaire* – MSR), led by Eugène Deloncle, Déat put much of his effort into turning his party into the only official organisation to represent the whole of French collaborationists. He failed in this, even if he was active in the pursuing of goals increasingly similar to those of Nazism. It was in such a context that he even participated in the founding of the Legion of French Volunteers Against Bolshevism (*Légion des volontaires français contre le bolchévisme* – LVF), a militia that would fight in the German invasion of the USSR. Nevertheless, in spite of the failure of this party, Déat still retained the status of an influent figure in French nationalist circles, and in 1944 he became Minister of Labour and National Solidarity in the Vichy Regime. In the last months of the war, Déat fled with other members of the government-in-exile to the German city of Sigmaringen, and right before the fall of the Nazi regime he took refuge in Italy, where he came to die in 1955 while still hidden.

## Marcel Déat amid the ideological struggles of his time

Let us first note that Déat's fascist configuration emerged when the battle for meaning was rampant among the organisations and individuals who, for some reason, saw in the Vichy regime a platform for advancing their political views or who expected that the collaboration with Nazi Germany would bring better prospects for France than resisting against the invasion. Far from being the only collaborationist who aspired to a political career, the leader of the RNP, in fact, wasn't even the only leader who preached collaborationism from a fascist perspective, for also in this he had at least the competition of Jacques Doriot and his PPF. Besides, in France, Collaborationism was not limited to the political Right, for it also included some Left-Wing groups.[4] There was thus a fierce and complex battle for meaning that involved a great number of individuals, organisations and ideologies. In this context, the main political battles mainly revolved around the concept of 'National Revolution', which became the motto of Pétain's Vichy and coud be interpreted in many different ways.

According to Paxton, the several groups which competed for political and ideological space included: several minority Radical Right groups and individuals who followed the path previously opened by the 1934 demonstrations (some of them having participated in them), which included La Rocque's PSF; traditionalists like Lucien Romier, who dreamed of a comeback to the supposed purity of a rural life; what Paxton calls 'experts', that is, those who defended a neutral public administration within the context of a state devoid of ideology (these included, for instance, Yves Bouthillier); and the Left-Wing collaborationists, who included people like the socialist Charles Spinasse and Trade Union Leaders, many of them seeing in the defense of Vichy a synonym of militancy for peace (an attitude which was mainly due to the desire of stopping a war that could bring the same destruction as the 1914–18 conflict).[5] We shall note that, according to Paxton's distinction, Déat (like Doriot and ex-Radical Bergery) belongs to the first group of rightist radicalism for, albeit his leftist past and independently of the way how he saw himself, his political path had clearly moved him closer to a fascist position. The fourth group, the collaborationist left, includes people whose views could still be termed left wing at the time of collaboration or who belonged to Left-Wing organisations.

It was this, therefore, the context in which Déat's ideology first emerged, a context of fierce competition among the right (and even among the left) for the reconfiguration of an ideology capable of guiding and influencing a regime that had just come into being and was the result of a defeat in war. As it was already mentioned, he formed his RNP in 1941. One year later, the role that the party should play was discussed during a meeting of its national council on 12 July 1942. Following this, from 18 July to 4 September, the leader of the RNP would publish a series of articles in the newspaper *L'Oeuvre* in which he exposed his vision about the national renewal of France and the importance of the party. These texts were later collected in a book titled *The Unique Party* (*Le Parti Unique* – PU). As it can by now be guessed, this is precisely the book that will be here used in order to disentangle the conceptual configuration of Déat's ideology. Since it came out precisely at the time when, according to Burrin, he had completed his process of nazification, it will be interesting to analyse the tenets of his ideology at the moment when he began to see Nazism as a positive force to be followed in his country.[6] Besides, it will allow us to spot some of the rearrangements that were possible within the scope of fascist ideology in a context in which the French Right (and not only the Right) was influenced by the politics of the very regime that had occupied their country.

# The conceptual core of *Le Parti Unique*

## *The national community, the French empire and the state*

An important part of Déat's ideological goals must be attained within the scope of the National State, which leaves no doubt as to the centrality of the concepts of Nation and State. Just like in the case of the generic configuration, there is here a holistic conception that is best perceptible through the use of the concept of 'Community', which is a word that Déat himself uses several times throughout the text. This vicinity between the Nation and 'Community' is one of the features that distinguishes the configuration of this leader. All the changes that he wants to carry out in society have at their basis the goal of making the members of the community gain conscience of the collectivity to which they belong.

The organic community, therefore, represents the homogeneous collectivity within which the individual must be inserted. In Déat's view, only when the individual is connected to this national collectivity and to the culture and values that they represent it is possible to exist a fruitful contact between people from different civilisations. After rejecting liberal and communist decontestations of 'Internationalism', Déat states that:

> It is another thing the meeting between a Wiseman from the Far East and a western philosopher worthy of that name. In the condition that each of them refuse to change their nature, which is the only way to understand the other humanly. Also the only way to turn culture into a nourishment, instead of a fancy, a camouflage or a varnish.[7]

According to him, it was only by accepting the culture to which one belongs that it becomes possible to get in touch with other cultures while maintaining a unique identity of one's own.

However, the concept of 'Community' does not mean that Déat does not make use of ideas of blood unity, even if the concept of 'Race' does not have the same priority as in the case of Hitler's ideology. This leader clearly states that 'our people, more than others, has the need of a biological renewal [...] for the purity of the race is a primary condition for all demographical recovery'.[8] Most evidently, the Jews become a symbol of evil for they are also seen as the mastermind behind Anglo-Saxon liberalism and Russian bolshevism (though this connection never becomes so obsessive as in the case of the German leader). The Jews are, according to the leader of the RNP, a wandering people that represents the biggest menace to all nations, since their main goal is to destroy unity and cohesion. As he says, 'the problem, the only problem, is therefore to make French people understand the necessity of systematic and resolute defense against Jewish infiltration'.[9] The task of nationalist should thus be that of showing to workers and peasants the 'true' nature of Jewish conspiracies, for many French were still unaware of the supposed dangers posed by the infiltrations of the group that Déat characterises as 'parasites'.

The core concepts of Empire and State also interlink with the Nation. As to the former, Déat's configuration does not include neither the concept of 'Expansionism' nor the desire to conquer new territories. However, this concept is nevertheless present and has in its vicinity the adjacent concept of 'Maintenance and Revalorization of the Empire' that France already possesses. This aim of maintaining the Empire is expressed when the leader of the RNP writes about the necessity of educating French citizens so that they know the history of past conquers and learn how to cherish them as an important component of the Nation. According to him,

> it is necessary to make the French relearn their history and restitute to them the sense of magnitude. It is necessary to teach them, if they never knew, to love those lands watered by the blood of theirs. And to instill in them the resolution to not let them get stolen by England and the United States. Therefore, to defend what is still in our possession, starting with Western Africa.[10]

As one can see, the possessions held by France shall be valued as important parts of the national territory and the struggle for which Déat is calling also includes the defense of these lands against Anglophone enemies. Furthermore, it is also possible to find in these texts a clear mention to a concept that can be described as 'radical change in the nation's relationship with other powers', since this leader believes that his country must play an important role in the new rejuvenated Europe that is being created by Hitler. In his own words, 'the hope that France has a great role to play in the new Europe we do not have any shame in proclaiming'.[11] That such a role implied the defeat of his own country against the invader does not seem to disturb him in the least.

As to the core concept of State, this shall be an instrument which has the goal of uniting the different elements of the Nation. Déat describes the State as the 'keeper of order and authority', the instrument which has the function of guiding the National community and which is compared to a gardener that fulfills the mission of rearranging his flowers. 'Until the new order, one needs a gardener, which is, once again, the state', he says.[12] According to him, the comparison with the gardener is best suited than comparing the State to a policeman, for the gardener must prepare the land in a non-violent way so that a new life can grow. In a certain way, so he seems to believe, there is an agreement between the plant and the gardener that takes care of it. Likewise, in a way that resembled that of the gardener, the State must create an agreement between itself and the people that live under it in order to organise and direct the national community. The figure of the gardener connotes the paternalistic idea of the State that Déat wants to transmit.

Apart from the adjacent concept of 'Order', there is also the idea that the State must be strong, even if Déat tries to clarify that the State 'does not aim at dictatorship in the classical sense of the word. It wants a strong state, not a tyrannical one'.[13] Apparently, the State shall command but not in a despotic manner, and shall limit itself to the use of strength to the extent that it is necessary to impose a communitarian spirit within the Nation. However, no less relevant is the concept of 'Totalitarianism', which refers to the control of the community by the State and the subjugation of private matters to the interests of the Nation. The author of *Le Parti Unique* sees totalitarianism as the 'regime that reunites what was kept separated', thus conciliating the individual with the national community.[14]

It is also worth discussing the functions that the State will have when led by a party like Déat's. According to him, a State animated by the ideology of such a party should include a Ministry of Propaganda controlled by it. Putting such a competence in charge of the party is justified since this is a sensitive question, crucial to instill the National ideology among the masses. This ministry shall not deal with 'information in itself [...] but general propaganda, the type that is not simply governmental apology, the type that aims at the overall orientation of opinion'.[15] Déat also envisions to create a National Relief (*Secours National*), an organism different from the bureaucracy of traditional administrations, with the aim of helping the Nation in times of need.

However, the leader of the RNP does not wish to destroy all the present functions of the State, since this should retain some of its ancient apparatus even after the eventual takeover by a revolutionary nationalist party. For instance, when it comes to elections, Déat still reserves some space to universal suffrage since he believes that democratic electoral processes are too well regarded by the French community to be totally abolished. 'It is perfectly vain to imagine that one can indefinitely deprive the French of the use of the ballot paper' he says. After all, 'they took up arms a certain number of times to acquire that right, which was essentially illusory under the ancient regime'.[16] Rather than eliminate some electoral practices of liberal democracies, Déat aims to make them truly effective under a new type of regime, the only one which can actually materialise the promises of the ancient democratic regime. This is a rather interesting point for it departs from what is written by most fascists, since the majority of them refused to accept the idea of a universal suffrage that in any way resembled liberal democracies. However, we shall not let this feature deter us from continuing analysing Déat's work as that of a fascist. After all, his acceptance of universal suffrage is a very limited one, and he is very explicit in saying that all the promises made by Liberalism in relation to free elections were irremediably destined to fail. It was as if fascism, in his view, was best suited to achieve the goals that liberal democracy had proposed but was not able to put into practice due to its flaws.

In this context, Déat accepts that, apart from the candidates who belong to the party, each electoral process could also be composed of candidates which run without any partidary affiliation. This would minimise the internal divisions and competitions among the national community while reserving some space to a certain freedom of choice. Déat's idea is that electoral choices be based on programs of immediate action and on the quality of the people involved in them. Besides, there would be corporative organisms and municipal councils destined to solve concrete problems without the interference of universal suffrage. Elections could also be held to choose the members of county councils and to a national council which would have the function of watching over the interests of the general community.

One last topic related to the concept of State is the discussion of the type of regime to which the National Revolution should give origin: in this context, Déat discusses if this regime should be a republic or a monarchy. He concludes that his country is no longer a Royalist Nation and even organisations like the *Action Française* do not have significant support among the people. For this reason, assuming that French people will no longer accept a king, he defends that the new regime shall be classified as a Republic. Like he says, 'the French people will better accept the future regime if it has the name of Republic'.[17] However, this republic will be different from the previous ones for it will supposedly give the people a chance to participate in it (truly fulfilling the false promises of liberal democracy): it will be a republic to which must be added the word 'Communitarian'. Such 'Communitarian Republic' is meant to be directed towards the needs of whole Nation and not just a part of it.

### *Corporatism and class conciliation*

The concept of Corporatism interlinks with the concepts of Nation and State and holds the key to understand how Déat envisioned the social transformation that had to occur within the community. This concept has both a political and an economic dimension. As to the political transformations, they refer to the creation of new forms of representation that include the creation of a national council performing tasks that resemble those of a Senate. As to the economy, the leader of the RNP defends the creation of Chamber of Corporations which would represent professions on a national and county level. Economic corporatism is thus conceived by Déat as a system of 'Communities of Work' ('Communautés de Travail'). The adjacent concept of 'Dirigisme' also appears, as it happens in many other variants of fascist ideology, because Déat envisions a system that 'does not tolerate anymore that the economy escapes the state'.[18]

Once again, one finds the concept of 'Class Conciliation' in the vicinity of this core concept, because Déat aims at harmonizing the interests of employees and employers and subjugate them to the interests of the community. Rather than 'Workers', the concept that helps Corporatism to gain a specific meaning is 'Producer' and, to a lesser extent, that of 'Consumer'. Déat's new form of socialism would only be possible when 'the social prize contains in itself the just remuneration of all producers from all rungs and permits them to acquire their part in other productions'.[19] Rather than preaching class struggle as the way to emancipate the working class, Déat sees this corporate solution as the best form of making employees work in the interests of the Nation and at the same time conquer a fair place in the chain of production and consumption. What Déat wants is national solidarity instead of class solidarity.

He does not reject the concept of 'Private property', for 'all property is legitimate insofar as it is not detrimental to the common interests, more strongly so if it is useful'.[20] However, the National community should be able to restrain the interests of employers whenever they endangered it and the possibility that workers gain increasingly greater control of their workplace is also not ruled out by Déat. Furthermore, corporations should also include the representation of other social classes since the community is not limited to industrial workers: the middle classes, that is, small and medium employers will be able to have their fair share of representation, 'under the condition that they reject an obsolete individualism and that the unity permits them to access new forms of rational administration'.[21] Likewise, the peasantry (which represented a large part of the French population) and its interests should also be taken into account.

### *The totalitarian revolution and internationalism*

Several times throughout the texts that compose *Le Parti Unique,* its author affirms his Revolutionary goals and refuses to see fascist ideology as a reactionary one. As with the other core concepts, the concept of Revolution interlinks with the concept of 'Community', for the transformation envisioned by Déat must focus on the regeneration of the Nation as a whole and not just on one specific social class or group. The Revolution has a national scope and therefore interlinks with the concept of Nation but also with that of State, since one of its main goals is the 'reconquest of sovereignty, at the same time that it is a renovation of the state and the instauration of a totalitarian order'.[22] Some of the usual adjacent concepts are also present in this configuration, and that is the case, for instance, of the 'Cult of Youth', since there is a constant opposition between the 'Old' and 'Youth', with the latter being conceived by Déat as the age of heroic deeds and vitalism.

The importance of the youth is such that the party cannot neglect their education, since 'it is not conceivable that the young, who are the future, and without whom this great effort has no tomorrow, escape the influence of the pioneers of the revolution'.[23] Subjected to the same divisions that divide the rest of the community, young people must also make an effort to unite and quit rivalries between them. This is where the party comes in, for it shall also have the function of creating a holistic and undivided youth, by conducting their social training and political education, However, Déat refuses to accept the idea that the party will promote fanaticism among the young, while also refusing to believe that this type of education could create an amorphous and irrational youth.

Two more concepts are found in the vicinity of Revolution, 'Totalitarianism' and 'New Man' and, this time, these two seem to interlink more than usually due to the use of the of term 'Total Man' ('Homme Total'). This man will be one who is integrated in a community where antagonisms are overcome and the individual reconnects with the whole. The 'Total Man' is always inserted in a collectivity for 'the new order will not permit that the individual be accepted as a being apart from the group to which he normally belongs: family, township, profession and finally nation'.[24] And he also asks: 'what becomes of him, this individual on whom our retarded thoughts lean with a painful tenderness? He becomes a person'.[25] The concept of 'Person', already perceptible in other configurations, appears once more in interlinkage with the concept of 'New Man'.

The belonging of one individual to a certain group will not suffocate his potential but will rather make him turn into a 'Person', it will make him gain a new conception of its own humanity and place in the world. Man shall become a true person when he is connected to his community and understand its values, spirituality and history. This is conceived by Déat as a true humanism, a concrete humanism and not an abstract one (which was the only one that the old liberal regime could offer). As he says, 'it is thus that [...] he shall pass from the individual to the person. For he will belong to the small societies where he learns to be a man, to societies which are more natural than artificial, with the contact with the soil and tradition'.[26] This conceptualisation closely resembles the one that was found, for instance, in Primo de Rivera and, being the 'Person' a part of a wider process of national synthesis that also included 'Class Conciliation, this represents one further argument to make us rethink the concept of Corporatism in our final chapter.

Another important aspect of Déat's Revolution is that its scope far surpasses the limits of the French Nation. This leader believes that there is a Revolution taking place all over Europe and that its leader is Adolf Hitler: it is the entire European continent that is rejuvenating itself and not just France. Thus, the regeneration of his country is inserted in a wider process of renovation in which various different nations shall have a role to play. In order for France to acquire a prominent position in this new Europe that is rising out of the ashes, it was necessary to start a process of palingenetc renewal that would be similar to the one already in march in a country like Germany. This adherence to a European conception of regeneration does not lead to a rejection of French nationalism for 'choosing Europe is not the same as abandoning France, quite the contrary. It shall rather lead to the discovery of the new mission of France in a Europe freed from bolshevism and liberal capitalism'.[27] This conceptualisation can, therefore, be seen as a consequence of the emergence of a fascist configuration at a time when the Nazi invasions were already taking place (including the invasion of Déat's country). In such a context, this fascist leader was forced to interpret the Nazi domination of French (which he supported) in accordance with nationalist principles, something which at a first glance woud seem impossible to do. The solution for this problem was conceiving the regeneration of his own Nation as only a part of something that transcended France and in-which Nazi Germany was a fundamental part. Déat could, thanks to this line of reasoning, find arguments to defend the Nazi invasion while still holding French Nationalism as highly valuable and necessary.

*Authority, violence and order*

As it is common in fascist morphologies, the concept of Authority, besides interlinking with the State, is also connected to adjacent concepts and ideas such as 'Hierarchy', 'Obedience' and 'Discipline', which is noticeable when Déat writes that 'discipline and selection will be the rule' in the party.[28] The concept of 'Elites' also appears and it refers to the most spiritually elevated members of the National community, the 'purest and toughest', who are ready to conduct the destinies of the State and of the Nation. A future Nationalist State guided by the Party should participate in a process of selection of the new elites, for they would be found among the militants that are 'grabbed by a high ideal, so high that they will be able to conceive it and give themselves to it'.[29] Such Elites 'by its origins and tendencies, shall express France', which means that elites can come from every social background as long as they represent the most valuable members of the community.

The adjacent concept of 'Leader', in its turn, refers to the utmost authority in the Nation, the one who should lead the Revolution. At the top of the hierarchy, the chief must act with great responsibility and wisely survey the true will of his subjects. Rejecting democratic forms of selecting a leader, the Corporate State must be constructed in such a manner as to permit the leader to be in touch with the masses and conduct them with their consent. 'No chief should be elected', he says, 'all of them should be chosen. But according to true merit, and according to their proven capabilities, not according to fantasy and favor or in a spirit of clientele'.[30] This is obviously a conception that totally rejects the typical processes of choosing representative elites that are common in liberal democracies. Déat intends to replace such processes for a more direct type of selection (loosely based on something called 'merit') with the assumption that this will permit a closer relationship between the people who is led and the chief who leads.

The concept of Violence interlinks with Authority because, in the vicinity of the former, one finds the usual notions about discipline and obedience. The members of the RNP are therefore called 'militant soldiers' who are committed to the National cause and have the duty to fight against enemies. According to him, 'the party must somehow be a sort of an army, even if its action is not of a military faction: he must be constantly on his guard, always ready to attack or rip, and it would be naïve to believe that his legionaries and militiamen will not have to give their lives in occasions of possible extreme danger'.[31] However, if Violence is to Déat a natural part of life (as it happens with all the other leaders that we saw), there is also an instrumental value in it. In this regard, Violent action has a practical goal to achieve in the National community: the repression of the enemies. The existence of militias within the Party is justified by this necessity to neutralise the supposedly dangerous elements of the community.

However, the concept Violence, just like Revolution and Authority, has always in its vicinity the concept of 'Order', for Déat does not see the type of violent actions that he defends as a destructive force. In his view, it is precisely this concept of 'Order' that distinguishes fascist violence from the anarchic and destructive Violence which is used by the enemies of the Nation and must be prevented with a supposedly orderly Violence. As he says, 'such is the iron law of every revolution, even and mostly when it is about doing it in order and recurring to an intelligent force that is aimed at avoiding explosions of anarchic violence'.[32] The idea of 'Order' is present even when the adjacent concept of 'Eliminationism' comes to the fore, since even the most merciless elimination of enemies must obey to orderly principles. For this reason, purifying the Nation is a eugenically and necessary task, and Déat goes as far as defending concentration camps. Even in this case, however, he tries to present such solution in a more palatable way by comparing it to a medical procedure.

Déat's invective against the supposed enemies reaches its highest peak when he writes a passage against the corrosive influence of Gaullism, which he defines rather loosely and including in it both leftist and rightist ideologies, as long as they are fighting the war on the side of the Allies. 'Gaullism is everywhere, whether it proceeds from a bourgeois conservatism or a pseudo-revolutionary ideology, be it the late flower of democracy or the rotten fruit of international affairs', he says. Déat believes that Gaullism is infiltrated in every place of the Nation and of the Empire, and that it is conspiring and sabotaging the National enterprise in the war, since 'it is in every civil administration, in the police, in the army, it spreads in the non-occupied zone, it poisons northern Africa and the A.O.F., it vibrates in the occupied zone'. And he continues, characterizing Gaullism as an opportunist enemy that can make alliances with everyone with the goal of defeating French Nationalism:

> He goes from the slang to the preparation of anti-government coups. It filters in the press, in spite of the minister of information and its censorship, it travels through the corridors of the hotels turned into ministry, it is served as an aperitif, it is savored in the revelries of the black market, it bears alternatively or at the same time the signs of false patriotism and

those of the international Jewelry, it is, according to the moment and the environment, Sovietophile, anglophile, americanophile, he invokes for patron and guarantor either Churchill or Stalin, unless it is Roosevelt.[33]

## Other important features of the configuration

### The party

The discussion about the Party that shall lead the State acquires an obvious relevance that seems absent from the configuration of the other leaders so far. This is evident from the very title of this work. Let us note, however, that the decontestation of this concept strongly contrasts with the way how liberal ideologies conceptualise the existence and function of political parties. The Party should not be a simple 'groupping of men' ('groupement d'hommes'), representing a faction within society or playing a role in the political struggle. In the same way, 'the party is not a juridico-mystical scaffold, invented to distract the French from their stomach concerns'.[34] The party must not be guided by the Marxist-Leninist notions of the vanguard of the proletariat and it shall not manufacture false ideologies based on misconceptions that would only serve to distract the French. Opposing all these, Déat conceives this Party as an instrument of the National Revolution that must fulfill the task of connecting the popular masses with their leaders. Rather than playing a role in a competitive political system, the Party must be used to help bringing an end to competitiveness and unite the community.

The very creation of the Party can be considered as a Revolutionary act in itself, 'the one that will influence all the other and make them possible'. Furthermore, the Party must be present in all aspects of the communitarian life and inspire it with a revolutionary spirit. Vaguely resembling Marxist-Leninist notions, Déat also uses the word 'Vanguard' to describe the Party, but the proximity with the concept of Nation distinguishes this conceptualisation of the National vanguard from the one that is found in Leninist ideology (that is, the Vanguard of the Proletariat). The function of the party is to be ahead of the Nation, awaking its people when they seem to be asleep and anticipating the future and what is best for the Nation.

In an attempt to clarify the meaning of concepts, Déat thoroughly distinguishes the roles of the State, Government and Party. The Party cannot be confused with the two other concepts because its function shall not include that of governing or administer the Nation (even if the leader of the State must also be the leader of the party). Nevertheless, that does not mean that the party should not enliven the State with a revolutionary spirit and orientation. The function of the party must be one of ideological inspiration and the State apparatus shall not be exempted from such task. Aware of the conflicts that can occur between the party and the government (which can happen, for instance, when the Party is given the function of taking charge of propaganda), Déat tries to clarify which should be the function of each. Thus, among other functions, the Party shall also have its own Planning Office (*Bureau du plan*) and a Study Office (*Bureau d'études*).

At this point, it is here argued that this concept of 'Party', which in other fascist configurations seem to be less preponderant, acquires in this book a relevance that allows for it to be considered a core concept. All the other concepts in this book somehow relate to the concept of Party and their meaning and interlinkages can only be fully understood if one bears in mind that this book was written with the main goal of justifying the formation of a single Party and explaining its function within a new type of regime. Be it uniting the Nation, inspiring the State, controlling a Corporatist economy or forming the new Authoritarian elites, the Party is almost always in the vicinity of all other core concepts.

We also argue that the historical context in which these texts appeared is the factor that explains the presence of this concept in a position closer to the core. Déat wrote PU at a time when he was trying to influence the path of a regime that he saw as too conservative and lacking a single party. With the supposed collapse of Liberal democracies and the defeat of France against the Nazis, the time had come to construct a new alternative that, so he believed, the Vichy regime was not yet offering. Furthermore, Déat also had the clear goal of surpassing his competitors among the Right and be the one leading a Revolutionary regeneration, and for this reason he needed to put forward a coherent program capable of supplementing those of his rivals. According to Cointent, 'to Déat, it's about overtaking the Doriots and Bergerys, associating them to his great design: collaboration with Germany. For that, it is necessary to offer that Germany, that he believes to be socialist, the spectacle of a reinvigorated France, recovered from its illusions. That is the role of the Party'.[35] Therefore, in the context of the ideological struggle with which Déat was dealing, it was fundamental for him to develop a theory of the State and of the Party and thoroughly describe how it should lead the Nation. That is the main goal behind the book that we scrutinised.

*Peripheral concepts*

As one can expect, the concept of 'Liberty' is also a marginal one in Déat's configuration, since it is a secondary goal when compared to the construction of the Totalitarian State in which the individual is reunited with the community. Furthermore, 'Liberty' is understood as something that can only truly exist when this reinsertion has taken place, for the individualist freedom of Liberalism is a false promise that can never be fulfilled. 'Liberty', so Déat believes, is what exists when the New Man acts in accordance with the interests of the groups to which he belongs. As to the perimeter, it is possible to spot in it all the themes and discussions about the function of the Party in society and in the State. For this reason, the main perimeter concept in these texts can be summarised as 'the functioning and role of the party'.

## Permeability and rejections

Déat's permeability with Socialism seems to be more pronounced in the concept of 'Social Justice' and its description of an economic system in which workers would have a greater control of the productive process, even if this did not entail the abolition of private property. Thus, the idea of performing changes in the management of companies and attain some level of economic social justice approximates Déat to other configurations coming from socialist ideologies, which is also noticeable in his opposition to trusts and the call for the annihilation of their power (which does not mean, of course, that his configuration fits into a type of socialist ideology). It is true that the concept of 'Social Justice' appears in some fascist configurations that were analysed thus far, but perhaps with the exception of Rolão Preto and Primo de Rivera, it is not possible to find in them such a relevance when it comes to ideas of economic equality and labour rights. It seems reasonable to argue that the political path taken by Déat after he abandoned the SFIO never ceased to be vaguely influenced by socialist notions of equality, even if they now interlinked with the concept of 'Community' and were inserted in a configuration typical of fascist ideology.

However, one shall not forget to mention Déat's rejections, noting that, despite this quasi-socialistic permeabilities, he does reject revolutionary Communism on the basis that this is a false revolution and a false form of Socialism. It is the concept of 'Community' that moves Déat's decontestation of Revolution away from the one that is found in Marxism, because the leader of the RNP rejects the idea of a social transformation associated with just one class. The rejection of Liberalism and liberal democracy is also evident when he affirms the necessity of fighting against parliamentarianism, in this way achieving 'the rupture with a certain political past, the will not to relapse in certain ruts and to build the new'.[36] The repudiation of the liberal republic and its institutions is also patent in his opposition to Masonry, which he included in the group of enemies that endanger the Nation. In sum, he concludes that 'liberalism tears consciousness apart, arouses the revolt of man against himself and against society, dissociates the State, pulverizes the nation, maintains a permanent and unappeasable fight between the various zones of institutions'.[37]

This rejection of Liberalism, as it is here argued, is most evident in the decontestation of the concept of State. This decontestation, in our view, is also one of the keys that helps to explain why Déat felt the necessity to rearrange a new configuration, different from traditional socialism, first with his adherence to the so-called 'Neo-socialism' and later with this attraction for fascism. Individualism is seen by Déat as an undesirable consequence of the conceptualisation of the State as a non-interventionist entity. Therefore, he criticises his former socialist colleagues (like Charles Spinasse, whom he addressesdirectly in his articles) for having been coopted by liberal permutations and for having an irrational fear of State power. Déat rejects both the decontestations of non-interventionism (that one finds in liberal configurations and also in liberal forms of socialism) and the notion of 'totally free contracts' that appears in the works of anarchists like Proudhon (of course, he also rejects the Marxist conception in which the State is seen as an instrument for a dominant class to perpetuate its power).

Déat sees the State as the main guardian of the contracts that are stablished between the different elements of the Nation (mostly in labour relations), because any contract where the State has not intervened from the beginning is doomed to failure and to turn into anarchy. He even mentions pejoratively the type of social contracts that had been established in the last years between employer organisations and trade unions in Sweden (the Saltjobaden agreement in 1938) and France (the Matignon Agreements in 1936 during Léon Blum government). According to him, it is certain that, if the State does not enforce its law and controls this social contracts from their very beginning, soon one of the parts of the contract will scorn the agreement and act according to its own interests, leading the Nation and its economy to a situation of anarchy.

Decontesting the State in opposition to Marxist and Liberal conceptions, Déat, as we know, reconfigured his ideology several times throughout the 30s. According to Bastow, Déat's deviation from Marxist socialism 'led to a reconceptualization of the state, no longer perceived as necessarily an instrument of class domination, but as a site of a political contestation (...) this suggested the possibility of a transformation to socialism via the state in a capitalist regime'.[38] Thus, Déat's view of the State can help explaining why he ended up being a fascist, or at least why he became disillusioned with the types of Socialism that existed in France, and began to search for a new alternative. When his fascist configuration was finally fully formed, this search for a new definition of State had encountered a definitive meaning due to its proximity with the concepts of Nation and Community.

Déat also rejects Gaullism for he sees it as a form of treason against the Nation. Furthermore, there is also a rejection of other forms of conservative nationalism, which is manifest due to the use of the concept of Revolution. As he writes, 'there is a nationalism of the besotted, a chauvinism typical of captains of clothing, which serves as a ragged cover for Gaullism and wait-and-see operations?'.[39] This form of nationalism is one that the leader of the RNP rejects for its chauvinism and reactionary content (besides the fact that it is the type of nationalism held by Gaullist supporters): it is the interlinkage between Revolution and Nation that leads to the rejection of other ideologies belonging to the Conservative Right.

### *Contradictions: nationalism and internationalism*

Some of the contradictions that one finds in Déat's ideology are also noticeable in other fascist configurations, such as the contradiction between 'Individual' and 'Collectivity', which is solved with the use of the concepts of

*Marcel Déat and the French RNP* 179

'Totalitarianism' and 'Person', since Personality refers to the individual that is reinserted in the community. The contradiction between 'Populism' and 'Elitism' is somehow mitigated by the conception of the Party as an instrument that facilitates the communication between the masses and the leader, even if it also serves to create new 'Elites'.

However, the main contradiction in Déat's ideology is the one that opposes Nationalism to Internationalism. It can seem rather inconsistent that this leader defends French Nationalism and at the same time calls for the collaboration with the German occupier. Likewise, his vision of the Nazi regime as an inspirational model for France seems not to fit with the image of a nationalist militant, at least not at first sight. How is it possible, then, to be a French Nationalist while at the same time seeking inspiration in an international phenomenon such as a fascism and, even worse, defending that a foreigner power had the right to invade one's own country? Such contradiction, as already mentioned, ise solved with Déat's idea of the Revolution as an event with a European scope. This means that he integrates French Nationalism in something that is taking place all over Europe (the fascist Revolution), in which France had to participate in order to regain its greatness. Thus, in his view, collaborating with the occupants and defending Nazism does not implicate the abandonment of French Nationalism.

According to him, 'never has such a field of investigation offered itself to French thought: it has a new Europe to discover and to understand, and it has to situate itself in a rejuvenated historical perspective, an original interpretation in order to create specific French tasks in this unique universe'.[40] In the new world that was being created with the Nazi invasions, France should have the task of finding its new mission, its rightful place, and thus play an important role in the new society. One of the most original features of Déat's nationalism is precisely the idea that rebuilding the unity of the Nation was a task to carry out in a larger context of European regeneration. More than just French Nationalism, the leader of the RNP supports a unification of several different European Nationalisms, each of them maintaining its identity and contributing to the preservation of the civilisational values of Western Europe against Communism and Liberalism.

If this apparent contradiction between the concepts of Nation and 'Internationalism' could have led to a tension within the morphological structure of his ideology, this conciliation between the role of the French Nation and the role of the European Fascist Revolution not only solves the contradiction but also allows for a decontestation of Nation which stands out from other fascist leaders. The renovation of France is as necessary as the renovation of an entire continent, and Adolf Hitler has already begun the latter. Believing that a fascist Europe would surely suffer from the absence of a renewed France, Déat successfully reconciles his Nationalism with the necessity of supporting a war provoked by the German invader. In face of this, he seems to have no problems in reassuring the reader of his faith in France while being a collaborationist.

## Concluding remarks

We chose to deal with the leader of the RNP because we thought it was important to study a fascist who wrote in the 40s, when WWII had already begun and the two main fascist regimes had been serving as a guide for a long time. Furthermore, Déat was not writing at a far distance from the war but rather as an inhabitant of a country that had actually been invaded by Germany, which renders him even more interesting. Thus, besides this international context, Déat also witnessed political turmoil in his own country, for there was an actual authoritarian regime that he still hoped to influence and make it move into a fascistized direction. With the fascist regimes serving as inspiration, he was able to have a much more detailed conception about how the State and the fascist Party should be structured and the functions that they should have. This is the reason why there is a passage of the book in which he even explicitly mentions concentration camps, something that is not referred in in any other leader that we have analysed so far.

Nevertheless, it is still possible to find components which relate to his core ideology and not to contextual influences. That is the case of the adjacent concept of 'Community', which appears in the vicinity of many other core concepts. This concept means that the type of Socialism that he still believes to defend is ultimately different from other types of socialism, which focus on the working class and not on the Nation. The community is a homogeneous entity in which the individual must feel inserted and which must be defended against dangerous disruptive elements. Déat only accepts as viable the forms of socialism that are based on the well-being of such a community. Let us finish by saying that the fact that one can find in this configuration some notions coming from his previous socialist militancy does not mean that this is not a fascist configuration: this concept of 'Community' and others like 'New Man' and 'Racism' only make sense if inserted within a fascist ideological content, and such a content is exactly what this configuration reveals.

## Notes

1. Soucy, in his turn, also considers France to be a successful place for fascism, even though, as noted by Passmore, he uses a broad definition of fascism that makes him include in this group organizations like the *Action Française* and Coronel La Rocque's *Croix de Feu*.
2. That was the case, for instance, of Jacques Doriot, *La France ne sera pas un pays d'ésclaves* (Paris, Les Oeuvres Françaises, 1936).
3. Translated by the author from the original in French: 'Sa nazification était pour l'essentiel achevée à la fin de l'été 1942, et c'est dans cet état que le trouva le débarquement allié en Afrique du Nord' Burrin, *La Dérive Fasciste*, 403. All the other translations of this chapter are made by the author.
4. 'The support for Vichy of Socialists such as Charles Spinasse and Paul Faure and of trade unionists such as René Belin, Minister of Labour from the beginning of the regime until July 1942, reminds us that the cooperation between left and right

Marcel Déat and the French RNP    181

was not unprecedented in Third Republican politics [...] Historically, relations between conservatives and the left had taken many forms'. Kevin Passmore, *The Right in France: From the Third Republic to Vichy* (Oxford, Oxford University Press, 2014), 355.

5 'A much larger minority reacted to the growing threat of war with more militant pacifism. The left, remembering its role in 1914, had good reason to fear another "union sacrée" that, as Bergery said, would prevent continuing the struggle against their own economic aristocracy by diverting workers' energies into war'. Robert Paxton, *Vichy France 1940–1944* (New York, Columbia University Press, 2001), 276.

6 According to Burrin, this goal had already entered his ideology even before the full fascization of its features since, 'During the summer of 1940, Déat had shown the signs of a creeping fascisation, which still lacked essencial elements of development. To a certain extent, he remained faithful to neo-socialism, having found in the post-defeat something of his original inspiration. Basically, in the 30 s his aspiration had been to form and lead a communitarian and united nation, free from artificial divisions of ideologies and parties'. In the original, it says, 'au cours de l'été 1940, Déat avait manifesté les signes d'une fascisation rampante, à laquelle faisaient encore défaut des éléments essentiels de développement. Dans une certaine mesure, il restait fidèle au néo-socialisme, ayant retrouvé dans l'après-défaite quelque chose de son inspiration originale. Au fond, dans les annés 30 son aspiration avait été de former et de diriger une nation unitaire et communautaire, débarrassée des divisions artificielles des ideologies e des parties'. Burrin, *La Dérive Fasciste*, 385.

7 'Autre chose est la rencontre entre un sage d'Êxtreme-Orient, et a penseur d'Occident digne de ce nom. À condition que chacun se refuse à changer sa nature, ce qui est a la seule manière de comprendre l'autre'. Marcel Déat, 'Le Parti Unique' in Philippe Randa, Ed., *Documents Pour l'Histoire*, Vol.1, (Paris, Éditions Déterma, 1998 [1942]), 36.

8 'Notre peuple, plus que d'autres, a besoin de se refaire biologiquement [...] que la pureté de la race est la condition première de tout redressement démographique'. Ibid., 84.

9 'Le Problème, l'unique problème est donc de faire comprendre au people français la nécessité d'une défense systématique et résolue contre les infiltrations Juives'. Ibid., 83.

10 'Il faut réaprendre aux Français leur histoire et leur redonner le sens de la grandeur. If faut leir enseigner, s'ils n'ont jamais su, à aimer ces terres arrosées du sang des leurs. Et faire naître en eux la resolution de ne pas les laisser voler par L'Angleterre et les États-Unis. Donc de defender ce qui est encore en notre possession, à commencer par l'Afrique occidentale'. Ibid., 67.

11 'Que la France ait un grand role a jouer dans la nouvelle Europe, nous n'avons aucune vergogne à en proclaimer l'ésperance'. Ibid., 67.

12 'Jusqu'à la nouvel ordre, il y faut un architecte, il y faut un jardinier, qui est, encore une fois, l'État'. Ibid., 47.

13 'Car le Parti unique ne vise pas à la dictature, au sens classique de ce mot. Il veut un État fort, non point tyrannique'. Ibid., 47.

14 'Un régime qui remet ensemble ce qui était séparé'. Marcel Déat'. Ibid., 47.

15 'Non pas l'information proprement dite [...] mais la Propagande géenerale, celle qui n'est pas simplement apologétique governamentale, celle qui vise à l'orientation d'ensemble de l'opinion'. Ibid., 47

16 'Il est parfaitement vain d'imaginer qu'on va pouvoir indéfiniment priver les Français de l'usage du bulletin de vote. Ils ont pris les armes un certain nombre de fois pour conquérir ce droit, qui était essentiellement illusoire et dangereux sous l'ancient regime'. Ibid., 59.

182  *Marcel Déat and the French RNP*

17 'Les Français accepteront mieux le régime de demain, s'il garde le nom de République'. Ibid., 63.
18 'Qui ne tolère plus que l'économie échappe au prises de l'État'. Marcel Déat'. Ibid., 32.
19 'Le prix social contient en lui la juste rémunération de tous les producteurs à tous les échelons et leur permet d'acquérir leur part des autres productions'. Ibid., 32.
20 'Tout propriété est légitime dans la mesure où elle n'est pas nuisible à l'intérêt commun, à plus forte raison si elle est utile'. Ibid., 86.
21 'Sous la condition qu'elles s'arrachent a un individualisme périmé, et que l'union leur permette d'accéder à des formes rationnelles d'administration'. Ibid., 83.
22 'La révolution est reconquête de la souveraineté, en même temps qu'elle est rénovation de l'État et instauration d'une ordre totalitaire'. Ibid,75.
23 'Il n'est pas concevable que la Jeunesse, qui est l'avenir, et sans laquelle ce grand effort serait sans lendemain, échappe à l'influence de la révolution'. Marcel Déat'. Ibid, 48.
24 'L'ordre nouveau ne permettra plus que l'individu soit accepté comme un être séparé du groupe, de tous les groupes auquel il appartient normalement: famille, commune, profession et enfim nation'. Ibid, 35.
25 'Que devient-il, cet individu sur lequel nos penseurs attardés se penchent avec une tendresse douloureuse? Il devient une personne'. Ibid., 35.
26 'C'est ainsi [...] qu'il passera de l'individu à la persone. Parce qu'il appartiendra à des petites sociétés où se fera son apprentissage d'homme, à des sociétés naturelles plus qu'artificielles, au contact du sol et de la tradition'. Ibid., 35.
27 Ibid., 75.
28 'Mais discipline et selection seront de règle'. Ibid.,40.
29 'Puissent-ils être empoignés par un haut ideal, aussi haut qu'ils sauront le concevoir, et s'y donner'. Ibid., 41.
30 'Cette élite, par ses origines et ses tendances, devrait exprimer la France'. Ibid., 41.
31 'Mais le parti sera en quelque manière une armée, même si son action n'est pas de forme militaire: il devra être constamment sur ses gardes, toujours prêt à l'attaque ou à la riposte, et il serait bien naïf de croire que ses légionnaires ou ses miliciens n'auront pas à donner de leur personne en des occasions peut-être singulièrement périlleuses'. Ibid., 40.
32 'Telle est la loi de fer de toute révolution, même et surtout quand il s'agit de la faire dans l'ordre et de recourir à une force intelligente et dirigée pour éviter les explosions de la violence anarchique '. Ibid, 40.
33 The whole text of this passage is the following: 'Le gaulisme est partout, qu'il procède d'un conservatisme burgeois ou d'une idéologie pseudo-révolutionnaire, qu'il soit la fleur tardive du démocratisme ou le fruit pourri de l'affairisme internationale. Il est dans toutes les administrations civiles, il est dans la police, il est dans l'armée, il s'étale en zone non occupée, il empoisonne l'Afrique du Nord et l'A.O.F., il vibrionne en zone occupée. Il se traduit par des freinages et des malfaçons, par des sabotages et des ajoutements, par des conciliabules et des conjurations. Il va de la fronde salonnarde à la préparation des coup de main antigouvernementaux. Il filtre dans la presse, malgré le ministère de l'information et sa censure, il chemine à travers les couloirs des hôtels transformes en ministère, il se deguste à l'apéritif, il se savoure dans les ripailles de marché noir, il porte tour à tour ou à la fois les signes du faux patriotisme et ceux de la juiverie internationale, il est, selon le moment et le milieu, soviétophile, anglophile, américanophile, il invoque pour patron et garant aussi bien Churchill que Staline, à moins que c ene soit Roosevelt'. Ibid., 111.
34 'Le parti n'est pas un échafaudage juridico-mystique, inventé pour distraire les Français de leurs préoccupations stomacales'. Ibid., 15.

35 'Pour Déat, il s'agit de prendre de vitesse les Doriot et les Bergery, en les associant a son grand dessein, la collaboration avec l'Allemagne. Pour cela, il faut offrir à cette Allemagne, qu'il veut croire socialiste, le spectacle d'une France revigoré, revenuee de ses illusions. Ce sera le role du Parti Unique'. Jean Paul Cointent, 'Marcel Déat et le Parti Unique (Été 1941)', *Revue d'Histoire de la Deuxième Guerre Mondiale*, 91, 2.
36 'L'antiplarlamentarism signifie rupture avec un certain passé politique, la volonté de ne pas retomber dans certaines ornières et de construire du neuf'. Déat, 'Le Parti Unique', 71.
37 'Le liberalism écartele les conscience, suscite la révolte de l'homme contre lui-même et contre la societé, il dissocie l'État, il pulverize la nation, il entretient entre les diverses zones d'institutions une querele permanente et inapaisable'. Ibid., 71.
38 Steve Bastow, 'Inter-war French fascism and the neo-socialism: the emergence of a third way' in David J. Howarth, David R. Howart, Aletta J. Norval, Yannis Stavrakakis, Eds., *Discourse Theory and Political Analysis: Identities, Hegemonies and Social Change* (Manchester, Manchester University Press, 2000), 38.
39 'Il y a un nationalisme d'obsédées, un chauvinisme de capitaines d'habillement, qui servent de couverture loqueteuse aux opérations attentistes et gaullisantes'. Déat, 'Le Parti Unique', 65–66.
40 Ibid. 67.

## List of References

Atkin, Nicholas, *Pétain* (London, Longman, 1997).

Bastow, Steve, 'Inter-war French fascism and the neo-socialism: the emergence of a third way' in David J. Howarth, David R. Howart, Aletta J. Norval, Yannis Stavrakakis, Eds., *Discourse Theory and Political Analysis: Identities, Hegemonies and Social Change* (Manchester, Manchester University Press, 2000).

Brunet, Jean-Paul, *Jacques Doriot: Du Communisme Au Fascisme* (Paris, Balland, 1982).

Burrin, Philippe, *La Dérive Fasciste: Doriot, Déat, Bergery, 1933-1945* (Paris, Éditions du Seuil, 1986). See also Pascal Ory, *Les Collaborateurs* (Paris, Éditions du Seuil, 1980).

Cointent, Jean-Paul, 'Marcel Déat et le Parti Unique (Été 1941)', *Revue d'Histoire de la Deuxième Guerre Mondiale*, 91, 1973, 1–22.

Cointent, Jean-Paul, *Marcel Déat: Du Socialisme au National-Socialisme* (Paris, Perrin, 1998).

Dard, Olivier (ed.), *Georges Valois, Itineraire Et Receptions* (Bern, Lang, Peter, Ag, Internationaler Verlag Der Wissenschafte, 2011).

Déat, Marcel, *Perspectives Socialistes* (Paris, Valois, 1930).

Deniel, Alan, *Bucard et le Francisme* (Paris, Éditions Jean Picollec, 1979).

Doriot, Jacques, *La France ne sera pas un pays d'ésclaves* (Paris, Les Oeuvres Françaises, 1936).

Jenkins, Brian and Chris Millington, *France and Fascism: February 1934 and the Dynamics of Political Crisis* (London, Routledge, 2015).

Passmore, Kevin, *The Right in France: From the Third Republic to Vichy* (Oxford, Oxford University Press, 2014).

Paxton, Robert, *Vichy France 1940–1944* (New York, Columbia University Press, 2001).

Payne, Stanley, *A History of Fascism: 1914–1945* (Madison, University Press of Wisconsin, 1995).

Rémond, René, *La Droite En France de 1815 à Nos Jours. Continuité et Diversité d'une Tradition Politique* (Paris, Aubier, 1954).

Soucy, Robert, *French Fascism: The First Wave, 1924–1933* (New Haven, Yale University Press, 1986).

Sternhell, Zeev, *Ni Droite Ni Gauche. L'idéologie Fasciste En France* (Paris, Éditions du Seuill, 1983).

# 8 Benito Mussolini and Italian Fascism

## The creation of a new conceptual configuration

Benito Mussolini gained his notoriety as the first charismatic fascist leader who was successful in his search for political power. The regime that he led between 1922 and 1943 is usually seen as the most paradigmatic case of a Fascist State, and in its era, it spread its influence to many different countries and impacted the ideological competitiveness that was taking place in them, mainly in the political right (but not only). Likewise, Mussolini's final appearance in the stage of world politics, with his body hanging upside down and vexed by an enraged crowd, also seems to be the symbol of the definitive decay and rejection of fascist ideology. Mussolini can thus be seen as symbol of the development of fascism, having played a role in its appearance, consolidation and extinction. For more than twenty years, since the March on Rome brought him to power on 27 October 1922, to the days when he led the so-called Italian Social Republic (also known as the Salò Republic), Mussolini was like a guide and inspiration for every fascist movement outside Italy, even if the coming of Hitler to power in the 30s defied his supreme authority. It is therefore difficult to conceive a study on the ideology of fascist leaders that does not take the Italian 'Duce' into account.

However, even if we focus only (as we intend to do) on the movement phase of Italian Fascism, we still find some difficulties that seem hard to overcome, not only because of the lack of a definitive text like *Mein Kampf*, but mainly because the ideological content of this movement (and Mussolini's thought, for that matter) changed rapidly during this epoch of ideological formation. Thus, from 23 March 1919, when the Fascist Movement was first created, to the day of the March on Rome, the ideological configuration of Mussolini and that of other fascists went through a process of constant reconstruction. In this context of recurrent reconfigurations, it is almost impossible to find a definitive moment on which to focus to disentangle a fixed ideological conceptual core. For this reason, as it will be further explained in the next sections, in this chapter we propose to follow a different approach. Instead of focusing on a single text in order to disentangle one sole conceptual configuration, we shall select several moments in the history of the fascist movement in order to verify how the configuration was altered and rearranged in those years. But first, let us learn more about Mussolini and his movement, as well as about the political milieu of his time.

## Benito Mussolini, fascism and the political milieu of Italy in the 20th century

Benito Amilcare Andrea Mussolini was born on 29 July 1883 in the Italian commune of Predappio, in the region of Emilia-Romagna. His father, Alessandro, worked as a blacksmith and was known in the region where he lived for his leftist ideas, being influenced both by anarchism and the Italian nationalism of figures like Giuseppe Mazzini and Giuseppe Garibaldi. Mussolini's rebellious youth was undoubtedly impacted by the political affiliations of his father, even if the influence of his catholic mother, Rosa, played a counterbalancing role. From a young age, Mussolini adhered to Left-Wing ideas, joining the Italian Socialist Party (*Partito Socialista Italiano* – PSI) in 1901. When he later moved to Switzerland, trying to escape military service, he continued with his socialist activities and calling for strikes, which eventually led to him being imprisoned.

His rise in the ranks of the party continued over the next decade and, at the beginning of the 10s, already back in Italy, he had become one of the most outstanding members of the most revolutionary wing of the PSI. [1] In this context, the future fascist leader vehemently opposed the Italian war in Libya, which was fought against the Ottoman Empire and was seen by him as a form of imperialistic aggression. After that, he had an effusive performance in the party congress of 1912, in Reggio Emilia, when denouncing the reformist wing of the party (especially the members of this faction who had defended the war, like Ivanoe Bonomi), and thus, contributing to the so called maximalist wing of the party (the most revolutionary one and similar to the Bolsheviks in Russia) to become the dominant one. A few months after this congress, he even became the editor of the newspaper *Avanti!*, in that way consolidating his notoriety as a revolutionary socialist.

However, as it is known, it is not for his militancy in socialism that Mussolini acquired his worldwide fame in the 20th century. The turning point in his political career came in 1914, with the beginning of World War I. Initially, Mussolini supported the official position of his party, which was once again opposition to the war, and he also looked approvingly to the riots that took place in June of 1914, after the killing of anti-militarist protesters. However, in October of that same year he published in *Avanti!* an article that went by the name of 'From absolute neutrality to active and working neutrality", in which it became clear that his opinions had unexpectedly changed and that he was coming closer to support Italian interventionism in the war. According to him, the conflict could be an opportunity for the working class if it resulted in the defeat of the reactionary powers of Germany and Austria, thus creating the conditions for the advancement of the interests of the proletariat.

This new position led to his expulsion from the PSI and marked the beginning of a new phase in Mussolini's political path, one that would end with him becoming the worst enemy of his former socialist comrades. In the times that followed, he continued militating for his country to enter in the war, further developing his new nationalist views and even founding an interventionist newspaper, *Il Popolo d'Italia*, just a few weeks after leaving his former party, as well as an organisation which was called *Revolutionary Fasci for International Action* (*Fasci Rivoluzionari d'Azione Internazionalista*). A few months after the end of WWI, in which he eventually participated and was injured, he would form the *Italian Fasci for Combat* (*Fasci Italiani di Combattimento* – FIC), which is often seen as the first fascist organisation that there ever was.

This seemingly abrupt volte-face that led Mussolini to exchange international socialism for nationalism can easily be seen as one among many examples proving that the fascist leader was but an opportunist politician who was only interested in obtaining power for himself and did not show any real type of commitment to ideologies.[2] However, not all authors seem to think this way, which is the case of Renzo de Felici and Zeev Sternhell, both of whom note that, even during his socialist period, Mussolini already displayed heterodox ideological features. These were influenced by authors such as Friedrich Nietzsche and Vilfredo Pareto and persisted throughout his life, apparently proving that there was indeed some form of coherence in his political path, albeit all the shifts that it went through.

Emilio Gentili gives us a list of such ideological features: the conception of politics as a form of art; the transformation of ideas into myths; an ambivalent attitude towards the masses, which are both despised and seen as force of change; an elitist view of historical progress; the possibility of social palingenesis; and a pessimistic view of humanity.[3] A. James Gregor goes even further and states that what a study on Mussolini's ideology 'reveals is an evolving system of thought'.[4] In this historian's view, what Mussolini went through during WWI was a consistent evolution in his conception of how to perform a transformative revolution. His conversion to revolutionary nationalism was a logical evolution stemming from the conclusion that class struggle could no longer mobilise the masses. For our purposes, as it is already known, we will approach Mussolini's ideology by taking its content seriously and, given what has already been said in the introduction of this book about the ideology of fascism, this can be stated without further ado.

Let us now go back to the FIC, which was formed in Milan on 23 March 1919 in a reunion that took place at the *Piazza di San Sepolcro*. This group soon became famous for his violent punitive attacks which had as their main enemy the members of the Socialist Party, even if sometimes militants of other parties were also victims. It was during this period that the word 'Fascism' became common use, most of the times being connoted with violent actions. As the movement grew stronger and conquered support among the small landowners in the northern and center parts of Italy, it also became more conservative than during its initial phase. Soon, the idea of a government led by Mussolini, or at least one which counted with his support, started to be seen as a feasible one by an Italian elite facing political crisis. This became more obvious after November 1921, when the Fascist movement was officially turned into the *National Fascist Party* (*Partito Nazional Fascista* – PNF) in a Congress held in Rome. In spite of all the violence that the Fascists perpetrated in different parts of the country (like Bologna), Mussolini would eventually come to power in October 1922, after a fascist mass demonstration that led the King Victor Emanuel III to accept him as the country's prime minister and which became known as the 'March on Rome'.

The regime that lasted until 25 July 1943 passed through different phases, each with different degrees of radicalisation, but it is generally assumed that the turn towards what one could call a totalitarian state only happened after the so called 'Matteotti affair' in 1924 and the speech of 6 January 1925.[5] After this event, Mussolini eventually silenced the most radical factions within the party (led by Roberto Farinacci), and the syndicalist faction (to which belonged people like Edmondo Rossoni) also lost most of the preponderance that it still had. Influenced by the nationalist ideology of Alfredo Rocco and other members of the *Italian Nationalist Organization* (*Associazione Nazionalista Italiana* – ANI), the fascist regime developed a fully formed ideology that helped it to find its political legitimacy. Years later, during the 30s, Party Secretary Achille Staracce would lead the regime into a new radical phase and, after the invasion of Ethiopia of 1935, the rapprochement with Nazi Germany became more evident, mostly due to the adoption of racist laws. The entering of the country in World War II marked the beginning of the end for Mussolini and his regime and, in 1943, he would be deposed after a meeting of the Fascist Grand Council. After that, the fascist leader became the head of the ephemeral Italian Social Republic, which was but a puppet state of Nazi Germany, as the country plunged into civil war between fascists and anti-fascists. However, as the conflict was leading to the defeat of the Axis, Mussolini's fate was already sealed: he was executed on 28 April 1945 and his body was exhibited in the manifestation of public hatred that we already mentioned.

However, one shall not make the mistake of looking at Mussolini without taking into account the political milieu of this time and the struggles for meaning that were taking place. Looking at this political milieu, we can find out which political concepts and themes were being discussed and influenced the emergence of fascism. Thus, even before WWI, we encounter a redefinition of the concept of Nationalism in an organisation like the Radical Right Italian Nationalist Association (Associazione Nazionalista Italiana – ANI), which held an organicist and elitist view of the Nation, while displaying at the same time a deep contempt for liberal institutions. This organisation included people like Enrico Corradini, who saw Italy as a

'Proletarian Nation', thus believing his country to be a victim of powerful empires that did not allow it to form its own Empire. This new nationalism can be seen as a reconceptualisation of rightist themes with leftist vocabulary (notably the use of the word 'Proletarian'). On the other hand, coming from the Left, we find the Revolutionary Syndicalists, who progressively abandoned their leftist ideology and came to view the Nation as the main concept behind Revolution, envisioning the construction of an economic system capable of uniting all the producers and not only workers. Among the most important Revolutionary Syndicalists, we find people like Sergio Pannunzio, Filippo Corridoni and A.O. Olivetti, and many others whose political path somehow shares similarities with the one that was being followed by Mussolini. Furthermore, other groups of intellectuals, such as the one linked to *La Voce* (to which belonged the writer Giovani Papini), dealt with themes such as moral decay and the creation of a 'New Man'. Around the same time, the Futurists, led by Filippo Tomaso Marinetti, praised war and violence as a creative phenomenon.

In this context, WWI brought an impactful change in Italian politics, and this included a process of conceptual redefinition in the thought of many people on the Left. Among them we find Mussolini himself, who began to see the potentialities of Nationalism as a catalyst for social change. When the conflict ended, several organisations of veteran soldiers known as the *Arditti* were active in violent actions against what they thought to be traitors of the nation. As Gentile notes, they based their activity on myths such as the idea that there was an aristocracy of the trenches formed by ex-soldiers ready to change Italian society, or the idea that the Italian victory was a *Vittoria Mutilata*, since the country had not received the portions of territory that it supposedly deserved. The *Arditti* also participated in the takeover of Fiume by Italian poet Gabriel D'Annunzio. The self-proclaimed State of Fiume, which lasted for a year, was also an important event for the Italian right, for D'Annunzio's style as a leader came to influence the early period of Fascism, mainly because of his speeches and liturgies (which included the so called Roman Salute) directed at the masses.

Having all this in mind, it is easy to see why the first phase of the Fascist movement of 1919 was marked by the influence of Futurists, the *Arditi*, Revolutionary Syndicalists and some former leftists who had militated for the interventionist cause. Thus, according to Garau, the metapolitical drive and the mentality of the movement came from the Futurists and the Arditti: it was a metapolitical drive prone to advocate radical nationalist change and a mentality that favoured direct violent action. This violent activity and love for creative destruction was completed by a doctrinal core containing concepts that initially came from the National Syndicalists, and this is why, this movement initially had a quasi-leftist tone in its appeals for the working class. From 1920 onwards, when Fascism began to gain support from the small landowners and attacking groups of the organised working class, the conceptual framework began to be influenced by more conservative elements, even if the violent mentality was still there.

## The conceptual reconfigurations of Mussolini during the formative years of Fascism

Having in mind all that we have previously said, we do not intend to untangle a definitive conceptual morphology of Mussolini's ideology, but rather grasp the transformations and reconfigurations that his conceptual core went through during the movement phase of Italian Fascism. The limits of our study, however, do not allow us for a thorough analysis of the evolution of his thought and, for that reason, we need to find some important landmarks in the history of the FIC, thus disentangling the conceptual configuration of that precise moment in time. This chapter will thus have a different structure from the previous ones and its purpose is rather to try to shed some light on the process of formation of Fascist ideology in a time when its conceptual configuration was still rapidly evolving. For this reason, we left Mussolini to the last chapter, even though the texts that we treat here were the first to appear.

In the following sections, we will therefore analyse four different moments in the history of the Fascist movement. The first one is the speech made by Mussolini when officially forming the FIC. After that, the next sections deal with speeches made in each of the three congresses of the *Fasci*: the first was delivered in Firenze on 9 October 1919; the second one on 24 May 1920 in Milan; and the third one in Rome on 9 November 1921. The last was also the occasion when the movement was officially transformed into a party. In each of these speeches we will try to untangle the main concepts and interlinkages appearing in Mussolini's speeches.

### *The founding speech of the Fasci Italiani di Combatimento and the political program of the Fasci*

The first phase of fascism is often termed the 'Fascism of San Sepolcro' or 'Sansepolcrismo', due to the name of the Milanese square where the first meeting was held. On 23 March 1919, the meeting, which was directed by Mussolini, was attended by people like Italo Balbo, Emilio de Bono, Michele Bianchi, Cesare Maria de Vecchi or Filippo Tomaso Marinetti. Later during the regime, these people were granted a special place in the ranks of the new hierarchies, due to their militancy of the first hour. The plans for the concretisation of this meeting were first published on the 2nd March 1919, in Mussolini's journal *Il Popolo d'Italia*. Two days before its holding, the official foundation of *Fascio di Combattimento di Milano* took place. During the meeting, that took place at the headquarters of Industrial and Commercial Alliance, Ferruccio Vecchi and Enzo Ferrari (not the famous entrepreneur) were the first speakers. Right after them, came Mussolini's turn. Let us then look at what the future *Duce* then said.

Right at the beginning, Mussolini tells his audience that he has no time to go down into details and that 'wanting to act, we take reality in its big lines without following it minutely in its details'.[6] Interestingly enough, his first words in the founding meeting relate to the necessity to act and to the scarcity of time for discussion. With the intention of going straight to the point, Mussolini divides his speech in three small parts, each of them beginning with a declaration of interests. The first declaration says:

> The meeting of March 23 addresses its first salute and its memory and reverent thoughts to the sons of Italy who have fallen for the greatness of the fatherland and the liberty of the world, to the mutilated and the disabled, to all the fighters, to the ex-prisoners who did their duty, and it declares to be ready to vigorously support the claims of material and moral order that will be advocated by the associations of fighters.[7]

Already in this first meeting of Fascism, we find the concept of Nation, since Mussolini praises the greatness of Italy after the country had come out victorious of the conflict in which it had engaged in the last years. Moreover, there seems to be a connection between the greatness of the fatherland and progressive values, for the ones who fought for the later seemed to have also fought for the former. At this time, there still seems to be in Mussolini's thought an idea that nationalism can be a force that helps bringing progress to the world.

Furthermore, we find the concept of Violence, interlinking with the adjacent concept of 'War'. In this context, WWI is seen as a force of progress, for it was fought with the goal of preventing the Hohenzollern and the Hapsburg from dominating the world. After the end of the conflict, the forces of reaction, so Mussolini says, had not assumed power in any place of the world. Quite the contrary, it was possible to note that, in every country, steps are being taken towards more complete forms of political and economic democracy. In sum, 'the war gave, despite certain details that may annoy the more or less intelligent elements, all that we asked for'.[8] As it is possible to conclude from this speech, World War I was an event that greatly impacted Mussolini and fascism as a whole. This was the conflict of which the Fascist leader had wanted to be part as well as an historical happening that had led him to reconceptualise and change his former political views. For this reason, it shall come as no surprise that many passages of his intervention at the Piazza di San Sepolcro are dedicated to discussing the legacy of the war and the impact that it still has among the participants in that meeting.

One should also note that the concept of 'War' somehow appears to interlink with the concept of 'Progress', which also happens in other fascist permutations, but in this case we still find some interlinkages that seem not to fit what we already know about generic fascism. Thus, in a way that still resembled Communism and Socialism, Mussolini connotes reaction with the old aristocratic families of Europe and with the regimes that allowed no democracy. In the same way, the leader shows that he hasn't got totally rid of Marxist language and thought when referring the necessity to evaluate the 'qualitative' changes brought by the war. However, the idea that some kind of spirituality might contribute to the greatness of war, which is a feature of fully formed fascism, already comes to surface when the leader states that 'we can affirm in all security that the country is bigger today, not just because it reaches Brenner [...] not only because it goes to Dalmatia. But Italy is bigger [...] because we had the experience of this war inasmuch as we wanted it; it was not imposed on us'.[9]

Besides, another important feature of fascism is already present: the praise for those who fight, which is noticeable in the eulogy for the ones who have fallen in the war, giving their life for a higher cause. In a description that already comes close to the forms of Integral Nationalism of later fascists, the future Duce wants to include in his evocation all those who died: the savants and the ignorant, the great generals and the infantrymen. Among the ones who deserve fascist praise, we find Mussolini's former comrades, whom he considers to be the representatives of the 'wonderful youth who went to the front and there remained'.[10] He talks of people like Corridoni, Reguzzoni, Vidali, Deffenu or Serrani whose cult can be seen as a precursor of the cult of later figures like Ion Mota, Horst Wessel or Matias Montero.[11]

After this, the second declaration says:

> The meeting of March 23 declares opposition to imperialism from other peoples which cause damage to Italy and eventually to Italian imperialism in the detriment of other people; it accepts the supreme postulates of the Society of the Nations, which purpose the integration of each of them, integration that as far as Italy is concerned must be made in the Alps and the Adriatic with the claim and annexation of Fiume and Dalmatia.[12]

Mussolini thus rejects a type of imperialism that is characterised by what he terms barbarity (which is, according to him, the German type of imperialism).[13] Different methods make different imperialisms and the one chosen by Italy shall not be an uncivilised kind of imperialism that oppresses other nations. Nevertheless, one should not think that Mussolini has any qualms against imperialism in itself, for 'imperialism is the grounding of life for every people who tends to expand economically and spiritually'.[14] And he adds that 'we [Italians] want our place in the world, we have the right to it'. Thus, in spite of the apparent rejection of 'barbarism', there seems to be no doubt that imperialism is a fundamental component of the national enterprise that Mussolini envisions. In this aspect, his words do not differ much from latter fascists and, whatever criticism he dedicates to British or French or any other imperialism it is based on the fact that they imperil Italy's interests.

Finally, the third declaration states that 'the meeting of March 23 commits the fascists to sabotage by all means the candidates of the neutralists in all parties'.[15] In sum, these final words ignite the tempers against the main rivals of the Fasci, that is, the ones who stood against Italy entering the war or that simply reject the legacy of the war. Reiterating his pride for having fought in the conflict and stating that he would do the same if need be, Mussolini almost foreshadows one feature that would soon be a distinctive one in fascist methods: the political persecution of enemies. Even if, for now, all that he talks about is 'Sabotage' and not explicit Violence, his tone is still a menacing one.[16]

Several months after the gathering at San Sepolcro, on June 6, the journal *Il Popolo d'Italia* published the program of the *Fasci Italiani di Combatimento*. In a few words, this program summarises the goals of this movement, persistently repeating the words 'WE WANT' (*NOI VOGLIAMO*). Even if this text is not part of Mussolini's speech, it is still interesting to take a quick look at it. The goals of the FIC are divided into several sections, each of them relating to different aspects and fields where the movement wants to intervene. Among them we find the following sections:

– in the political problem: the fascists want universal suffrage; a decrease in the voting age to 18 years; the abolition of the Senate; the establishment of a National Assembly in order to discuss the constitution of the state; the formation of technical National Councils in the areas of Labor, industry, transportation, social hygiene, communications, etc.

– in the social problem: the fascists want an eight-hour work schedule; a minimum wage; the participation of labour representatives in the technical functioning of Industry; the entrusting of industrial management to proletarian organisations; the reorganisation of the railways and the transport sector; the revision of the law on invalidity insurance and the reduction of the retirement age from 65 to 55.

– in the military problem: fascists aim at the institution of a national militia; nationalisation of all weapons and explosive factories; a foreign external policy that values the place of Italy in the world.

– in the financial problem: heavy progressive taxes on capital that may resemble partial expropriation; the seizure of assets from religious congregations; the revising of war supplies treaties and the seizure of 85% of the war profits.

As we can see, many of the claims contained in this political program are very distinct from what is usually seen as fascist, and even include components which had leftist leanings, such as the appeals for working class organisations to have greater control in factories. This is, therefore, an important sign that fascism at this early moment was still influenced by the goals of Revolutionary Syndicalists and other former leftists who had not yet completely rejected components of the ideologies they previously held.

### The inaugural speech at the first congress of the Fasci

The first congress of the *Fasci* took place in Florence in October 1919, after the enterprise carried out by D'Annunzio in Fiume had already begun. The first speech by Mussolini in this event was delivered on October 9 and was published in his newspaper *Il Popolo D'Italia* the following day. Speaking after the intervention by Gastone Gorieri (who had been mutilated in war) and the General Secretary of the Party, Umberto Pasella, the leader starts by apologising for not having prepared his speech. In the first place, he evokes his visit to Fiume and his thoughts on the situation and the leadership by D'Annunzio. According to him, the poet's enterprise is an accomplished fact and the powerful capitalist countries won't deny Italy's right to that territory for fear of provoking a war that no one wants. The concept of Empire thus indirectly surfaces in Mussolini's words since the acquisition of Fiume is seen as a right pertaining to Italians. In his view, it was only the cowardice of Italian politicians that forced D'Annunzio to conquer a piece of land that rightfully belonged to the country.

Mussolini then moves on to address the type of regime that shall be defended by FIC, stating that his organisation is anti-dogmatic and does not need to evaluate situations according to a set of preconceived principles, but rather according to the facts in real life. It is on this basis that the value of the monarchy or an eventual republic must be judged. He also says, apparently rejecting the Monarchy, that this 'has perhaps accomplished its function by seeking and partially succeeding in unifying Italy. Now it should be the task of the republic to unite it and regionally and socially decentralize it, to guarantee the greatness that we want in the whole of the Italian people'.[17] However, given the pragmatic principles that Mussolini himself admits to have, this apparent rejection of the monarchy shall not be taken too seriously (mostly if we have in mind that, later in its history, fascism ended up by accepting it and coexisting with it).

In the next part of his speech, Mussolini asserts his rejection of communists and its methods. While talking about the Socialist party, this leader rejects both the most revolutionary sections of this organisation (represented by Amadeo Bordiga) and the reformist ones (to which belongs Filippo Turati). In the first place, the rejection of this ideology is made on the grounds that socialists do not display enough physical strength and strength of character to aggrandise the Italian Nation: 'they do not like to fight, they do not want to fight, the iron and the fire scares them'.[18] Furthermore, they are not truly representatives of the Italian proletariat, who composes only a minority within the party and who displays a nationalist feeling and a strength of character that socialists do not have. He therefore seems to make an effort to distinguish the Italian working class from the party that claims to represent it, since the 'clique of mediocre politicians' cannot be confused with the movement of the proletariat, which has is own 'reason for living, development and fraternity'.

In another important moment, the leader of the Fasci states that 'We defend th Nation, the people as a whole', thus showing that, already in its first days, Fascism tended to see the 'People' as a homogeneous entity that identified with the Nation.[19] Lastly, Mussolini deals with the elections, discoursing about what is necessary to do in order to attain success in this electoral act. Recognizing that the *Fasci* are a new organisation lacking a base of support, he states that its political program does not represent its true essence. For that, in order to gain the support of the masses, they must not present just words to the people but accomplished deeds. And he then ends his speech by affirming his main goal: to honor the victory of Italy in the war. As he says:

> We eradicated an enemy empire that had come up to Piave and whose leaders had tried to assassinate Italy. We now have the Brenner, we have the Julian Alps and the Fiume and all the Italians from Dalmatia. We can say that between Piave and Isonzo we have destroyed an empire and determined the collapse of four autocracies.[20]

Once again, we find in this speech the interlinkage between the concepts of Empire and Nation as well as some notions still reminiscent of socialism that lead him to see the defeat of reactionary regimes as an important event.

In sum, there seems to be four main themes in this speech: territorial expansionism, the type of regime that the *Fasci* should support, the rejection of communism and the actions that were necessary in order to conquer the masses. In it, we already find some of the concepts that should later be a part of our preliminary conceptual configuration of fascism, including the idea of the Empire as a necessary outcome of national grandeur, and the rejection of communism and socialism based on the belief that they lure the working class. The pragmatic side of fascism is also evident, namely in the moment when Mussolini states his opinion about the monarchy and the republic not on the basis of a core set of definitive values, but rather on a pragmatic evaluation of what the Nation supposedly needs in a certain moment in time. This pragmatic interest for action also comes to the fore in the call for an electoral campaign focused more on accomplished facts rather than on a political program.

### *The inaugural speech at the second congress of the Fasci*

The Second Congress of Fascism was held in May 1920 in the city of Milano. This was a time when the fascist movement was beginning to gain some support among the rural regions of the Po Valley, but was still far from coming near to achieve actual political power. For our purposes, it is important to look at the introductory speech by Benito Mussolini. Right in the beginning, the Fascist leader mentions once again his interest in actual deeds, stating that words can be acts too. A she says, 'let us therefore suppose and make all the words pronounced here today are the potential actions of today and the real ones of tomorrow'.[21]

Right after that, we find two important concepts, which are usually present in fascist configurations: 'War' and 'People'. Evoking the passing of five years since the interventionist manifestations, Mussolini states that 'the cause of intervention in those weeks of May was not espoused by the socalled bourgeoisie, but by the healthiest and best part of the Italian people'.[22] He believes therefore that entering the war was a desire felt by Italian people as a whole (including the working class) and that the sentiment felt by the masses was not just the product of a maneuver by the Italian ruling class, clearly showing that he has departed from his former socialist views that see imperialist war as a tool used by the bourgeoisie. As he says, 'no one can think that the thousands of citizens that, in those days of May, followed Corridoni, were all bourgeoisie' (note the reference to Corridoni once again).[23]

Continuing talking about the war, Mussolini reasserts that having entered the conflict was a wise decision for, in spite of the maltreatment by the Allies and the cowardice of Italian politicians, war brought to Italy what it was supposed to: victory. In the following sentences, the Fascist leaders deals with the concept of 'People', more precisely with the working class, praising both rural and industrial workers who produce the goods that Italy needs. In this context, he clearly states that 'we therefore do not disregard manual work' and 'we do not represent a standpoint of reaction'.[24] This part of his speech deals with the goal of bringing back the working class to the nationalist cause and makingit reject socialist and communist ideas. He insists that his fight is only against the Socialist Party and its defeatist ideology but not against workers themselves, something recurrent in many other fascist leaders. His attitude towards the Italian people is then expressed in the following words, 'we can't however go against the people because it was the people who fought the war. The peasants who today move to solve the agrarian question cannot be regarded by us with antipathy'.[25]

Displaying an apparent sympathy for the Italian poorest classes, Mussolini also praises the role of the Fascists in preventing the communists from taking power and avoiding that Italy knew the same faith as Russia. Recognizing then that the Nation may be in a state of lassitude after the war and after the attempt of takeover by the Bolsheviks, the Fascist leader still affirms his belief that soon the conflict will be fairly judged by the people. In this context, he says that 'within some time the psychology of the people will be changed and all or a great part of the Italian people will recognise the moral value of the victory; all the Italian people will honor their fighters and will fight the governments that did not want to guarantee the future of the nation'.[26] The speech then ends with a last paragraph in which Mussolini praises the value of the *arditi* and their courage while fighting for Italy at the risk of their lives.

In sum, what we find in this short speech is that a great relevance is given to the concepts of 'People' and Violence (which is expressed in Mussolini's praise for the war and for the grandeur that it can bring to the Italian Nation). We see a conception of the Nation as an entity that shall not be divided by class struggle and, at the same time, a desire not to separate the working class from national enterprises, which is also accompanied by a rejection of the idea that nationalist values belong only to the bourgeoisie. The opposition between 'Elitism' and 'Populism' is somehow evident, even if not directly. Mussolini seems to have no qualms in affirming both his admiration for the masses (who are capable of fighting for the Nation) and the elites constituted by the *Arditti*, who represent the best elements within the people.

### *The founding of the PNF*

The movement founded by Benito Mussolini witnessed an incredible growth in the year of 1920, when the social unrest led to an increasing of support among landowners in the northern regions of Italy. This in its turn led to a bigger influence of conservative thinking in the fascist movement, but one must not forget that the contradictions and rivalries between different factions were still there. When the leadership of Mussolini himself was being called into question, mostly by local leaders known as 'Ras', the unrest within the movement was enough to justify the gathering of a fascist congress (actually, the third) in Rome, between the 7th and 9th of November, 1921. It was in this congress that the FCI was officially transformed into the National Fascist Party. In the context of our study, it is relevant to verify what Mussolini said in his speech on November 8, an intervention in which he talked about the new program of the fascists.

Right in the beginning of his declarations he says: 'let us move on to the most feasible aura and claim our program, for which I am willing to battle without company'.[27] The first important step for him, therefore, is to mention the different political organisations that existed in Italy and see what distinguishes them from Fascism. In the lines that follow, Mussolini mentions the anarchists (whose coherence and condemnation of bolshevism he apparently admires), the communists (whose advocacy for class dictatorship he rejects) and the socialists (whose party 'is based on misunderstandings and makes us sick' with Mussolini even suggesting that not even Filippo Turati believes in his party anymore). This time, when opposing the Marxist conception of the State, he claims not to reject a dictatorship and a strong State, as long as it is based along the lines of the Nation and not class. As we can see, Mussolini's conceptions of the State by this time resembles those of the other fascist leaders and that of the generic configuration.

After this, he mentions the Republican Party, whose liberal traditions and national heroes like Mazzini and Garibaldi deserve Mussolini's respect. For this reason, the fascists can integrate some Mazzinian concepts in their ideology, but cannot forget that Republicans too are 'troubled by crisis'. However, while acknowledging the legacy of Republican liberalism, he rejects its concept of 'Democracy', for it seems to be no longer a valid option for an Italy where the masses are not interested in the electoral process. As he states, 'among eleven millions of electors, only six come to vote and often for alcoholic or monetary reasons'.[28] Because of this, democratic parties are like 'captains without soldiers.' At this point, we can notice in Mussolini a certain contempt for the masses and a skepticism in their capacity to participate in society (something that is common to most fascist ideologues).

Lastly, Mussolini mentions the Popular Party, whose sense of discipline seems to ape the fascist movement. This party is also an enemy of fascism because there are still many supporters of neutralism in it. He even compares it to bolshevism, stating that the *Popolari* can be seen as a kind of Migliolino Bolshevism (a reference to the Christian syndicalist Guido Miglioli), due to its work in sabotaging national enterprises. Judging from these statements, there seems to be no party with which the fascists fully agree.

After this first part, in which Mussolini displays what he is opposed to, that is, the rejections of fascism, the speech comes to the part where the leader reveals the positive features of his political ideology. Not surprisingly, the first concept that appears is that of Nation, with Mussolini praising the grandeur of Italian history and its people:

> The Italian people have a great history. It is enough to come down to Rome to feel that twenty or thirty centuries ago it was the center of the world and the Italians of the last centuries were great in arts, literature and business. From its people the genius of Dante and Napoleon expressed.[29]

The Nation is the starting point in Mussolini's conceptual morphology, and he himself acknowledges this when he says that 'we start from the concept of nation, which is a fact that for us cannot be erased neither overtaken'.[31] Furthermore, the 'People' interlinks with the Nation and is seen as a unity that cannot be divided, which is why this leader opposes any type of separatism. He also says that 'Fascism must want that within the borders there are no more Venetians, Romagnoli, Tuscans, Sicilians and Sardinians; but Italians, only Italians'. [32] That this unity of the 'People' is a precondition for the greatness of Italy to be achieved is a feature that resembles future fascists, namely Primo de Rivera. In another passage, Mussolini also vehemently rejects Marxism and the division of the 'People' according to class, since 'Class Struggle' is a fable and 'Proletariat and bourgeoisie do not exist in the history; they are both rings of the same formation'.[33]

This praise for the Nation is also accompanied by a complete rejection of the concept of 'Internationalism', for 'we are in antithesis against all internationalisms'.[34] Such Internationalism represents a dangerous utopia that can only imperil the survival of Italy. The dream of building an international humanitarian union is 'not based on reality' and is not desired by the people and for that reason it cannot be adopted either with a Wilsonist liberal point of view or with bolshevist revolutionary principles.

Starting with the Nation, Mussolini then arrives at the concept of State, which in his view must always be identified with the Nation. The whole world experiences a crisis of the State (at least the liberal decontestations of the State), says Mussolini, and for this reason 'it is necessary that the State rediscovers its authority', for only thus can the descent into chaos be avoided. This is why fascism is needed (at this point Mussolini strongly resembles Mosley and its defense of fascism as the solution for a national crisis). In relation to the regime, if in the past the fascist movement defended the establishment of a Republic, that seems not to be the case anymore: whether Italy should have a monarchy or a republic is a question about which fascism should remain neutral in principle, eventually supporting one of those regimes according to the national necessities of the moment (as he already had said in a previous speech that we analysed).

Nevertheless, when it comes to economic matters, one notices that the concept of Corporatism does not seem to be present in Mussolini's words. In fact, while definitely rejecting any kind of socialist conception of economy (and stating that he definitely left his socialist past behind him), Mussolini seems to be incredibly close to ultra-liberal views: the State should have a minimal role when it comes to guiding the economy and not transform itself into an autocratic and monopolist State. It should leave to private property the role of making the national economy evolve. The difference with the other fascist leaders that we analysed is striking, for all of them, even when rejecting the monopolist State and conceding a role to private initiative (or even in the cases that do not make much use of the concept of Corporatism), still thought that it was necessary for the State to serve at least as a guide in harmonising the different elements in the productive process. The rejection of the main tenets of the Charter of Carnaro (which had outlined the first Corporatist system in Fiume) may be one more sign that Mussolini was not yet ready to place Corporatism at the core of such an important public intervention.

The concepts of Authority and 'Elitism' also appear when Mussolini talks about the masses and their role in history. 'There are those who say: history is made by heroes; others say it is made by the masses', he affirms.[35] What we find once again is the opposition between the concepts of 'Populism' and 'Elitism', with Mussolini stating that he opts for a point of view that is in the middle of these two interpretations: both the people and heroic elites can contribute to the making of history, depending on the occasions. Nevertheless, leaders have a special role to play in the reinvigoration of the Nation since they must educate the masses, raising their intellectual level and improving their skills. One of these individual heroes who deserve the praise of Mussolini is Gabriel D'Annunzio, the poet who had recently tried to annex the region of Fiume.

The concept of Empire is not addressed in length, but Mussolini praises Francesco Crispi and his imperialistic thinking towards the Mediterraneum. He also eulogises former types of economic imperialism and states that 'Those peoples who one day, deprived of their will, shut themselves up in their house, are the ones who are going to die' (in this point, he comes close to what later will be found in La Dottrina el Fascismo).[36] it is possible to note that Mussolini believes that the historical times in which the Italian Nation had lived its best moments was when it had tried to expand its influence abroad, even if at times this was expressed through some type of economic imperialism that had the goal of expanding trade rather than with actual conquering of land. As to the concept of Violence, it makes its appearance when Mussolini indicates that he still sees wars as events that can bring about positive changes. However, he says that 'we don't exalt war for war's sake, just like we don't exalt peace for peace's sake. We exalt that war that in 1915 was wanted by the people, by us, against everyone'.[37] World War I thus remains in Mussolini's view as a supreme event that united all the Nation and was supposedly wanted by the whole of its people. It is the prototype of the type of conflict that can help to reinvigorate the Nation and create a national awareness among the masses that would not emerge otherwise. Lastly, what would later be called the Fascist Revoution is already noticeable when the Fascist leader talks about a 'spirituality' that is necessary to make Italians proud of belonging to their Nation. Such 'spirituality', as he acknowledges, may very well be found in the Charter of Carnaro, even if Mussolini rejects its concrete proposals.

As we shall see in the next section, this is the speech in which we find the configuration that comes the closest to our generic configuration, since almost all relevant concepts make their appearance. This may therefore be seen as a sign that the process of formation through which fascist ideology was going was reaching its conclusion.

## Concluding remarks

This analysis of Mussolini's speeches is, as we know, different from what we have done in the previous chapters. In this chapter, we did not deal with a single text but rather with several moments in which the Italian leader spoke to the masses. In such occasions, Mussolini's goal is not to display a doctrinal core but rather to instill in his audience a will to further believe in the fascist cause. Therefore, we shall have in mind that in these texts we find examples of invectives to action and early attempts of using myths to mobilise the masses. That is seen in the moments when Mussolini evokes the war as an event of grandeur, as something that the masses will sooner or later acknowledge as a truly heroic happening. In these myths and calls to action, we find what Garau calls the metapolitical drive and the mentality of the Fascist ideology. However, in our analysis, we focused more on Mussolini's doctrinal core and the concepts that were part of it, just like we did with the other fascist leaders.

What we tried to do was to shed a glimpse on the process of ideological reconfiguration in the formative years of fascist ideology, when Mussolini had not yet formed a complete conceptual morphology, and was still struggling to find a path for the movement that he founded a few years after ceasing to be a socialist. This earlier stage of the movement explains why we find themes that seem to belong to other ideologies, for instance, when Mussolini justifies WWI in a way that the interventionist left could also use: it served to stop the spreading of reactionary and aristocratic regimes in Europe. We argue that, from the moment of the foundation of Fascism, and in spite of all the reconfigurations that were still to happen, it is possible to find in Mussolini's ideology some of the main concepts and interlinkages that are part of Fascist ideology, namely the interlinkage between the concepts of Nation and Empire, as well as the use of the concept of Violence, mainly through the reference to war and to the grandeur that WWI brought to Italy.

However, it is in the last speech that, when dealing with the formation of the Party, it is possible to disentangle a much more coherent and fully formed fascist morphology. In it), Mussolini presents to his listeners a coherent political ideology that can be compared with our preliminary generic configuration. By doing so, we can conclude that, by 1921, all the core concepts seem to be present in Mussolini's thought: Nation, State, Empire, Violence and, in a certain way, even Revolution. There is, however, one important exception: the concept of Corporatism. Nevertheless, we argue that, even in regard to it, Mussolini already made use of the concept of 'Class Conciliation', which we found in several other leaders. After all, even in speeches delivered before the foundation of the party, the fascist leader had already shown his preoccupation with the idea of bringing back the working class to the nationalist cause and fight the influence that socialism had over it. In the last speech, he goes as far as denying 'Class Struggle', and then, to praise the 'People' as an indivisible unity. Thus, even if it is true that the concept of Corporatism in Italian Fascism only acquired its most influential decontestation during the regime phase (mostly thanks to the contribution of the ANI and its ideologues), it is also true that the rearrangements of Mussolini's ideology from the very beginning carried with them the necessity for this concept to be inserted. It is the goal of creating a holistic Nation and a holistic people, unaffected by class divisions, that can make us understand why Corporatism would definitely come closer to the core of Fascism during the regime. The implications that this brings to our configuration will finally be discussed in the next chapter.

## Notes

1 During his socialist years, Mussolini met some important figures of 20th century socialism, including Angelica Balabanov, and reportedly even Vladimir Lenin. It seems that the leader of the Russian Bolsheviks later lamented that Italian socialists had lost him to fascism.

2 The view that Mussolini was more interested in power than in ideas is also held by the following authors: Dennis Mack Smith, *Mussolini: A Biography* (New York, Borzoi Book, 1982); Richard J. Bosworth, *Mussolini* (Oxford, Oxford University Press, 2002).

3 The words by Gentile are worth quoting in its entirety. In his view, Mussolini's ideology included: 'a) A vision of politics subjectively conceived as art, meaning as an individual intuition of appropriate circumstances to be molded by the politician's will; objectively simply as a show of force and a clash of interests and ambitions; b) the transformation of ideas into myths, in the Sorelian sense of the word, or into key ideas as in Le Bon, in order to excite the passions of the crowds, to acquire their allegiance and push into taking action; c) contempt for the masses, but with a realistic evaluation of their political importance in modern society, not believing in their ability to change into autonomous forms of collective awareness; d) a vision of history as a cycle of hierarchies, aristocracies and elites, fundamentally made up of energetic and wilful minorities without any precise goal for their evolution; e)the possibility of social palengenesis or revolutions made possible by great leaders, viewed as in Nietzsche as new men, living and operating beyond and above the accepted rules of morality; f) pessimistic and skeptical views of humanitarian and social values, about the nature of man viewed as in Machiavelli, to be drawn towards evil if they are not subjected to a superior power dominating them and imposing the order of a State'. Emilio Gentile, *The Origins of Fascist Ideology: 1918–1925* (New York, Enigma Books, 2005 [1975]), 3.

4 A. James Gregor, *Young Mussolini and the Intellectual Origins of Fascism* (Berkeley, University of California Press, 1979), xi.

5 This refers to the kidnapping and killing of Socialist deputy Giacomo Matteotti a few days after he had accused the fascists of committing electoral frauds in a speech in the Italian parliament.

6 Translated by the author from the original in Italian: 'Vi dico subito che non possiamo scendere ai dettagli. Volendo agire prendiamo la realtà nelle sue grandi linee, senza seguirla minutamente nei suoi particolari'. Benito Mussolini, 'Atto di nascita del fascismo' in Edoardo Susmel and Duilio Susmel, Eds., *Opera Omnia*, Vol.XII (Firenze, La Fenice, 1961), 321.

7 'L'adunata del 23 marzo rivolge il suo primo saluto e il suo memore e reverente pensiero ai figli d'Italia che sono caduti per la grandezza della Patria e per la libertà del Mondo, ai mutilati e invalidi, a tutti *i* combattenti, agli ex-prigionieri che compirono il loro dovere, e si dichiara pronta a sostenere energicamente le rivendicazioni d'ordine materiale e morale che saran propugnate dalle associazioni dei combattenti'. Ibid., 321.

8 'La guerra ha dato, malgrado certi dettagli che possono urtare gli elementi più o meno intelligenti, tutto quello che chiedevamo'. Ibid., 322.

9 'Da questo punto di vista noi possiamo affermare con piena sicurezza che la Patria oggi è più grande: non solo perché giungé al Brennero -dove giunge Ergisto Bezzi a cui rivolgo il saluto *(ovazione)* – non solo perché va alla Dalmazia. Ma è più grande l'Italia anche se le piccole anime tentano un loro piccolo giuoco; è più grande perché noi ci sentiamo più grandi in quanto abbiamo l'esperienza di questa guerra, inquantoché noi l'abbiamo voluta, non ci è stata imposta, e potevamo evitarla'. Ibid., 322.

10 'Questa gioventù meravigliosa che è andata al fronte e che là è rimasta'. Ibid., 322.

11 Former Revolutionary Syndicalist Fillipo Corridoni adhered to leftist interventionism after the beginning of the world conflict. Having died during the battle, he later became one of the most important symbols of the Fascist regime,

often evoked as an example of a fallen soldier who gave his life for the Italian nation.
12 'L'adunata del 23 marzo dichiara di opporsi all'imperialismo degli altri popoli a danno dell'Italia e all'eventuale. imperialismo italiano a danno di altri popoli; accetta il postulato supremo della Società delle Nazioni che presuppone l'integrazione di ognuna di esse, integrazione che per quanto riguarda l'Italia deve realizzarsi sulle Alpi e sull'Adriatico colla: rivendicazione e annessione di Fiume e della Dalmazia'. Benito Mussolini, 'Atto di nascita del fascismo' Ibid., 323.
13 Two days before, on the 23rd of March, Mussolini had already stated at the Piazza di San Sepolcro that 'our action will be against every form of dictatorship that can only lead to a new manifestation of barbarity; and our revolution, if inevitable, shall have a Roman and Latin imprint, without the tartaric or muscovite influence'*.* 'La nostra azione sarà contro ogni forma di dittatura che non potrebbe sboccare che *in* una nuova manifestazione di barbarie; e la nostra rivoluzione, se sarà inevitabile, deve avere impronta romana e latina, senza influenze tartariche e moscovite'.
14 'L'imperialismo.è il fondamento della vita per ogni popolo che tende ad espandersi economicamente e spiritualmente'. Benito Mussolini, 'Atto di nascita del fascismo'. Ibid., 323.
15 'L'adunata del 23 marzo impegna i fascisti a sabotare con tutti i mezzi le candidature· dei neutralisti di tutti i Partiti'. Ibid., 323.
16 Note that the first punitive expedition by members of the *Fasci* would take place few days later against the headquarters of journal *Avanti!*.
17 'La monarchia ha forse compiuto la sua funzione cercando ed in parte riuscendo ad unificare l'Italia. Ora dovrebbe essere compito della repubblica di unirla e decentrarla regionalmente e socialmente, di garantire la grandezza che noi vogliamo di tutto il popolo italiano'. Benito Mussolini, 'I Diritti della Vittoria' in Edoardo Susmel and Duilio Susmel, Eds., *Opera Omnia,* Vol.XIV (Firenze, La Fenice, 1961), 52.
18 'Essi non amano battersi, non vogliono battersi, il ferro e il fuoco li spaventa'. Ibid., 53.
19 'Noi difendiamo la nazione, il popolo nel suo complesso'. Ibid., 53.
20 'Noi abbiamo debellato un impero nemico che ·era giunto fino al Piave ed i cui dirigenti avevano tentato di assassinare l'Italia. Noi abbiamo ora il Brennero, abbiamo' le Alpi Giulie e Fiume e tutti gJi italiani della Dalmazia. Noi possiamo dire che tra Piave e Isonzo abbiamo distrutto un impero e determinato il' crollo di quattro autocrazi'. Ibid., 54.
21 'Supponiamo dunque e facciamo sì che tutte. le parole pronunciate qui oggi siano delle azioni potenziali dell'oggi e reali del domani'. Benito Mussolini, 'Discorso Inaugurale al Secondo Congresso dei Fasci' in Edoardo Susmel and Duilio Susmel, Eds., *Opera Omnia,* Vol.XIV (Firenze, La Fenice, 1961), 466.
22 'la causa dell'intervento nelle settimane del maggio non fu sposata dalia cosiddetta borghesia, ma dalla parte più sana e migliore del popolo italiano'. Ibid., 466.
23 'Perché nessuno può pensare che le migliaia di cittadini, che, nelle giornate di maggio, seguivano Corridoni, fossero tutti dei borghesi'. Ibid., 466.
24 'Non dunque spregio al lavoro manuale [...] noi non rappresentiamo un punto de reazioni'. Ibid., 467.
25 'Noi non possiamo però andare contro ii popolo, perché è il popolo quello che ha fatto la guerra. I contadini che oggi si agitano per risolvere il problema terriero non possono essere da noi guardati con antipatia'. Ibid., 466.
26 'Ma fra qualche tempo la psicologia del popolo sarà mutata e tutto o gran parte del popolo italiano riconoscerà il valore morale e materiale della vittoria; tutto il

popolo italiano onorerà i suoi combattenti e combatterà quei Governi che non volessero garantire l'avvenire della nazione'. Ibid., 466.
27 'Eleviamoci a più spirabili aure e padiamo del nostro programma, sul quale sono disposto a battermi senza quartiere'. Benito Mussolini, 'Discorso Inaugurale al Secondo Congresso dei Fasci' in Edoardo Susmel and Duilio Susmel, Eds., *Opera Omnia,* Vol.XVII (Firenze, La Fenice, 1961), 216.
28 'Sopra undici milioni di elettori, sei soli vanno. a votare e spesso per ragioni alcooliche e pecuniarie'. Ibid., 218.
29 'Il popolo italiano ha una grande storia. Basta. scendere a Roma per sentire che venti e trenta secoli fa era il centro del mondo e· gli italiani riei secoli passati furono grandi nelle arti, nelle lettere e nei commerci. Dal loro popolo espressero il genio di Dante e di Napoleone'. Ibid., 222.
30 'Il fascismo deve volere che dentro i confini non vi siano più veneti, romagnoli, toscani, siciliani e sardi; ma italiani, solo italiani'. Ibid, 218.
31 '*Noi* partiamo dal concetto dì nazione', che è per noi un fatto, né cancellabile, né superabile'. Ibid, 223.
32 'Il fascismo deve volere che dentro i confini non vi siano più veneti, romagnoli, toscani, siciliani e sardi; ma italiani, solo italiani.' Ibid., 218.
33 'Proletariato e borghesia non esistono nella storia; sono entrambi anelli della stessa formazione'. Ibid., 220.
34 'Siamo quindi in antitesi contro tutti gli internazionalismi'. Ibid., 218.
35 'C'è chi· dice anche: la storia è fatta dagli eroi; altri dice che è fatta dalle masse'. Ibid., 224.
36 'Quei popoli che un giorno, privi di volontà, si rinchiudono in casa, sono quelli c,he si avviano 'alla morte'. Ibid., 218.
37 'Non esaltiamo la guerra per la guerra, come nòn esaltiamo la pace per la pace. Noi esaltiamo quella guerra che nel 1915 fu voluta dal popolo; da noi, contro tutti!!' Ibid., 223.

## List of References

Adamson, Walter L., 'Modernism and Fascism: The Politics of Culture in Italy, 1903–1922' in Michael Neiberg,, Ed., *Fascism* (London, Routledge, 2006), 1–32

Bosworth, Richard J., *Mussolini* (Oxford, Oxford University Press, 2002).

Bosworth, Richard J., *Mussolini's Italy: Life Under the Fascist Dictatorship, 1915–1945* (London, Penguin Books, 2007).

Burgwyn, H. James, *The Legend of the Mutilated Victory: Italy, the Great War, and the Paris Peace Conference, 1915–1919* (Westport, Greenwood Press, 1993).

Carsten, Francis Ludwig, *The Rise of Fascism* (Berkeley, University of California Press, 1982).

Cassels, Alan, *Fascism in Italy* (London, Harlan Davidson, 1985).

Clark, Martin, *Mussolini* (London, Routledge, 2005).

Felice, Renzo di, *Mussolini Il Rivoluzionario, 1883–1920* (Torino, Einaudi, 1965).

Fonzo, Erminio, *Storia Dell'Associazione Nazionalista Italiana (1910–1923)* (Napoli, Edizioni scientifiche italiane, 2017).

Gallo, Max, *Mussolini's Italy: Twenty Years of the Fascist Era* (New York, Macmillan, 1973).

Garau, Salvatore, *Fascism and Ideology: Italy, Britain and Norway* (London, Routledge, 2015).

Gentile, Emilio, *The Origins of Fascist Ideology: 1918–1925* (New York, Enigma Books, 2005 [1975]).

Gregor, A. James, *Young Mussolini and the Intellectual Origins of Fascism* (Berkeley, University of California Press, 1979).
Leeden, Michael, *D'Annunzio: The First Duce* (London, Routledge, 2001).
Leeds, Christopher, *Italy Under Mussolini* (Hove, East Sussex, Wayland, 1988).
Lyttelton, Adrian, *The Seizure of Power: Fascism Ini Italy, 1919–1929* (London, Routledge, 2009).
Milza, Pierre, *Mussolini* (Roma, Carocci, 2000).
Morgan, Philip, *Italian Fascism, 1915-1945* (London, Palgrave Macmillan, 2003).
Morgan, Philip, *The Fall of Mussolini: Italy, the Italians, and the Second World War* (Oxford, Oxford University Press, 2008).
Moseley, Ray, *Mussolini: The Last 600 Days of Il Duce* (Lanham, Taylor Trade Publications, 2004).
Musiedlak, Didier, *Mussolini* (Paris, Les Presses de Sciences Po, 2004).
Mussolini, Benito, 'Atto di nascita del fascismo' in Edoardo Susmel, and Duilio Susmel,, Eds., *Opera Omnia*, Vol. XII (Firenze, La Fenice, 1961), 321–327.
Mussolini, Benito, 'I Diritti della Vitoria' in Edoardo Susmel, and Duilio Susmel, ,Eds., *Opera Omnia*, Vol. XIV (Firenze, La Fenice, 1961), 50–55.
Mussolini, Benito, 'Discorso Inaugurale al Secondo Congresso dei Fasci' in Edoardo Susmel, and Duilio Susmel, ,Eds., *Opera Omnia*, Vol. XIV (Firenze, La Fenice, 1961), 466–471.
Payne, Stanley, *A History of Fascism: 1914–1945* (Madison, Wisconsin University Press, 1995).
Pini, Giorgio and Duilio Susmel, *Mussolini: L'Uomo e l'Opera* (Firenze, La Fenice, 1953).
Smith, Denis Mack, *Mussolini: A Biography* (New York, Borzoi Book, 1982).
Sternhell, Zeev, *The Birth of Fascist Ideology* (Princeton, Princeton University Press, 1994).

# 9 Final considerations about the conceptual configuration of generic fascism

Having come this far, we are now prepared to move on to the last phase of this study, which consists of a general reflection that includes the conclusions at which we have arrived in each chapter. All the leaders that have been analysed will now be evoked once again in order to allow for a redefinition of our first conceptual approach, which can thus be put to test. Therefore, in the next sections we will discuss the core concepts of our configuration and try to verify if the status of central features that we previously attributed to them can be confirmed. We shall also not forget to mention the following points: important interlinkages highlighted by our reading of the leaders; adjacent concepts that we may have overlooked in our first configuration; marginal concepts; concepts that explain either permeability or rejection between fascism and other ideologies, and the main tensions and contradictions of the fascist morphology. If it is needed, we will alter our first configuration, redefining core or adjacent concepts, and after doing that, we will try to arrive at a definition of fascism that is based on core concepts. This shall consist of a phrase that reunites all the concepts of the generic configuration, bringing them together with the purpose of making our definition of fascism easier to understand. We shall also note that, since most of the important information about fascism was presented throughout the book, this chapter will rely less on secondary sources and rather base itself on the core primary sources that were used throughout the last seven chapters.

### The core concepts of fascism

Most of the concepts introduced in the first generic configuration clearly belong to the core of fascist ideology and cannot be left out without it being transformed into something else. There is absolutely no doubt, for instance, that the Nation is at the core of fascism, since all the leaders dwell on it and place it at the centre of all their preoccupations. For this reason, the goals of every leader somehow relate to the Nation and to some type of social transformation to be performed in it: even Adolf Hitler, who uses the concept of 'Race' more frequently, shows that that this is the key concept for comprehending his visions about the evolution of society: 'first, I became a nationalist. Second, I learned to understand and grasp the true meaning of history'.[1] Oswald Mosley is also as clear as one can be when he says that 'we are essentially a national movement, and if our policy could be summarized in two words, they would be *Britain First*'.[2]

Even in the case of Benito Mussolini, when he had just founded the first fascist movement and had not yet formed the conceptual configuration of his new ideology, we notice his complete dedication to the cause of Italian nationalism and to the goal of restoring the greatness of Italy. This is, therefore, a clear sign that this concept was part of fascism from its very beginning, which attests for its importance and centrality in the morphology. Likewise, in the case of Marcel Déat, who was writing during the Nazi occupation of his country , there is an effort to conciliate his broader European views with French nationalism and to prove that 'choosing Europe is not the same as abandoning France, quite the contrary'.[3]

One of the most important concepts that appears in the adjacency of this core concept is 'Organicism', for the Nation must be 'organized as the human body' and 'every part fulfils its function as a member of the whole, performing its separate task, and yet, by performing it, contributing to the welfare of the whole', as it is quoted in the book by Mosley.[4] The hypothesis that this is an adjacent concept of the Nation was outlined in the first configuration and seems now to have been confirmed after the reading of leaders like Francisco Rolão Preto, in whose configuration 'Organicism' acquires a particularly relevant role. Some configurations make use of a concept that resembles this one and which is 'Holism', that is, unity and homogeneity. The importance of this concept is noticeable whenever fascist leaders state to have the goal of creating a national unity that is not disturbed by internal conflicts and divisions. In José Antonio Primo de Rivera, for instance, this adjacent concept expresses itself when the leader refers to Spain as a 'unity of destiny', but it is in Corneliu Codreanu that it acquires its most idiosyncratic meaning. According to this leader, the Nation is a spiritual and metaphysical entity that surpasses space and time and encompasses 'all Romanians, alive and dead, who have lived on this land from the beginning of history and will live here also in the future'.[5] Related to the holistic conceptions of the Nation, one finds the concept of 'People' in many of the leaders, including in Hitler (who writes about the 'Volk') and Mussolini (who even gave the name of *Il Popolo d'Italia* to his newspaper). A leader like Déat, for instance, prefers to use the word 'Community' instead, but this has a meaning that is very similar to that of 'People' in the generic configuration.

Given that adjacent concepts fulfil the task of delimiting the meaning of core concepts, the three concepts that were just presented make us conclude that the fascist type of nationalism is a 'organic, holistic and populist nationalism'. However, these features may not have the same preponderance in all the configurations. Even though our analysis of a single work for each leader does not allow us to draw very in-depth conclusions, it is possible to notice that 'Organicism' was not highlighted in the chapter dedicated to Adolf Hitler, which does not mean that it is not possible to find organicist conceptions in his book but rather that the conceptions of the 'holistic folk' have a greater prominence in his permutation of fascism.[6] In this context, it is interesting to outline the hypothesis of discerning two important varieties of fascism based on the main adjacent concept that surrounds the Nation, which can either be 'Organicism' or 'Holistic Folk'. Belonging to the former, we find Mosley, Rolão Preto, Primo de Rivera and Déat; while the latter includes the case of Hitler (since we have not carried out a thourough analysis of Mussolini, we canot be sure about him). Such a hypothesis does not presuppose that the two concepts are mutually exclusive but rather that a different prominence is given to each in the different varieties. Nevertheless, this is a hypothesis that, to be confirmed, would require a more thorough reading of fascist sources, not just those of the leaders, and for this reason we will do nothing more than outlining it here and hope to latter confirm it in a future research. Let us only state that it would be tempting to include Codreanu in the same variety as Hitler, since he also makes use of racist and biologist conceptions. However, his focus on spiritual and metaphysical matters places him apart from all other leaders and rather inserts him in a unique variant of fascist ideology.

Lastly, we shall pay attention to the concept of 'Race', which was also referred in the generic configuration, and which is used by several leaders even if with different degrees of proportion, including Codreanu, and Déat. However, it is in the case of Hitler that one finds the configuration in which this concept is given the highestpriority. In no other leader, not even Codreanu, one finds such explicit racist conceptions acquiring a closer proximity to the core. At times, Hitler even seems to replace Nation for 'Race', which could mean that his configuration acquires such a distinctive figure that it cannot really be considered a permutation of fascism. However, we argue that that is not case and that the prominence given to racism does not mean that Hitler leaves aside the concept of Nation, but rather that the Nation is defined according to racial principles. In this sense, if one wonders what to do with the concept of 'Race' in the conceptual configuration of fascist, the best answer is that it is a marginal concept that many times comes closer to the core. Racism is somehow always present in fascist ideology, even if only implicitly and even if it sometimes does not seem relevant enough to define the core features of some permutations. In the end, the concept of the 'People' as a homogeneous entity is clearly prone to let itself be permeated by the concept of 'Race', and for this reason, we will sometimes see it having a much important role, not only in the permutations that make use of it from the very beginning but also in the variants that ended up by bringing racism closer to the core even if it was not there at the start (which is the case of Italian Fascism, which in the 30s adopted a racist view of society).

Moving on, one finds that the concept of State is also a core one, for all the leaders dedicate some thought to it and see it as a fundamental component of the new society that they aim tocreate. The State, which in the words of Déat is a 'keeper of order and authority', is the instrument that has the function of conducting and organizing the life of the Nation in accordance with organic principles. In the words of Rolão Preto, it must 'conduct the gears of the national life'.[7] For this reason, the State is compared to a gardener in the case of Déat and to an arbiter in the case of Rolão Preto, while maintaining in its adjacency concepts such as 'Organicism', 'Holism', 'Order' and 'Dirigisme', as we also saw in our generic configuration. As to the concept of 'Totalitarianism', even though it is explicitly referred by Déat , we shall, after all, leave it aside and rather discuss some of it simplications when talking about the concept of Corporatism (even if not explicitly using the word 'Totalitarianism').

In the case of Hitler, there is a close interlinkage between 'Race'/'Volk' and State, and sometimes this may seem to indicate that, in his ideology, this concept is not truly a central one but rather a concept that is adjacent to the Nation and the 'Race'. For the rest, the Nazi leader conceives the role of the Racial State in a manner that is different from that of other leaders and specifically sees it as a tool that shall serve not only to harmonise the Nation but mostly to zeal for the interests and survival of the Aryan race. In his words, 'the fundamental principle is that the State is not an end in itself but the means to an end' and 'it will be the task of the People's State to make the race the center of the life of the community'.[8] Coming to the conclusion that the State is not central in Hitler's ideology could have impactful consequences to our generic configuration, for it would be enough proof that this is not a core concept. Nevertheless, we do not propose to leave this concept aside and further assert that, even in the case of Hitler's morphology, the State can be analysed as a crucial element, since his conceptualisation is clearly in line with that of other fascists that dedicate some time to discuss the failure of the liberal state and the necessity of replacing it with a stronger and more powerful State apparatus (even if in the case of Nazism the concept of 'Race' is always in its adjacency). In the end, it is possible to conclude that all fascists somehow eulogised State power and that this was one of their fundamental characteristics, and that Hitler is not an exception to this.

Three other core concepts of the generic configuration shall be now briefly mentioned, for their status as fundamental features of fascism is easy to demonstrate: they are Revolution, Authority and Violence. They all make their appearance in every configuration (even Mussolini) , sometimes in a very similar manner. Thus, in relation to the concept of Revolution, all the leaders insert in its vicinity the adjacent concepts of 'Palingenesis', 'New Man' and 'Cult of Youth'. That the goal of the fascist Revolution is the creation of a new heroic and virile type of human being is perhaps best noticeable in Codreanu, when this leader says that 'from this legionary school a new man will have to emerge, a man with heroic qualities; a giant of our history to do battle and win over all the enemies of our Fatherland'.[9] As to 'Palingenesis', this idea is so recurrent in every configuration that it hardly needs any further comment. Perhaps the best example of such a sense of decaying, if we exclude Mosley, is given to us by Primo de Rivera, when he describes the supposed decadence of the Spanish high classes in the last centuries and uses it as a symbol of the crisis of the Nation. In his view, the modern 'señoritos' are a 'degeneration of the 'señor', of the noble that wrote, and until very recently, the best pages of our history'.[10]

As to the concept of Authority, it appears in the leader's morphology to denote a very hierarchical view of society, in which elites and a charismatic leader always have a role to play in guiding and educating the masses. For this reason, one can reassert that the concepts that one finds in the adjacency of Authority are 'Hierarchy', 'Elites' and 'Leader'. It is because of the concept of Authority that Déat writes that 'discipline and selection will be the rule' in his party.[11] But perhaps the most elitist of all the leaders that we saw was the Spanish Primo de Rivera, who at times displays his contempt for a people that is not capable of carrying out a national Revolution without the guidance of prescient leaders that are part of a 'determined minority'.[12] One of the most original features of the elitist conception of fascism is that this ideology does not purpose to defend the perpetuation of the elites that already exist, since it rather aims at creating a new elite, formed by heroic men that can sometimes have humble origins but can nonetheless ascend to the highest positions thanks to what Codreanu sees as a process of 'social selection' of elites.

The importance of Violence is also straightforward., Its functions in the generic configuration can be simplified by saying that it can display three dimensions, each of them interlinking with one main adjacent concept: Violence as a device to be used against the enemies of the Nation, in which case it has in its adjacency the concept of 'Eliminationism'; Violence as a force of creation and regeneration, in which case it interlinks with the adjacent concept of 'Palingenesis'; Violence as a principle that explains the fascist worldview, in which case it has in its vicinity the adjacent concept of 'Social Darwinism'. The eliminationist side of fascist leaders reaches its most virulent features in Hitler, thanks to the prominence that is given to the concept of 'Anti-Semitism' in his morphology. The German leader comes close to literally defend the physical elimination of this supposed racial enemy, but in this feature he is closely followed by Corneliu Codreanu, who also frequently defends the use of violent methods against Jews.[13] That Violence shall also play a part in the palingenetic transformation of the Nation can be seen, for instance, when Mosley writes about the fascist Revolution and says that "in such a situation, new ideas will not come peacefully; they will come violently, as they have come elsewhere'.[14] However, the most interesting feature of fascist Violence is when this concept reveals itself to be at the basis of their conception of society. For

## Final considerations about the conceptual configuration 211

instance, it is because he sees the world as a place of struggle between good and evil, that Codreanu starts his book by saying that he is writing in the middle of a battle. But this characteristic is nowhere as evident as in the case of Hitler, who sees struggle as a component of human life that is instilled by nature itself. He even says that 'man must realize that a fundamental law of necessity reigns throughout the whole realm of Nature and that his existence is subject to the law of eternal struggle and strife'.[15]

However, the concept of Corporatism seems to be a more complex one. It is undeniable that this concept became particularly important during the regime phase of Italian fascism and that it was one of the main reasons why this ideology came to be admired and imitated in many other places of the world, including Latin America.[16] Nevertheless, as we saw, some variants of fascism make a less relevant use of this concept, which is the case of Hitler, but also of Codreanu. Not unsurprisingly, these are also the configurations in which the adjacent concept of 'Organicism' is less relevant and in which racist notions are more prominent. This may indicate that the permutations that tended to conceived the people as some kind of 'Holistic Volkish' homogeneous community might be less prone to adopt the idea of Corporatism.[17] Such an organic type of economic and political representation would perhaps still seem too pluralistic to be conciliated with such a view of the people.[18] Nevertheless, to our purposes, what matters is to admit that this leaves us in a difficult position, for the absence of corporatist notions in two important permutations is sufficient to conclude that this is not a true core concept of fascism. If it were so, it would have to be used by all varieties of the ideology in a relevant way, even if with different decontestations. Therefore, we are forced to leave this concept out of the generic configuration, but we still aim at finding another one to replace it and fulfills a similar function in the fascist morphology.

One possible solution would be 'Class Conciliation', because every fascist leader in our analysis asserts his goal of bringing back the working class to the national community and of ending class conflict in order for the Nation to become truly indivisible. This feature does not change independently of the permutation displaying a more organicist or a more 'Volkisch' conception, since it is a necessary goal in either case. In this sense, Corporatism is one of the most frequent solutions proposed to deal with this question of 'Class Conciliation', but not the only one. To create a society that is not divided by class strife is, therefore, one of the most important aims of fascism, or at least of interwar fascism, and it is a feature that can hardly be left out of the picture since every leader in our analysis puts much of his effort into explaining why the working class and their employers must conciliate their interests within the scope of national interests. Even Mussolini, in the formative years of fascism, already reveals his preoccupation with such question, as well as does Hitler, who reserves entire passages of the first chapters of his book to describe the conditions of the working class and the perils that the German Nation might face because of their adherence to communism. Later, he also says that workers 'will have to recognize the fact that the economic prosperity of the nation brings with it their own material happiness' at the same time that employers 'must recognize that the happiness and contentment of his employees are necessary pre-requisites for the existence and development of his own economic prosperity'.[19]

However, we are not totally satisfied with the use of this alternate new concept, because the fascist goal of conciliating opposites within the Nation did not refer only to social classes and did not have only an economic component. For this reason, the goal of creating a State capable of creating a holistic Nation also included, among other aspects, the idea of conciliating the individual with the national collective and not just the working class with the bourgeoisie. This was pointed out by us whenever, throughout our analysis, we saw that the project of creating a national synthesis went beyond the idea of conciliating classes through Corporatism. This happened with Déat, but also with Hitler, when theywrote about 'Personality', which in the specifc case of Hitler represents the heroes whose individual deeds are put at the service of the racial community. However, the most evident example of this feature is perhaps found in Primo de Rivera, when he uses the concept of 'Personality' to refer to the new type of man that is reinserted in the community.[20] Thus, pinpointing the conciliation between classes, when, in fact, fascist aims to conciliate many other opposing features of society, might be a wrong choice for our conceptual configuration. For this reason, from now on, we will consider that fascism has at its core the concept of 'Conciliation', which has in its vicinity two important adjacent conceptss: 'Class Conciliation' (which is how fascism tries to solve the problems exploited by socialism) and 'Conciliation of the Individual with the Collective' (which is how fascism tries to solve the problems created by Liberalism and its individualism) or 'Personality'. 'Conciliation', for fascists, could therefore display a wide range of possible meanings and adjacent concepts, depending on the features of the society in which a specific variety could emerge. Thus, in a way, even Primo de Rivera's rejection of separatisms can be seen as an unfolding of such a concept.

It may be true that 'Conciliation' may not seem at first a typical political concept, but it is the best term for us to define this characteristic of fascism that refers to a process of *synthesis within the Nation* and which has the goal of bringing back together opposing features that should not have become opposites in the first place. In other words, 'Conciliation' exists because fascists aim to bring together what, in their eyes, should never have been separated and create a new unity and a new synthesis. Thus, in this book, the word 'Conciliation' is not used to suggest that fascists had anything in common with some type of liberal conciliation, nor is it suggested that, in practice, such 'Conciliation' did not often imply the use of force and Violence. It shall also be said that, from now on, Corporatism will be here seen as a marginal concept of generic fascism, one that, nonetheless, comes particularly closer to the core in many of its historical varieties, mostly in those that make much use the concept of 'Organicism' and choose Corporatism as the solution to the problem of class struggle. However, the varieties of fascism making considerable use of 'holistic volkish' views also aim at reaching conciliation within the national community, even if their proposal does not necessarily include the construction of a corporatist system.

As to the concept of Empire, it clearly seems to be a core one if we think of Hitler's ideology and his goal of conquering land in Eastern Europe. Besides, even in the early epoch of fascism, Mussolini saw imperialism as a fundamental feature of fascism, because 'imperialism is the grounding of life for every people who tends to expand economically and spiritually'.[21] Also in the case of Primo de Rivera, the initial points of the Falange said that 'we have the will to Empire. We affirm that the historical plenitude of Spain is the Empire'.[22] However, our hypothesis that Empire is a core concept in fascism seems harder to adopt right now because it seems absent from the texts by Rolão Preto that we read without this endangering his classification as a fascist leader. Once again, this shall be enough to conclude that Empire is not at the core of fascist ideas. Furthermore, if we intend to replace this concept with some other broader word playing a similar function, the choice is difficult to make, since it would have to be one capable of encompassing the following components: Hitler's expansionism; the valorization of an already existing Empire by Déat and Mosley; the reconquering of influence in the Hispanic world in the case of Primo de Rivera; and the concretization of the values of the 'Greater Romania' in Codreanu.

A concept such as 'international reconfiguration' is rather vague, while the 'reconquering of the international prestige of the nation' seems to be more of an adjacent concept of Nation than a core concept. Thus, and as we had already suggested that might happen, we simply choose to leave out this concept without replacing it with any other. From now on, therefore, Empire will be seen as a concept that is in the periphery of fascist ideology, even if in many variants it comes closer to the core and interlinks with the concept of Nation (such as in the case of Hitler's and Mussolini's ideology, the latter displaying imperialist ambitions even before fascism was fully formed). Nevertheless, in spite of our decision, we must not regret the inclusion of Empire in our first tentative configuration for it gave us an opportunity to analyse in more detail the varieties in which this concept is indeed closer to the core and plays a crucial role to understand the elements of a specific configuration, even if not of fascism as a generic phenomenon.

## Interlinkages

One of the interlinkages that seems to appear recurrently during the reading of these leaders is the one between the concepts of Nation, State and, in the cases in which it does appear, Corporatism. This is particularly evident in relation to Oswald Mosley and Francisco Rolão Preto, but the same could also be said about Primo de Rivera and Marcel Déat. The reason why this interlinkage is so recurrent relatesto the adjacent concept of 'Organicism', which surrounds these three concepts at the same time. Thus, if the Nation is an organic entity, the State is the instrument that must organise its life according to organicist principles and Corporatism is the actual political and economic system that reflects the organic features of the Nation. For this reason, we can conclude that such an interlinkage represents a core feature in some of the most important varieties of fascist ideology and that they can be grouped together as examples of a cluster of concepts that is paradigmatic in a main current of fascist thought. Another interlinkage, which appears in almost every leader, is the one that approximates the concept of State with that of Authority. This happens, because the State, with all its strong powers, has the function of inculcating in the masses the principles of obedience and leading the sovereign Nation with as much strength as possible. However, we shall note that this is only one of the dimensions that the concept of Authority displays and that it also stands on its own as a concept that represents a principal that is fundamental to understand how fascists saw important aspects of society, that is, as a very hierarchical place. Other important interlinkages include, for instance, Revolution, Violence and Nation, as well as Revolution and Authority (in cases such as those of Primo de Rivera and Rolão Preto).

**The adjacent concept of order**

One of the additional adjacent concepts that we could include in the conceptual configuration is that of 'Progress', which in some variants is placed in the adjacency of Revolution. In the case of Hitler, for instance, this concept makes sense because it relates to how this leader envisioned the evolution of society and the role that racial struggle played in it. In his view, it was the Aryans that 'furnished the great building-stones and plans for the edifices of all human progress'.[23] As to the case of Rolão Preto, it relates to the idea of resuming a march towards the future that was lost during the liberal era, while in Mosley 'Progress' is positively seen as a force that creates new technological innovations.[24] However, the picture gets more complicated if we think that the fascist conception of time and evolution is complex and difficult to grasp. For this reason, we choose not to go into much detail in relation to this conception, but we do not leave out the possibility of carrying out a new research exclusively focused on the concept of Progress in fascist ideology.[25] For now, we can take the risk of assuming that fascists in general do use the concept of Progress in the adjacency of Revolution and that they see the progression of history as a march towards a new era in which the past is evoked in order to serve as a guide for the creation of a new future.[26]

*Final considerations about the conceptual configuration* 215

Thus, the main adjacent concept that we want to highlight is that of 'Order', which in our generic configuration wasplaced in the adjacency of State. Nevertheless, we are now in a position to note that the most interesting feature of this concept is that it also surrounds the concepts of Violence and Revolution, thus creating a meaning that at a first glance seems contradictory. Thus, even when fascists praise violent actions and the importance of struggle, they seem to have some kind of reverence for 'Order' as a principle of society that must be preserved at all costs. Not infrequently, fascists believe that their Violence serves the purpose of defending this principle of 'Order' for, even if for a moment it is capable of creating turmoil, its goal is that of avoiding the coming to power of elements that use a rather destructive and anarchic type of Violence. Such a conception is noticeable in Déat, Mosley and also in Codreanu, when he says that 'we provoked disorder ... but those disorders would stop the great disorder, the irreparable disorder'.[27]

Portuguese historian João Bernardo succinctly summarises this feature by saying that "fascism was a revolt in the order".[28] According to him, fascism was since its beginnings structured around two important and apparently contradictory axes: that of revolt (which had a more radical aspect) and that of respect for "Order" (which was related to a more conservative side of fascism). Thus, uniting these two principles, fascist ideology was constitute das a political force with two main drives, one leading to the radical transformation of society, and the other, to the maintenance of order . For this reason, we always find the concept of "Order" in the vicinity of Violence and this is one of the most distinctive features of fascist ideology.

**One marginal concept: liberty**

We already know that the concepts of Corporatism and Empire are peripheral concepts of generic fascism but that oftentimes they come closer to the core in some important varieties. However, 'Liberty' is a concept that, while not absent, remains in the margins of this ideology, being thus unsubstantial to the understanding of its core ideas. Furthermore, it is a concept that is decontested in a way that completely differs from the one that we find in practically every other ideology, mainly liberalism. To fascists, Liberty is something that can only be achieved after the extinction of the individualism that began with the coming of liberal societies. 'True' liberty can only be attained by the Personality that is reinserted in the society they belong. This view is noticeable, for instance, in Marcel Déat when talks about the type of 'regime that reunites what was kept separated' by liberalism.[29] It is worth noticing that Oswald Mosley seems to make an effort not to totally disregard individual freedom. He says that the private sphere of life shall always give some degree of Liberty to fascist militants and even states that one of the characteristics of a fascist society is 'Liberty in private life. Obligation in public life. In his public capacity a man must behave as befits a citizen and a member of the state [...] In private he may behave as he likes'.[30] However, this can easily be discarded as a mere theoretical statement that would be of no consequence to the practices of the regime, had the British fascist leader ever come to power.

## Permeability and rejections

In the permutations that make use of the concept of 'Social Justice', fascism does seem to permeate somehow with leftist and socialist ideologies. The permutations in which such feature is more evident are perhaps those of Rolão Preto and Primo de Rivera, the latter claiming that it is necessary for the people to have 'bread and justice'. However, such concept of 'Social Justice' is, for the most part, a marginal one in fascist ideology, and in the case of Hitler it is even subordinated to the concept of Racial Struggle. For this reason, it is clear that fascism does not belong to the political tradition of socialist ideologies, even if it also makes use of a very specific meaning of the concept of Revolution. Furthermore, socialism and communism are precisely the ideologies that fascism most vehemently rejects, mostly because they interlink the concept of Revolution with that of 'Class', something that fascist nationalism cannot tolerate. In the cases of the permutations that use racist conceptions, the leaders also tend to see 'Internationalism' and communism as a Jewish conspiracy destined to weaken the Nation. As to right wing ideologies, the permeability between them and fascism is more evident for they share some of the main preoccupations, including Nationalism. The one who dedicates more space to the discussion of right wing ideas is Hitler, who acknowledged his debt towards Lueger and Schönerer. However, as it was seen in the case of Rolão Preto and what he said about Salazar, the absence of the concept of Revolution in conservative ideologies is the main reason why fascists ultimately reject conservatism and other ideologies of the right. As to Liberalim, fascists rejected it because of concepts such as 'Democracy', 'Individualism' and, as we know, 'Liberty'.

## Contradictions and tensions

Finally, one must mention the main contradictions that are at the core of fascism. We already know that this is an ideology that is replete with tensions and contradictions and that one of its goals is even that of creating a synthesis of opposites, as it is stated by Mosley. Thus, among the many contradictions and tensions that we might point out is the contradiction 'Individualism'/'Collectivity' (which is solved with the concept of 'Personality') and Violence/Order, of which we talked about. However, there is still another contradiction that seems to be more difficult to solve: the one that opposes Populism and Elitism. It is generally assumed that fascism is an extremely elitist ideology, which we believe to be correct, given the role that this ideology gives to the concept of Authority and its adjacent concepts of 'Elites' and 'Leader'. Nevertheless, some populist themes and motives do

*Final considerations about the conceptual configuration* 217

make its appearance in the fascist morphology and become more evident each time that the people within the national community is eulogised as an entity capable of transforming society and possessing the strength and the purity to carry out a Revolution. In this context, and in spite of all their elitism, some fascist leaders at times seem to conceive that the people shall not only serve to be moulded by the elites (even though that certainly must happen), but that the leader also must learn to respect the people and its powerful will. It is true that the degree of populist features in fascism vary according to each leader and that, for instance, fascists like Primo de Rivera are particularly elitists, but it is also true that, in the case of Hitler, and in spite of all his contempt for the masses, he recognises that 'no great idea, no matter how sublime and exalted it may appear, can be realized in practice without the effective power which resides in the popular masses'.[31]

In this context, while not denying that fascism is, at its core, an elitist ideology, we do recognise that some populist tenets do enter its morphology and render it more contradictory at times. Thus, this is a tension that is never truly solved and that must be seen as the most important one in fascist ideology, even if we saw that, during the founding of the PNF, Mussolini tried to adopt a 'middle of the road' solution to this problem, by stating that both heroic individuals and the masses can contribute to the evolution of history depending on the occasions and on the circumstances. We also must state that, in our view, fascist populist tenets are not simply a tactic employed by parties in order to attain power and disguise their elitism. It is rather a feature that is a consequence of their conception of the people as an entity that must play a crucial role in the rebirth of nation.

## Concluding remarks: a definition of fascism

We can thus now summarise the main tenets of fascist ideology by referring that it includes the following core and adjacent concepts:

- Nation, which is delimited by the concepts of 'Organicism', 'Holism' and 'People'.
- State, which has in its adjacency the concepts of 'Organicism', 'Holism', 'Dirigisme' and 'Order'.
- Conciliation, which can be surrounded by the concepts of 'Class Conciliation' and 'Conciliation between Individual and Collectivity' (or simply 'Personality' to say it in a simpler way). The concepts of 'Organicism', 'Holism' also appear.
- Revolution, which has in its adjacency the concepts of 'Palingenesis', 'New Man' and 'Cult of Youth'.
- Authority, which has in its adjacency the concepts of 'Hierarchy, 'Elites' and 'Leader'.
- Violence, which interlinks with 'Eliminationism', 'Palingenesis' and 'Social Darwinism', as well as 'Order'.

218  *Final considerations about the conceptual configuration*

The most common interlinkages between core concepts are the ones uniting Nation-Corporatism-Conciliation and State-Authority. Race, Empire and Corporatism are concepts that are in the periphery of the ideology, but often come closer to the core in some important varieties, interlinking with Nation or Conciliation. The peripheral concept of 'Social Justice' (coming closer to the core in some varieties) and the core concept of Nation can make this ideology permeate with socialist and conservative ideologies, respectably, but fascists ultimately reject Socialism (because of its use of the concept of 'Class Struggle') and, though not as vehemently, Conservatism (because it does not incorporate the concept of Revolution). Liberalism, on its turn, is rejected on the basis of such concepts as 'Democracy', 'Liberty' and 'Individualism'. Some contradictions in this conceptual morphology are 'Individualism'/'Collectivity' (a contradiction which is solved), Violence/Order and Populism/Elitism.

Having said all this, all that is left for us to do in the context of this study is to try to create a phrase based on the core concepts that we have found, a phrase that can be considered as a definition of fascism. Remembering that we have left aside the core concept of Empire, we now have six concepts with which we can construct a definition. All we have to do is reunite all the concepts in order to say that: **Fascism is a type of Nationalism that aims to strengthen State power; conciliate the opposite parts within the national community; carry out a spiritual Revolution; sees Authority as a principle of organisation in society; and evaluates Violence in a positive way.**

## Notes

1 Adolf Hitler, *Mein Kampf*, Translated by Ralph Manheim (London, Hurst & Blackett LTD, 1939), 22.
2 Oswald Mosley, *The Greater Britain* (London, BUF, 1934), 19.
3 Marcel Déat, 'Le Parti Unique' in Philippe Randa, Ed., *Documents Pour l'Histoire*, Vol.1, (Paris, Éditions Déterma, 1998 [1942]) 375.
4 Mosley, *The Greater Britain*, 34–35.
5 Corneliu Codreanu, *For My Legionaries* (Madrid, Libertatea, 1976), 54.
6 The ideological differences between Nazism and other varieties of fascism are outlined in Klaus Newman, 'Interwar Germany and the Corporatist Wave, 1918–1939' in António Costa Pinto, Ed., *Corporatism and Fascism: The Corporatist Wave in Europe* (London, Routledge, 2017), 134. According to this text, organicist vocabulary was not, indeed, part of Nazi ideology, and as we shall see, this also has an impact on the importance of the concept of Corporatism.
7 Francisco Rolão Preto, 'Para além do Comunismo' in José de Melo Alexandrino, Ed., *Obras Completas* (Lisboa, Edições Colibri, 2015 [1932]), 208.
8 Adolf Hitler, *Mein Kampf*, 314.
9 Codreanu, *For My Legionaries*, 159.
10 José Antonio Primo de Rivera, *Obras Completas* (Madrid, Ed. Instituto de Estudios Políticos, 1976), 219.
11 Déat, 'Le Parti Unique', 40.
12 Primo de Rivera, *Obras Completas*
13 Hitler, *Mein Kampf*, 512; Codreanu, *For My Legionaries*, 192.

*Final considerations about the conceptual configuration* 219

14 Mosley, *The Greater Britain*, 181.
15 Adolf Hitler, *Mein Kampf*, 194.
16 To read more about Corporatist experiments in Latin America see Pinto, António Costa (ed.) *Latin American Dictatorships in the Era of Fascism: The Corporatist Wave* (London, Routledge, 2019).
17 To further legitimate such an assertion, we can quote what is referred by Pinto: 'the legionary leader Ion Mota stated, corporatism 'is entirely colourless from a folk point of view' and just after modification of the 'ethnic structure of the state' could be an option for Romania'. António Costa Pinto, 'Corporatism and Organic Representation in European Dictatorships' in António Costa Pinto, Ed., *Corporatism and Fascism: The Corporatist Wave in Europe* (London, Routledge, 2017), 134.
18 This point is refered in Stanley Payne, *A History of Fascism: 1914–1945* (Madison, University of Wisconsin Press, 1995), 10.
19 Hitler, *Mein Kampf*, 459.
20 Primo de Rivera, *Antologia*, 79.
21 'L'imperialismo.è il fondamento della vita per ogni popolo che tende ad espandersi economicamente e spiritualmente'. Benito Mussolini, 'Atto di nascita del fascismo' in Edoardo Susmel and Duilio Susmel, Eds., *Opera Omnia*, Vol. XII (Firenze, La Fenice, 1961), 323.
22 'Tenemos voluntad de Imperio. Afirmamos que la plenitud histórica de España es el Imperio'. Primo de Rivera, *Obras Completas*, 359.
23 Hitler, *Mein Kampf*, 226.
24 Preto, 'Para além do Comunismo', 196.
25 The best work about this topic is undoubtedly Roger Griffin, *Modernism and Fascism: The Sense of a Beginning under Mussolini and Hitler* (London, Palgrave Macmillan, 2007).
26 In the words of Roger Griffin, in fascism 'the past is to be remembered in order to regenerate the present and transform the future', 13. Roger Griffin, 'I am no longer human. I am a Titan. A god!' The Fascist Quest to Regenerate Time' in Matthew Feldman, Ed., *A Fascist Century* (London, Routledge, 2008).
27 Codreanu, *For My Legionaries*, 14.
28 João Bernardo, *Labirintos do Fascismo* (Porto, Edições Afrontamento: 2015), 13.
29 Déat, 'Le Parti Unique', 47.
30 Mosley, *The Greater Britain*, 51.
31 Hitler, *Mein Kampf*, 94.

## List of references

Bernardo, João. *Labirintos do Fascismo* (Lisboa, Afrontamento).
Codreanu, *For My Legionaries* (Madrid, Libertatea, 1976).
Dagnino, Jorge, Matthew Feldman and Paul Stocker, *The New Man in Radical Right Ideology and Practice, 1919-1945* (London, Bloomsbury, 2017).
Darré, Richard Walter, *Blut Und Boden Ein Grundgedanke Des Nationalsozialismus* (Berlin, Reichsdruckerei, 1936).
Déat, Marcel, 'Le Parti Unique' in Philippe Randa, Ed., *Documents Pour l'Histoire*, Vol. 1 (Paris, Éditions Déterma, 1998 [1942]), 36.
Eatwell, Roger, *Fascism: A History* (London: Penguin Books, 1997).
Feldman, Matthew (ed.), *A Fascist Century* (London, Routledge, 2008).
Felici, Renzo de, *Le Interpretazioni Del Fascismo* (Bari, Laterza, 2017 [1967]).

Finchelstein, Federico, *Transatlantic Fascism: Ideology, Violence, and the Sacred in Argentina and Italy, 1919–1945* (Durham, Duke University Press Books, 2010).
Gentile, Emilio, *Chi é Fascista* (Bari, Laterza, 2019).
Gentile, Emilio and Robert Mallett. 'The Sacralisation of Politics: Definitions, Interpretations and Reflections on the Question of Secular Religion and Totalitarianism', *Totalitarian Movements and Political Religions*, *1* (1), 2000, 18–55.
Gregor, James, *The Ideology of Fascism* (New York, Free Press, 1969).
Griffin, Roger, *The Nature of Fascism* (London, Routledge, 1993).
Griffin, Roger (ed.), *Fascism* (Oxford, Oxford University Press, 1995).
Griffin, Roger, *Modernism and Fascism: The Sense of a Beginning under Mussolini and Hitler* (London, Palgrave Macmillan, 2007).
Hitler, Adolf, *Mein Kampf*, Translated by Ralph Manheim (London, Hurst & Blackett LTD, 1939).
Kallis, Aristotle, *Fascist Ideology: Territory and Expansionism in Italy and Germany, 1922–1945* (London, Routledge, 2000).
Kallis, Aristotle, *Genocide and Fascism* (London, Routledge, 2009).
Kallis, Aristotle, 'The Regime-Model of Fascism: A Typology', *European History Quarterly*, *30*, 2000, 77–107.
Mann, Michael, *Fascists* (Cambridge, Cambridge University Press, 2004).
Matard-Bonucci, Marie Anne and Pierre Milza (eds.), *L'Homme Noveau Dans l'Europe fasciste (1922–1945)* (Paris, Fayard, 2004).
Morgan, Philip, *Fascism in Europe, 1919-1945* (London, Routledge, 2003).
Mosley, Oswald, *The Greater Britain* (London, British Union of Fascists, 1934).
Mosse, George, *The Fascist Revolution: Toward a General Theory of Fascism* (New York, Howard Fertig Pub, 1999).
Mosse, George L., *The Crisis of German Ideology: Intellectual Origins of the Third Reich* (New York, Grosset and Dunlap, 1964).
Mussolini, Benito, 'Atto di nascita del fascismo' in Edoardo Susmel and Duilio Susmel, Eds., *Opera Omnia*, Vol. XII (Firenze, La Fenice, 1961), 321–327.
Nolte, Ernst, *Three Faces of Fascism: Action Française, Italian Fascism, National Socialism* (New York, Holt, Rinehart and Winston, 1966).
Passmore, Kevin, *Fascism: A Very Short Introduction* (Oxford, Oxford University Press, 2014).
Payne, Stanley, *A History of Fascism: 1914–1945* (Madison, University Press of Wisconsin, 1995).
Pinto, António Costa (ed.), *Corporatism and Fascism: The Corporatist Wave in Europe* (London, Routledge, 2017).
Pinto, António Costa and Aristotle Kallis (eds.), *Rethinking Fascism and Dictatorship in Europe* (London, Palgrave Macmillan, 2014).
Primo de Rivera, José António, *Obras Completas* (Madrid, Ed. Instituto de Estudios Políticos, 1976).
Roberts, David D., *Fascist Interactions: Proposals for a New Approach to Fascism and Its Era, 1919–1945* (New York, Berghahn, 2016).
Sorel, Georges, in Jeremy Jennings, Ed., *Reflections on Violence* (Cambridge, Cambridge University Press, 1999 [1908]).

Sternhell, Zeev, *Ni Droite Ni Gauche. L'idéologie Fasciste En France* (Paris, Éditions du Seuill, 1983).

Sternhell, Zeev, *The Birth of Fascist Ideology* (Princeton, Princeton University Press, 1994).

Weber, Eugen, *Varieties of Fascism* (Florida, Krieger Pub Co., 1982 [1964]).

Woodley, Daniel, *Fascism and Political Theory: Critical Perspectives on Fascist Ideology* (London, Routledge, 2010).

# Conclusion

It is undeniable that the main progresses in the field of studies about fascism were made possible by the methodological option of taking its ideology seriously. However, and in spite of all the studies that have been written in the previous decades, we decided to take the risk of carrying out a new research based on the belief that a study exclusively focused on leaders of fascist parties might be a very valuable one and could contribute to shed some light about ideology. That is so because, as was argued in the introduction, the messianic message that was contained in the words of fascist leaders surely would reveal some of the most important tenets of fascist ideology. Furthermore, such a study would also have the added value of using the conceptual morphological approach, which focus on concepts and on the interlinkages of conceptual configurations in order to try to decode the meaning of ideologies. Such an approach would be capable of grasping both the stable content of a generic ideology at the same time that it was flexible enough to account for ideological fluidity, thus allowing for the study of specific permutations of fascism that emerged in the most varied national contexts.

From this starting point, we were capable of formulating a first Preliminary configuration of generic fascism that was based on the reading of secondary sources as well as some primary fascist sources. This way, this first configuration was composed by the concepts of Nation, State, Corporatism, Revolution, Authority, Violence and Empire. From the beginning, it was said that such configuration would be subjected to revision if the readings of texts by the leaders showed that it did not hold up to scrutiny. In the adjacency of these concepts, we also found other concepts such as 'Organicism', 'Holism', 'People', 'Race', 'Totalitarianism', 'Class Conciliation', 'Palingenesis', 'New Man', 'Elites', 'Leader', 'Eliminationism' or 'Irredentism'.

After that, the rest of the study consisted mainly in a close reading of the following leaders of fascist parties: Adolf Hitler, Oswald Mosley, Francisco Rolão Preto, José António Primo de Rivera, Corneliu Codreanu, Marcel Déat and Benito Mussolini. After all the readings, it became possible to rethink our first configuration and add some important conclusions. Namely, that the interlinkages between State and Authority and Revolution and Violence, among many others, are recurrent in most variants of fascism; that 'Liberty' is recurrently a marginal concept; that the adjacent concept of 'Order' is also particularly relevant; that fascism can sometimes permeate with socialist ideas due to concepts such as 'Social Justice' but that it ultimately rejects those ideologies for they make use of the concept of 'Class Struggle'; that, in spite of all the permeability, fascism rejects other conservative right-wing ideologies because they do not make use of the concept of Revolution; that fascism rejects liberalism mostly due to the concepts of 'Democracy' and 'Individualism'; and that the contradictions between Individual/Collectivity and Populism/Elitism are the most evident tensions in the fascist morphology, even if the former is eventually solved thanks to the concept of 'Personality'.

More importantly, we found that the concepts of Corporatism and Empire do not consistently appear in all leaders and for this reason cannot truly be considered as core concepts. We thus substituted the former for the concept of Conciliation and simply decided to leave out the latter. With this conclusion, it became possible to arrive at a definition of generic fascism that can simply be transcribed in the following phrase: fascism is a type of nationalism that aims to strengthen state power; conciliate the opposites within the nation into a cohesive unity; carry out a spiritual revolution; sees authority as a fundamental principle of society; and evaluates violence in a positive way.

At this point, it is important to note that this first study can be followed by more researches that also make use of the conceptual morphological approach. For instance, it would be interesting to use our final conceptual configuration in order to study other lesser known leaders, that way trying to confirm its validity further. Besides, it would also be interesting to use this approach to analyse the more dynamic side of fascist ideology: for instance, the interactions between fascism and other ideologies of the right. Starting from our chapter about Rolão Preto and the configuration that there emerged, it would be possible to read, for instance, António Salazar (who at the time was his most important competitor) and try to disentangle his conceptual configuration. That way, by comparing the configurations of these two leaders and highlighting ideological reformulations and permeability, one could have a better idea of how these two politicians influenced each other and the interactions that took place between fascism and conservatism in the Portuguese political milieu of the time. The potentialities of the conceptual approach when it comes to study both the fixity and fluidity of fascism shall not be downplayed, and believing this was one of the reasons that led to the writing of this book.

# Index

Acción Española, 119
*Action Française*, 162, 170
Alecsandri, Vasile, 144
Alexandrino, José de Melo, 94
Alfonsists, 118
Alfonso XIII, 118–19
Allardyce, Gilbert, 22
anti-Marxism, 22
anti-Semitism, 50, 54, 59–61, 64, 141, 150–2, 210
Antonescu, Ion, 141
*Apararea Nationala*, 142
Archangel Michael, 142
*Arditti*, 189, 196
Arrow Cross Party, 25
Aryan race, 34, 52–4, 61, 214
authority, 33–4, 173–4, 210
  charismatic, 3
  of heroic leader, 58–9
  ideological, 3
  interlinkages, 214
  legal, 3
  and revolution, 34
  traditional, 3
  and violence, 38, 82–4
*Avanti!* 186
Averescu, Alexandru, 142

Balbo, Italo, 190
Ballester, Gonzalo Torrente, 120
barbarism, 192
Basque Country, 122, 130
Battle of Cable Street, 73
*Beacons_Guidelines_Soul (Balizas_Directrizes_Alma)* (Preto), 97
Beer Hall Putsch, 49
Benn, Gottfried, 33
Bernardo, João, 215
Bessarabia, 142

*Beyond Communism (Para Além do Comunismo)* (Preto), 97, 106
Bianchi, Michele, 190
Black Shirts, 73
*Blood and Soil* (Darré), 34
Blum, Léon, 164, 177
Bobbio, Norberto, 104
Bolsheviks/Bolshevism, 61, 98, 108, 150, 196
Bono, Emilio de, 190
Bonomi, Ivanoe, 186
Bordiga, Amadeo, 194
Boulanger, 162
Bouthillier, Yves, 166
British Fascists, 72, 74
British Union of Fascists (BUF), 14
  Battle of Cable Street, 73
  creation of, 73
  dissolution of, 73
  Olympia Rally, 73
Brüning, Heinrich, 49
Bucard, Michel, 162
Bukovina, 142
Burleigh, Michael, 26, 66
Burrin, Philippe, 162, 165–6

Caballero, Ernesto Giménez, 119
Calinescu, Armand, 141
Carlists, 117–18
Carnation Revolution, 96
Carol II, 140–1
Catalonia, 122, 130
Catholic corporatism, 28
Celmins, Gustav, 36
Centre Party (*Deutsche Zentrumspartei – DZP*), 49
Chamberlain, Houston Stewart, 25
charismatic authority, 3
Charter of Carnaro, 199–200

*Charter of Labour* (*Carta del Lavoro*), 29
Chesterton, A.K., 31, 73
Chesterton, G.K., 73
Christian Social Party (Austria), 64
Churchill, Winston, 74
class conciliation, 28, 78, 99, 124, 142, 153–4, 170–1, 211
class struggle, 9, 87, 122, 201
Classic Ages, 127
Codreanu, Corneliu, 14, 139–57
  death of, 141
  early life, 139
  Greater Romania, 145–6, 213
  Guard of National Conscience, 139
  Iron Guard, 139–41
  Legion of the Archangel Michael, 140
  murder of Constantin Manciu, 139–40, 150
  *For My Legionaries* (*Pentru Legionari*), 14, 143–53
  National-Christian Defense League, 139
Codreanu, Corneliu, ideology of, 141–3
  anti-Semitism, 141, 150–2, 210
  authority, 148–9
  contradictions, 155–6
  corporatism, 153–4
  Cult of Death, 153
  eliminationism, 150–1
  elites, 148–9
  empire, 145–6, 213
  holist nationalism, 143–4
  leader, 148
  messianic leader, 142 nation, 207
  New Man, 147–8, 209–10
  palingenesis, 141–2
  permeability and rejections, 154–5
  race, 144–5
  rejection of communism and liberalism, 155
  social justice, 154
  violence, 149–50
Codreanu, Ion Zelea, 139
Cointent, Jean-Paul, 176
Cold War, 27
collaborationism, 165–6
Comintern, 163
communism, 64, 107–8, 155
  Déat's rejection of, 177–8
  Mussolini's rejection of, 194, 196
  rejection of, 216
communitarians, 170
community, 167–8, 177

conceptual morphological
  approach, 6–9
  and fascism, 9–10
  internal contradictions, 8–9
  permeability, 8
  priority, 7–8
  proportionality, 8
  proximity, 8
conciliation, 212
Conservative Party, 74
consumer, 78, 171
Conta, Vasile, 144–5
contradictions, 216–17
  Codreanu, 155–6
  Déat, 178–9
  Hitler, 65–6
  Oswald, 88–9
  Primo de Rivera, 132
  Rolão Preto, 109–10
corporate state, 28, 75–81, 97–102, 123–5
corporatism, 27–9, 39, 211, 213
  Codreanu, 142, 153–4
  Déat, 170–1
  Hitler, 62–3, 67
  integral, 110–11
  interlinkages, 213–14
  Mosley, 74, 77–8, 80
  Mussolini, 201
  Primo de Rivera, 118, 124–5
  and revolution, 81
  Rolão Preto, 96, 99, 102
Corradini, Enrico, 189
Corridoni, Filippo, 192, 196
Costa Pinto, António, 5, 28
Couceiro, Henrique de Paiva, 94
Councils of the National Syndicalist Offensive (*Juntas de Ofensiva Nacional-Sindicalista* – JONS), 117
Crispi, Francesco, 200
Croce, Benedetto, 21
*Croix de Feu*, 162
*Cruzada Nuno Álvares Pereira*, 94
Cult of Death, 153
Cult of Youth, 31, 58, 82, 103, 171
Cuza, A.C., 142, 144, 155

D'Annunzio, Gabriel, 189, 199
Darré, Walter, 34
de Felici, Renzo, 21
Déat, Marcel, 14, 162–80, 207
  death in exile, 165
  Legion of French Volunteers Against

Bolshevism, 165
  membership in socialist parties, 164
  Popular National Rally, 164-5
  socialist parties, 164
  support for Vichy regime, 164-5
  *The Unique Party* (*Le Parti Unique*), 14, 167-75
Déat, Marcel, ideology of, 165-6
  authority, 173-4
  class conciliation, 170-1
  collaborationism, 165-6
  community, 167-8
  contradictions, 178-9
  corporatism, 170-1
  elites, 173, 210
  empire, 168, 213
  internationalism, 167, 171-3, 178-9
  leaders, 173
  nationalism, 178-9
  neosocialism, 164, 177
  order, 174
  party, 175-6
  peripheral concepts in, 176
  permeability and rejections, 177-8
  person, 172
  rejection of Gauillism, 177
  rejection of liberalism and communism, 177-8, 215
  state, 168-9, 207
  totalitarian revolution, 171-3
  totalitarianism, 169
  violence, 173-4
Deffenu, Attilio, 192
Dégrelle, Léon, 30
Deloncle, Eugène, 165
Dirigisme, 26, 28-9, 77
Dobry, Michael, 4-6
*The Doctrine of Fascism* (*La Dottrina del Fascismo*) (Gentile and Mussolini), 11
Doriot, Jacques, 23, 26, 163, 165
Douglas, Allen, 34
Drace-Francis, Alex, 141
Drexler, Anton, 48-9
Drumont, Édouard, 25
Duca, Ion, 140

Eatwell, Roger, 3, 22, 24, 27, 31
eliminationism, 35, 84, 129, 150, 174, 210
elites and elitism, 34, 216
  Codreanu, 148-9, 155-6
  Déat, 173, 179
  Hitler, 65-6
  Mussolini, 197
  Primo de Rivera, 128, 132
  Rolão Preto, 109
Eminescu, Mihail, 141, 144
empire, 37-40, 213
  autarchic, 84-6
  Codreanu, 145
  Déat, 166
  Hitler, 60-1
  holistic, 123
  Mosley, 84-6
  Mussolini, 92
  Rolão Preto, 106-7
Ethiopia, 188
Everything for the Country (*Totul pentru Tara* – TPT), 140
Evola, Julius, 3
expansionism, 38, 60-1

Faria, Dutra, 95
Farinacci, Roberto, 188
*Fasci Italiani di Combattimento*, 20
fascism
  authority, 33-4
  and conceptual morphological approach, 9-10
  conceptual structure of, 206-18
  contemporary studies, 1
  core concepts of, 23-4, 206-13
  corporatism, 27-9
  definition of, 22
  definitions of, 21-2, 217-18
  empire, 37-40
  generic, *see* generic fascism
  interpretations of, 21-2
  minimum, *see* generic fascism
  nation, 23-5
  revolution, 30-2
  state, 25-7
  violence, 34-7
Fascist Grand Council, 29, 188
fascist interactions, 5
Felici, Renzo de, 21, 187
Ferenc, Szálasi, 25, 39
Ferrari, Enzo, 190
Ferro, António, 97
Filippo Corridoni, 189
First Republic (Portugal), 94
Fiume, 189
*For My Legionaries* (*Pentru Legionari* – PL) (Codreanu), 14
  conceptual core of, 143-53

holist nationalism, 143–4
  peripheral concepts in, 154
  violence in, 149–50
France
  fascist organisations, 162–3
  Gaullism in, 174–5
  Matignon agreements, 177
  nationalism, 179
  nationalism in, 174–5
  Nazi domination of, 172–3
  Vichy regime, 164
Francist Movement (*Mouvement Franciste* – MF), 162
Franco, General Francisco, 117, 119–20
Frankfurt School, 21
Freeden, Michael, 6–9, 11
French Popular Pary (*Parti Populaire Français* – PPF), 163, 165
French Revolution, 105
French Section of the Workers International (*Section Française de l'Internationale Ouvrière* – SFIO), 164
*Führerprinzip*, 33
futurists, 189

Garau, Salvatore, 1, 189, 200
Garibaldi, Giuseppe, 186, 197
Gaullism, 174–5, 177
General Strike of 1926, 74
generic fascism, 4–6, 20–40
  authority, 33–4
  conceptual structure of, 206–18
  core concepts of, 23–4, 206–13
  corporatism, 27–9
  definition of, 22
  empire, 37–40
  nation, 23–5
  revolution, 30–2
  state, 25–7
  violence, 34–7
Gentile, Emilio, 26, 187
Gentile, Giovanni, 3, 11
German Workers' Party (*Deutsch Arbeiterpartei* – DAP), 48
Gil-Robles, José Maria, 119
Giovenezza, 31
Gobineau, Arthur de, 25
Goebbels, Joseph, 36, 49
Gomes da Costa, Manuel, 95
Göring, Herman, 49
Gramsci, Antonio, 21
Great Depression, 49, 72, 78
Greater Britain, dominions, 85
*The Greater Britain* (Mosley), 14, 75–84
  autarchic empire in, 84–6
  authority in, 82–4
  corporate state in, 75–81
  peripheral concepts in, 86 revolution in, 81–2
  violence in, 82–4
Greater Romania, 145–6, 213
Gregor, A. James, 3, 22, 187
Griffin, Roger, 4, 9–11, 22–3, 30
Grundel, E. Gunther, 31
Guard of National Conscience (*Garda Constiintei Nationale* – GCN), 139

Hajdeu, Bogdan Petriceicu, 144
Haw Haw, Lord (William Joyce), 33
Hedilla, Manuel, 117
Heimwehr, 23
Hervé, Gustave, 162
Himmler, Heinrich, 49
Hitler, Adolf, 13, 48–67, 172, 206
  on the Aryan race, 52–4
  Beer Hall Putsch, 49
  collectivist view of society, 65 death, 20 early life, 48
  expansionism, 213
  on Jews, 54–5
  *My Struggle* (*Mein Kampf*), 14, 51–62
  and Nazi party, 48–50 violence, 210
Hitler, Adolf, ideology of, 5, 50–1
  anti-Semitism, 54–5, 60, 210
  authority of heroic leader, 58–9
  expansionism, 60–1
  irredentism, 60
  nationalism, 52
  people, 207, 217
  progress, 214
  race and racial struggles, 52–6, 208–9
  racial state, 56–7
  revolution, 57–8
  social Darwinism, 60
  survival of race, 60–1
  violence, 59–60
  vital space, 60–1
Hitler, Alois, 48
Hitler Youth, 31
holism, 24, 28, 52, 76, 81, 121, 124, 143, 207
holist nationalism, 143–4
homo corporativus, 32
homo economicus, 32
House of Commons, 77

# 228  Index

Hugenberg, Alfred, 50
Hungarian United Territories, 39
Hungarianism, 25
hybridization, 5–6

ideological authority, 3
ideological morphology, 9–10
ideologies
  minimum list, 2
  perspectives on, 1–2
*Ideologies and Political Theory: A Conceptual Approach* (Freeden), 6–9
*Il Popolo d'Italia*, 187, 190, 193, 207
Imperial Fascist League, 72
imperialism, 106–7, 192, 213
India, 74, 85
Industrial Revolution, 108
integral corporatism, 110
integral state, 98–9, 101–2
integralism, 24, 98
internal contradictions, conceptual morphological approach, 8–9
internationalism, 9, 88, 167, 171–3, 177–8, 216
Iorga, Nicolae, 142
Irish Blue Shirts (IBS), 32
Iron Guard (*Garda de Fier* – GF), 139
  Antonescu's alliance with, 141
  conflict with the authorities, 141
  mass mobilisation, 140
irredentism, 38–9, 60, 145
Italian Balilla, 31
Italian Fasci for Combat (*Fasci Italiani di Combattimento* – FIC), 20, 187
  First Congress, 194–5
  founding speech of, 187–93
  goals of, 193 program, 193
  Second Congress, 195–7
  transformation into National Fascist Party, 197–200
Italian National Fascist Party (*Partito Nazionale Fascista*), 15
Italian Nationalist Association (*Associazione Nazionalista Italiana* – ANI), 188
Italian Social Republic, 185
Italian Socialist Party (*Partito Socialista Italiano* – PSI), 186
Italy
  futurism in, 189
  March on Rome, 188
  Matteotti affair, 188
  Mussolini as prime minister, 188
  nationalism in, 188–9
  rapprochement with Nazi Germany, 188
  totalitarianism, 188
  war in Libya, 186

Javier de Borbón, Francisco, 118
Jesus Christ, 142, 147–8
Jews, 54–5, 150–2, 167
  anti-Semitism, 210
Joyce, William (Lord Haw Haw), 33, 73
Jünger, Ernst, 50
*Justice* (Preto), 107

Kallis, Aristotle, 5, 22, 38–9
Korneuburger Oath, 23
Kornprobst, Markus, 38

*La Dottrina el Fascismo*, 200
La Rocque, François de, 162, 166
*La Voce*, 189
Larsen, Stein Ugelvik, 2
Latran Treaty, 122
Latvia, 36
*Le Faisceau*, 26, 162
leader, 3–4, 33, 216 authority of, 58–9
  Codreanu, 148 Déat, 173
  heroic, 58–9 Hitler, 58–9, 65–6
  and masses, 65–6
  messianic, 142 Mosley, 83
  Primo de Rivera, 127–8
Lebensraum, 50, 61
legal authority, 3
Legion of French Volunteers Against Bolshevism (*Légion des volontaires français contre le bolchévisme* – LVF), 165
Legion of the Archangel Michael (*Legiunea Arhanghelului Mihail* – LAM), 140–1
legionary violence, 150
Lenin, Vladimir, 98
Leon XIII, 28
Lese, Arnold, 72
liberalism, 8, 64, 87, 104, 107–8, 122, 155
  Déat's rejection of, 177–8
  Primo de Rivera's rejection of, 131
liberty, 8, 63, 87, 89, 107, 130, 154, 176, 215–16
Libya, 186
Lindholm, Sven Olof, 31, 33, 36
Linton-Orman, Rotha, 72, 74
Ljotic, Dimitrije, 39

*L'Oeuvre*, 166
Lueger, Karl, 64, 216
Lusitan Integralism (*Integralismo Lusitano* – IL), 94, 96
Lusitan Nationalism (*Nacionalismo Lusitano* – NL), 94
Lyttelton, Adrian, 1

*Machtergreifung*, 49
Magistracy of Labour, 29
Magyar people, 25
Manciu, Constantin, 139–40, 150
Mann, Henrik de, 107
Mann, Michael, 22, 25
Manoilescu, Mihail, 27, 142
March on Rome, 20, 24, 34, 185, 188
margin, 8
Marin, Vasile, 140
Marinetti, Filippo Tomaso, 189–90
Marxism, 51, 65, 108, 131
masculinity, 32
Masonry, 177
material patrimony, 143
materialisation, 155–6
materialism, 109, 155–6
Matignon agreements, 177
Matteotti affair, 188
Mazzini, Giuseppe, 186, 197
McDonald, Ramsay, 72
Mediterraneum, 200
Michael I, 141
Michael the Brave, 142, 144, 148
Middle Ages, 127
Miglioli, Guido], 198
Migliolino Bolshevism, 198
*Milice Socialiste Nationale*, 162–3
miscegenation, 54
Monsaraz, Alberto, 95
Montero, Matias, 116, 129, 192
Morgan, Philip, 5
Mosley, Oswald, 14, 72–90, 207
 creation of British Union of Fascists, 73 early life, 72
 *The Greater Britain*, 14, 75–84
 New Party, 72–3 public/private contradiction, 88–9
 Union Movement, 73
Mosley, Oswald, ideology of, 74–5
 authority, 82–4
 class conciliation, 78
 corporate state, 75–81
 corporatism, 75–81
 eliminationism, 84

empire, 84–6, 213
 internationalism, 88
 liberty, 86, 89
 nationalism, 88
 pacificism, 84
 progress, 214
 rejection of communism and liberalism, 87
 rejection of liberalism and communism, 215
 revolution, 81–2
 violence, 82–4, 210
 virility, 83
Mosse, George, 22, 31
Mota, Ion, 37, 140, 154, 192
Moti people, 146
Mussolini, Alessandro, 186
Mussolini, Benito, 3–4, 11, 15, 105, 185–201, 207
 appointment as prime minister, 188
 on class conciliation, 211–12
 death, 20
 *The Doctrine of Fascism* (*La Dottrina del Fascismo*), 11
 early life, 186
 as editor of *Avanti!* 186
 execution of, 188
 expulsion from Italian Socialist Party, 187
 *Fasci Italiani di Combattimento*, 20
 founding of National Fascist Party, 197–200
 founding speech of *Fasci Italiani di Combattimento*, 187–93
 ideology, 190–200
 *Il Popolo d'Italia*, 187, 190, 193, 207
 inaugural speeches, 194–7
 in Italian Socialist Party, 186
 March on Rome, 20, 24, 188
 Matteotti affair, 188
 and World War I, 186
Mussolini, Benito, ideology of,
 authority, 199
 corporatism, 199
 elitism, 199
 empire, 194, 200
 internationalism, 198–9
 nation, 191, 195, 198
 people, 196–8, 207, 217
 progress, 192
 rejection of communism, 194, 196
 rejection of imperialism, 192, 213
 rejection of monarchy, 194

230  Index

state, 199
violence, 35, 191, 197, 200
war, 191–2, 196
Mussolini, Rosa, 186
*My Struggle (Mein Kampf)* (Hitler), 14, 51–62
  anti-Semitism in, 60
  authority of heroic leader, 58–9
  race and racial struggle in, 52–6
  racial state in, 56–7
  social Darwinism in, 60
  survival of the race in, 60–1
  violence in, 60
  vital space in, 60–1

Nasjonal Samling, 25
nation, 23–5, 207
  cleansing of, 36
  and eliminationism, 35
  and elites, 34
  and empire, 38
  historical mission, 120–3
  interlinkages, 213–14
  and revolution, 31
  spiritual dimension of, 143
  and state, 26, 29
National Council, 78
National Fascist Party (*Partito Nazional Fascista* – PNF), 188, 197–200
National Legionary State, 141
National Liberal Party (*Partidul National Liberal* – PNL), 140
National Popular Rally (*Rassemblement National Populaire*), 14
National Renaissance Force (*Frontul Renasterii Nationale* – FRN), 141
National Socialist German Workers' Party (*Nationalsozialistische Deutsche Arbeiterpartei* – NSDAP), 14, 49
national syndicalism, 109, 189
National Syndicalist Movement (*Nacional Sindicalismo* – NS), 14, 94–111
National Union (*União Nacional* – UN), 95
national vanguard, 175–6
National-Christian Defense League (*Liga Apararii National Crestine* – LANC), 139, 142
nationalism, 8, 23, 52, 88, 119, 177–8
  in Italy, 188–9
  romantic, 131–2

*The Nature of Fascism* (Griffin), 11, 22
Nazis and Nazism, 21, 34
  and corporatism, 62–3
  and creation of New Man, 57
neosocialism, 164, 177
New Man, 31–2, 37, 57, 81, 103, 147–8, 172, 176
New Party, 72–3
*Nicadori*, 140
Nietzsche, Friedrich, 187
Nolte, Ernst, 1
Nordic race, 25

*Obras Completas* (Primo de Rivera), 132
O'Duffy, Eoin, 32
Olivetti, A.O., 189
*Opera Omnia*, 15
order, 26, 86–7, 124, 174, 214–15
organicism, 24, 28, 76–7, 80, 98, 124, 207–8, 213–14
Ortega y Gasset, José, 131
Ottoman Empire, 186

pacificism, 36, 84, 164
Pais, Sidónio, 94, 105–6
palingenesis, 30–1, 81–2, 103, 127, 210
Pancu, Constantin, 139
Panunzio, Sergio, 3, 189
Papini, Giovani, 189
Pareto, Vilfredo, 187
party, 175–6
Passmore, Kevin, 24
Patriotic People's Movement (*Isänmaallinen kansanliike* – IKL), 28
Pavelic, Ante, 36
Paxton, Robert, 166
Payne, Stanley, 3, 22, 25, 30, 33, 37, 39, 119, 132
Pedro, António, 95
people, 24, 65, 207
*People's Observer* (*Völkischer Beobachter*), 24
People's Party, 142
peripheral concepts, 8
  in Déat's ideology, 176
  in *The Greater Britain* (Mosley), 86
  *The Greater Britain* (Mosley), 86
  in *For My Legionaries* (*Pentru Legionari* – PL) (Codreanu), 154
  in *My Struggle* (*Mein Kampf*) (Hitler), 63–4
  in Primo de Rivera's ideology, 130

in Rolão Preto's ideology, 107
in *The Unique Party* (*Le Parti Unique*) (Déat), 176
Perkon Krust, 36
permeability, 216
  Codreanu, 154-5
  conceptual morphological approach, 8, 13
  Déat, 177-8
  Hitler, 64-5
  Oswald, 86-7
  Primo de Rivera, 131
  Rolão Preto, 107-9
person, 172
personality, 65, 81, 103, 129-30, 132, 179, 212, 215
Pétain, Marechal, 164
physical patrimony, 143
Piazzesi, Mario, 34
Pinto, António Costa, 110
Popular Front, 164
Popular National Rally (*Rassemblement National Populaire* – RNP), 163, 166-7, 173-4
Popular Party (Italy), 198
populism, 65-6, 109, 132, 155-6, 179, 197
Preto, Francisco Rolão, 14
Primo de Rivera, José Antonio, 14, 116-33, 207
  conceptual core of, 120-32
  contradictions in, 132
  early life, 116
  formation of Spanish Falange, 116
  historical mission of nation, 120-3
  imprisonment, 117
  Sanjurjada collaboration, 116
Primo de Rivera, José Antonio, ideology of, 118-20
  class conciliation, 124
  corporate state, 123-5
  elitism, 128, 210
  elitist revolution, 128
  empire, 122-3, 213
  holism, 123
  leader, 127-8
  nation, 122
  palingenetic revolution, 126-7
  peripheral concepts, 130
  personality, 129-30, 212
  progress, 127
  rejection of liberalism and communism, 131
  social justice, 125
  violence, 129
Primo de Rivera, Miguel, 116, 131
priority, conceptual morphological approach, 7-8
private property, 171
producer, 78, 171
progress, 86-7, 104, 127, 132, 214-15
proportionality, conceptual morphological approach, 8
*The Protocols of The Elders of Zion*, 50
proximity, conceptual morphological approach, 8
Pugh, Martin, 74

Quisling, Vidkun, 25
*Quotations of Chairman Mao*, 11

race, 25, 52, 144-5, 206, 208
racial state, 56-7
racial struggle, 52-6
  and historical progress, 57-8
Radulescu, Ion Heliaede, 141
Ramos, Ramiro Ledesma, 117
Raven Thomson, Alexander, 28-9
Redondo, Onésimo, 117
rejections, 216 Codreanu, 154-5
  Déat, 177-8 Hitler, 64-5
  Mussolini, 192, 194, 196, 213
  Oswald, 86-7
  Primo de Rivera, 131
  Rolão Preto, 107-9
Renovación Española, 119
Republican Party (Italy), 197-8
*Rerum Novarum*, 28
revolution, 30-2, 102-5, 209-10
  and authority, 34
  elitist, 128
  and empire, 38
  and historical progress, 57-8
  interlinkages, 214
  palingenetic, 127
  totalitarian, 171-3
  and traditionalism, 109-10, 132
  and violence, 36
Revolutionary Fasci for International Action (*Fasci Rivoluzionari d'Azione Internazionalista*), 187
Revolutionary Social Movement (*Mouvement Social Révolutionnaire* – MSR), 165
revolutionary syndicalists, 189
Rexist movement, 31

Right Wong ideologies, 131
Roberts, David, 5, 27
Rocco, Alfredo, 188
Rolão Preto, Francisco, 94–111
　*Beacons_Guidelines_Soul*
　*(Balizas_Directrizes_Alma)*, 97
　*Beyond Communism (Para Além do Comunismo)*, 97
　death, 96
　early life, 94
　exile in Spain, 96
　*The Revoloution*, 95
　rivalry with Salazar, 96
　*Salazar and his Epoch (Salazar e a sua Época)*, 97
　two phases in political trajectory of, 94–5
Rolão Preto, Francisco, ideology of, 96–7
　authoritarianism, 105–6
　class conciliation, 99
　contradictions in, 109–10
　corporatism, 97–102
　Cult of Youth, 103
　integralism, 98
　national corporate state, 97–102 national revolution, 102–5
　organicism, 207
　palingenesis, 103
　progress, 214
　rejection of liberalism and communism, 107–9
　state, 209
　syndicalism, 100–1
　violence, 105–6
Romania
　anti-Semitism in, 150–2
　elections of, 1937, 140
　formation of, 142
　Greater, 145–6
　Jews in, 145, 150–2
　Moti people, 146
　terrorism, 140
Romanian Iron Guard *(Garda de Fier)*, 14
Romier, Lucien, 166
Rossoni, Edmondo, 188
Rousseau, Jean-Jacques, 127, 131
Ruiz de Alda, Julio, 116
Russia, 108 Bolshevism in, 61–2

sacrifice, 37, 60, 153
Salazar, António de Oliveira, 95, 109, 216
*Salazar and his Epoch (Salazar e a sua Época)* (Preto), 97

Salgado, Plinio, 4
Saltjobaden agreement, 177
Sandu, Traian, 140, 155
Sanjurjada, 116
Sansepolcrismo, 190
Sardinha, António, 96
Schijf, Huibert, 216
Schmitter, Philippe, 28
Schönerer, Georg Ritter von, 64, 216
*Schutzstaffel* (SS), 49
Second Spanish Republic, 118
Seigo, Nakano, 4
Sima, Horia, 141
Simojoki, Elias, 28
social Darwinism, 58–60
Social Democratic Party *(Sozialdemokratische Partei Deutschland* – SPD), 49
social justice, 101–2, 110–11, 125, 131, 154, 177, 216
social question, 63, 96, 109
socialism, 122, 216 democratic, 8
neosocialism, 164, 177 soldier, 36
Socialist Party of France *(Parti socialiste de France)*, 164, 166
*Socialist Perspectives (Perspectives socialistes)* (Déat), 164
Socialist Republican Union *(Union socialiste républicaine)*, 164
soldier socialism, 36
Sorel, George, 36, 162
Spain
　Civil War, 117 empire, 123 Second Republic, 118 separatist regions, 122
Spanish Confederation of Autonomous Right *(Confederación Española de Derechas Autónomas*-CEDA), 119
Spanish Falange *(Falange Española* – FE), formation of, 116 merger with Councils of the National Syndicalist Offensive, 117
Spanish Falange of the Councils of the National Syndicalist Offensive *(Falange Española de las Juntas de Ofensiva Nacional Sindicalista)*, 14
Spanish Falange of the JONS *(Falange Española de las JONS)*, 117
Spengler, Oswald, 50, 127
Spinasse, Charles, 166, 177
Spirito, Ugo, 3, 31
spiritual patrimony, 143
spirituality, 155–6, 200

Stalinism, 23
Staracce, Achille, 188
state, 25–7, 168–9, 208
  corporate, 28, 75–81
  interlinkages, 213–14
  and nation, 26, 29
  organic, 28
Stelescu, Mihae, 140
Stephen the Great, 142, 144, 148
Sternhell, Zeev, 22, 187
Strasser, Gregor, 25, 49
Strasser, Otto, 25
Streel, José, 31–2
*Sturmabteilung* (SA), 49
Sweden, 177
Swedish National Socialist Party
  (*Svenska nationalsocialistiska partiet* -
  SNSP), 32

Third Reich, 20, 50
Third Way, 27
Thomason, Alexander Raven, 73
Tinoco, António Lepierre, 95
Total Man, 172
totalitarianism, 21, 26–7, 76, 89, 169, 172, 209
traditional authority, 3
traditionalism, economic, 100, 104, 107, 109–10
Traditionalist Spanish Phalanx of the
  Councils of the National Syndicalist
  Offensive (*Falange Española
  Tradicionalista y de las Juntas de
  Ofensiva Nacional Sindicalista*), 117
Transylvania, 142, 146
Turati, Filippo, 194, 197
*The Twelve Principles of Production* (*Os
  Doze Princípios da Produção* – DPP)
  (Preto), 95

Union Movement, 73
*The Unique Party* (*Le Parti Unique*)
  (Déat), 14, 166
  authority in, 173
  class conciliation, 170–1
  conceptual core of, 167–75
  corporatism in, 170–1
  empire in, 166
  internationalism in, 171–3
  national community in, 167–8
  order in, 174

  party in, 175–6
  peripheral concepts in, 176
  state in, 168
  totalitarian revolution in, 171–3
  violence in, 173–4
USSR, 74
Ustash movement (Croatia), 36

Valdecases, Alfonso Garcia, 116
Valle de los Caídos, 119
Valois, George, 26, 162
Vecchi, Cesare Maria de, 190
Vecchi, Ferruccio, 190
Vichy regime, 164
Victor Emanuel III
  (King of Italy), 188
Vidali, Vittorio, 192
violence, 34–7, 210
  and authority, 38, 82–4
  Codreanu, 149–50
  Déat, 173–4
  Hitler, 59–60
  interlinkages, 214
  Mosley, 82–4
  Primo de Rivera, 129
  Rolão Preto, 105–6
virility, 32, 37, 83, 106
vital space, 61
Volk, 24
*Volk*, 50
*Volkisch* culture, 24–5
Von Hindenburg, Paul, 49
Von Papen, Franz, 49
Von Schleicher, Kurt, 49
Von Schönerer, Georg
  Ritter, 64

Webb, Sidney, 87
Webb. Beatroce, 87
Weber, Eugen, 1, 22, 30
Weber, Max, 3
*Weltanschauung*, 51–2, 58
Wessel, Horst, 192
World War II, 1, 36
Young Blueshirt, 32
youth, 31, 58, 82, 103, 171
Yugoslav National Movement – United
  Militant Labor Organization
  (*Združena Borbena Organizacija Rada
  – Zbor*), 39